White Ros.

THE ASSOCIATION FOR SCOTTISH LITERARY STUDIES

NUMBER THIRTEEN

THE ASSOCIATION FOR SCOTTISH LITERARY STUDIES

ANNUAL VOLUMES PUBLISHED BY SCOTTISH ACADEMIC PRESS

1971 James Hogg. *The Three Perils of Man*. Ed. Douglas Gifford.

1972 *The Poems of John Davidson*. Vol. I. Ed. Andrew Turnbull.

1973 *The Poems of John Davidson*. Vol. II. Ed. Andrew Turnbull.

1974 Allan Ramsay and Robert Fergusson. *Poems*. Ed. Alexander M. Kinghorn and Alexander Law.

1975 John Galt. *The Member*. Ed. Ian A. Gordon.

1976 William Drummond of Hawthornden. *Poems and Prose*. Ed. Robert H. MacDonald.

1977 John G. Lockhart. *Peter's Letters to his Kinsfolk*. Ed. William Ruddick.

1978 John Galt. *Selected Short Stories*. Ed. Ian A. Gordon.

1979 Andrew Fletcher of Saltoun. *Selected Political Writings and Speeches*. Ed. David Daiches.

1980 *Scott on Himself*. Ed. David Hewitt.

1981 *The Party-Coloured Mind*. Ed. David Reid.

1982 James Hogg. *Selected Stories and Sketches*. Ed. Douglas S. Mack.

1983 Sir Thomas Urquhart. *The Jewel*. Ed. R. D. S. Jack and R. J. Lyall.

THE ASSOCIATION FOR SCOTTISH LITERARY STUDIES

GENERAL EDITOR — DOUGLAS MACK

Sir Thomas Urquhart of Cromarty

THE JEWEL

Edited
with an introduction and commentary
by
R. D. S. JACK AND R. J. LYALL

SCOTTISH ACADEMIC PRESS

EDINBURGH

1983

First published in Great Britain, 1983
by Scottish Academic Press Limited,
33 Montgomery Street, Edinburgh EH7 5JX.

Introduction and Notes
© 1983, R. D. S. Jack and R. J. Lyall

ISBN 0 7073 0327 3

British Library Cataloguing in Publication Data

Urquhart, *Sir* Thomas
The jewel. — (The Association for Scottish
Literary Studies; 13)
I. Title   II. Jack, R. D. S.   III. Lyall, R. J.
823'.4[F]   PR3736.U6

Printed by Clark Constable (1982) Limited, Edinburgh

CONTENTS

ACKNOWLEDGEMENTS

The Editors are grateful to all those who have filled gaps in their knowledge revealed by an author whose learning was too encyclopedic and eccentric for this specialised age, and in particular to Dr Alex Agutter (Department of English Language, University of Edinburgh), Mr A. J. Aitken (Editor, *Dictionary of the Older Scottish Tongue*), Dr Alexander Broadie (Department of Moral Philosophy, University of Glasgow), Mr R. M. Cummings (Department of English Literature, University of Glasgow), Dr Frances Dow (Department of History, University of Edinburgh), Dr John Durkan (Department of Scottish History, University of Glasgow), Professor R. W. Hepburn (Department of Philosophy, University of Edinburgh), Mr Allan Hood (Department of Humanity, University of Edinburgh), Mr J. G. Howie (Department of Greek, University of Edinburgh), Dr Michael Lynch (Department of Scottish History, University of Edinburgh), Mr J. Derrick McClure (Department of English, University of Aberdeen), Dr Betty I. Sharpe and Professor Peter Walsh (Department of Humanity, University of Glasgow), and Dr Jennifer Wormald (Department of Scottish History, University of Glasgow); also to Mr Alastair Cherry and Miss Townley of the National Library of Scotland, who prepared a full bibliographical description of the 1652 edition of *The Jewel*. Dr Lyall is also indebted to the trustees of the Ross Fund in the University of Glasgow, who made possible a visit to the Beinecke Rare Books Library, Yale University, New Haven, to examine the Urquhart materials in the Osborn Collection. Our thanks are due to the librarians there and elsewhere who gave valuable professional assistance.

INTRODUCTION

I

On 3 September 1651 the Royalist army, under the command of the claimant to the throne and consisting principally of Scottish forces, was heavily defeated at Worcester by the Parliamentary army led by Cromwell and Charles Fleetwood. The Scottish contingent, which had been on the march for more than three weeks when it entered the city of Worcester on 22 August, was already suffering from low morale as a result of its failure to attract English reinforcements along the way; and it was outmanned, outgunned, and tactically out-thought by Cromwell's army. The defeat was decisive, bringing to an end both the military effort of the Royalists and the Scottish attempt to influence English politics, and it had the further effect of driving Charles II into exile. Four thousand Scottish prisoners were taken to London, whence many of them were gradually allowed to return to their own country, leaving the commanders and the most ideologically committed Royalists still in custody at the turn of the year.

Among the Scots who thus found themselves in an English prison was Sir Thomas Urquhart of Cromarty, a consistent supporter of the Royalist cause. He was committed with eighteen other Scottish prisoners to Windsor Castle on 16 September,[1] and he almost immediately began petitioning the Council to grant him his freedom. As the work here edited makes manifest, Urquhart was no ordinary prisoner. He started by hinting that he could offer something 'for the advantage of this nation', an overture which led the Council on 25 September to request one of its committees to investigate Urquhart's claims and to report back.[2] The terms of its report are unfortunately not preserved, but Urquhart, apparently present in person from day to day, continued to press for his release.[3] Eventually, on 14 July 1652, he was allowed to return to Scotland for five months — later extended by another six weeks — to attend to his personal affairs.[4] By that time, no doubt, he had found the leisure to complete *The Jewel*, which appears to have been published while he was still in London.

It is not too hard to guess the nature of the advantageous project with which Urquhart attempted to negotiate his freedom. Its promise is the eponymous Jewel, and forms the connecting link in the *Logopandecteision*, published the following year. Urquhart's claim to have developed a Universal Language, a perfect logical instrument which would revolutionize the world of learning, presents, as we shall see, a number of problems of interpretation; but there seems to be little doubt that he was indeed attempting to lay it (in all seriousness, presumably) before the Council of State three weeks after the battle at Worcester. The exposition of its underlying principles and more striking characteristics, published in slightly varying versions in both *The Jewel* and *Logopandecteision*, must have been one element of the fragments of Urquhart's literary manuscripts which, according to his own account, survived the destruction: he states that what survived was merely seven sheets, containing 'but a parcel of the preface he intended to premise before the grammar and lexicon of an universal language'. It seems unlikely that everything else in the volume was in fact written from scratch in the aftermath of the battle, and it is even more difficult to credit Urquhart's claim that his lost material amounted to $116\frac{1}{2}$ quires, almost 3,000 sheets.[5] That his fertile imagination could create at formidable speed seems to be beyond question; but it could also exaggerate in a manner worthy of Rabelais, whose works were already well known to Urquhart and may in part already have been translated by him. At the very least, much of the enormous volume of esoteric and diverse learning manifested in the works published after Worcester must have been absorbed by Urquhart earlier in his career, and were probably available to him in some form in the winter and spring of 1652.

Sir Thomas Urquhart's life had already been unusually eventful, even for a seventeenth century laird. By his own account, he was born the eldest child of Sir Thomas Urquhart of Cromarty and Christian Elphinston some five years after their marriage; since there is independent evidence that this marriage took place in 1606, we can with some confidence place his birth in 1611. He was, therefore, eleven years of age when he matriculated at King's College, Aberdeen in 1622, his regent being Mr Alexander Lunan.[6] As was commonly the case in his day, he seems not to have proceeded to take a degree, but the wide Classical reading and lively intellectual curiosity which are reflected in his later works perhaps owed a good deal to the teachers he met during his years as an undergraduate in Aberdeen: among the Aberdonian teachers praised in the pages of *The Jewel* he remembers his tutor William Seaton, 'a very able preacher truly and good scholar'.[7] Like many gentlemen of his time, he travelled abroad to extend his education, and there is no further reference to him in the Scottish records for more than a decade. His writings contain several references to his travels in France, Italy and Spain which may go back to this period, and it may also have been in this phase of his career that he established the foundations of that collection of books he later compared to 'a compleat nosegay of flowers, which in my travels I had gathered out of the gardens of above sixteen several kingdoms'.[8]

It is the gathering financial crisis afflicting Sir Thomas Urquhart senior which begins to dominate the story in the mid-1630s. We cannot tell how long the problems had been accumulating, but by the summer of 1636 Urquhart senior began to lose control of the family estates. Four years before, he had borrowed from a neighbour, William Rig of Adernie, the sum of £20,000. Unable to repay the debt, he sold to his creditor on 29 June 1636 £2,000 worth of annual rent of the lands of Cromarty, Davidstoun and elsewhere, to be offset against the money he owed.[9] Other creditors quickly descended, perhaps sensing the possibility of a total collapse of Urquhart's affairs, and within the week James Cuthbert of Draikies and Robert Leslie of Findrassie (the latter to distinguish himself as the most hawkish of the pursuers of the Urquhart assets, and to earn himself a special place in the works of the younger Sir Thomas) had gained control of further groups of lands.[10] The apprisings continued into the autumn, and it must have seemed that the entire estate was about to disappear into other hands.[11] Whether because of the threat to their patrimony or for other causes, the elder Urquhart's sons now fell out with him as well: in December 1636 they resorted to violence, 'putting violent hands on the persone of... their father, taking him captive and prissoner, and

3

detening him in sure firmance within ane upper chalmer, callit the Inner Dortour, within his place of Cromertie' for the period of five days. After securing his freedom their father instituted legal proceedings against Thomas and his younger brother Alexander, but the Justiciary Court was able to achieve a settlement without formal penalties.[12] The struggle between the Urquharts and their creditors, however, was not so easily resolved, and in July 1637 another neighbouring landowner, Patrick Smith of Braco, secured a hold on various Urquhart lands.[13]

By this time, moreover, a still more serious remedy had been sought by Sir Thomas' creditors: on 25 January 1637 he was outlawed by the Privy Council at the instance of Alexander Dunbar of Westfield and Katherine Dunbar, widow of David Brodie, over a debt of five thousand merks of principal and a thousand merks of expenses plus interest.[14] He was still an outlaw when the Council considered the matter again on 16 March but he had one important card still to play, and four days later he was granted, by Charles I in Westminster, a Great Seal letter protecting him for one year 'from all dilligence at the instance of his creditors'.[15] This royal protection was confirmed by the Scottish Council on 1 June,

> having tane to thair consideration the trew grounds and motives whereupon the said protection was grantit, and respecting therewithall the honest and worthie disposition of the said Sir Thomas himselfe, throw whois default or neglect nane of the burdens now lying on his hous hes fallin out but the undewtifull cariage and behaviour of his children hes procured the same.[16]

By 25 July the dispute between Sir Thomas and his sons was resolved, but nothing in the evidence tells us the nature of the 'undewtifull cariage and behaviour' on the part of the younger Thomas and his brother which caused the Council to absolve their father of responsibility for his desperate financial plight. Nor does the author of *The Jewel*, for all the praise which he bestows upon his father, allude to this judgement, rather attributing his downfall to his 'too strict adherence to the austerest principles of veracity'.[17]

4

There was to be no recovery from this series of misfortunes during the lifetime of the elder Sir Thomas, or in that of his eldest son, but their domestic affairs were soon transcended by what must have seemed an even greater political calamity. The publication of a new Scottish prayer-book in the summer of 1637 triggered a campaign of anti-episcopal resistance in the Scottish Church, culminating in the circulation of the National Covenant from February 1638.[18] The position of Urquhart and his family, firmly on the king's side and opposed to the Covenant, is indicated by the chronicler James Gordon, who notes that the Episcopalian faction in the north included 'in Rosse, Sir Thomas Urquhward, Sheriff of Cromertie, with his following, but they environed with Covenanters, their neighbours'.[19] Religious differences thus reinforced the relations between the Urquharts and their neighbours, already unfriendly as a result of financial strains. According to John Spalding, Sir Thomas Urquhart was urging support for the rival 'King's Covenant' at Ellon on 8 May 1638, by which time a confrontation between the presbyterians and the strong Royalist faction in Aberdeenshire was becoming imminent.[20] 'The young laird of Cromartie', now about twenty-seven, played a central part in a small but significant incident: having been robbed of a quantity of arms by some Covenanting lairds, he took part in a counter-raid on 10 May, in the course of which there was some shooting and a man was killed. This, says Spalding, 'wes the first blood that wes drawin heir sen the begining of this covenant'.[21] On 14 May, the Royalists attacked the Covenanting party at Turriff, with some further loss of life. Intermittent fighting continued in the area during May, and on the 23rd young Urquhart joined with the Bishop of Aberdeen and other leading northern Royalists in sailing for England.[22] His commitment to the Royalist cause was thus firmly made, three years before the outbreak of the English Civil War.

Towards the end of the year, Urquhart would appear to have established himself at the court of Charles I. In a revealing but neglected passage in *The Jewel*, he tells us that he was present when the manuscript of Spottiswoode's *History of the Church of Scotland* was presented on the day after the author's death by the Bishop of Ross to the king.[23] Since Spottiswoode is known to have died on 26 November 1639, it follows that Urquhart was a member of the court circle by that date. It is no doubt in this light that we should read *Apollo and the Muses*, the manuscript collection of no fewer than 1,103 epigrams now part of the Osborn Collection in the Beinecke Library at Yale, which its author claims to have written in thirteen weeks and which is dated 1640.[24] Unlike the published *Epigrams: Divine and Moral*, which appeared the following year, those in manuscript tend to be somewhat racy in character, and they perhaps reflect Urquhart's pretensions as a Cavalier wit; it is certainly noteworthy that each of the ten books of *Apollo and the Muses* is dedicated to a different noble courtier, thus providing a checklist of the author's prospective patrons.[25]

By his own testimony, Urquhart was knighted by Charles I at Whitehall on 7 April 1641.[26] Later in the same year (since the author is described as 'Knight' on the title-page), he published *Epigrams: Divine and Moral*, compiled in three books and dedicated to the Marquis of Hamilton. The unpublished, *risqué* epigrams are scarcely literary masterpieces, but these 134 short poems have the edge for dullness. They do, however, provide confirmatory evidence that in the last days of Charles' court before the outbreak of war, this Scottish aspirant to the throne of Apollo — he is so presented in an engraving by W.S., perhaps intended as an illustration to *Apollo and the Muses*[27] — was seeking to establish himself as a literary figure. We can only guess what his fellow-courtiers made of his fanciful imagination.

The following year, he was called away by the death of his father, whose ultimate concern had apparently been the financial welfare of his unfortunate son and heir. His own statement is that his father died in August 1642, but there is independent evidence to suggest that he was already dead by 14 June, and it may be that Urquhart's memory failed him on this point.[28] There is also a difficulty about his reference to having spent 'some few years' abroad after having returned to Scotland to set his affairs in order, since he would appear to have been living in London in May 1644, barely two years after his father's death. On 9 May of that year, he was assessed for a forced loan of £1,000 when Parliament was attempting to finance its army, and when he failed to pay up it was ordered that he should be brought into custody. He appealed to the Scottish Committee, and nothing more is heard of the matter; but the documents indicate quite clearly that he was at this time resident in Clare Street, London.[29] It is evident that we must not place too much reliance on the autobiographical details which Urquhart offers us!

It was perhaps while he was still living in London that he produced *The Trissotetras*, a trigonometrical work which was printed by James Young in 1645 'for the benefit of those that are mathematically affected' and dedicated to his mother, the dowager lady of Cromarty.[30] Scholarly and fantastic in almost equal measures, and owing much to the example of John Napier of Merchiston, this opaque treatise suggests that its author had abandoned the pursuits of the courtier (hardly a profitable calling in 1645) for the world of learning. Soon afterwards, he abandoned London for what remained of his estates in the north of Scotland, where he once more took up residence. Although he seems thus to have been able to avoid the greater part of the conflict of the Civil War, it is clear that his retreat was scarcely peaceful. He continued to have great trouble with his creditors, led by Leslie of Findrassie, and his Episcopalian views brought him into controversy with three prominent members of the local clergy. His hereditary claim to the Sheriffdom of Cromarty was prejudiced by the apprising of the title and the estate of Cromarty by Sir Robert Farquhar of Mounie on 31 March 1647. While he continued to claim both, they eventually passed after his death to Sir John Urquhart of Craigfintry, his cousin, who bought them from Farquhar and who was calling himself John Urquhart of Cromarty by December 1657.[31]

During the period of compromise between Royalists and the Scottish Presbyterians which began with the 'Engagement' between Scottish parliamentary leaders and King Charles, agreed at Christmas 1647, Sir Thomas Urquhart played his part in organizing a Scottish army to secure the return of the king to London: he served on the committee of war for Cromarty and Inverness which was set up by Parliament on 18 April 1648.[32] The expedition was, however, doomed, and the Scottish forces were destroyed at Preston in August; the influence of the Engagers perished with the 2,000 who died in the battle, and a parliament dominated by the shadow of Cromwell himself disqualified the Engagers, Royalists and other 'wrongdoers' from holding public office. A week later, on 30 January 1649,

Charles I was executed. Almost immediately, Thomas Mackenzie of Seaforth, Sir Thomas Urquhart of Cromarty and other Royalist lairds began an uprising, seizing Inverness and attempting to take control of all the northern counties. John Willcock believed that the style of Urquhart is apparent in the letter written to the Commissioners of the General Assembly by the northern rebels, and it may well be that he was justified:

> Yet we find, that evill willers and envyous vnderminers, in a singular and praetextuous way aiming at our ruine, doe spend the quintessence of their witts to find out means whereby, under specious pretences of the publick ... to extermine ws with povertie, and by inventing fresh occasions to make ws odious, and bring ws vpon fresh stages vnder the base name of Malignancy.[33]

The learned style and the elaborate rhetoric are certainly reminiscent of the author of *The Jewel*, and although Urquhart was not a signatory to the letter, it seems probable that he had a hand in its composition. Quite certainly his is the letter addressed to the Moderator of the General Assembly, Robert Douglas, on 14 November, in which Urquhart offers to make good his wrongdoings during the insurrection of May, and asks the Church's terms (Appendix I, p. 43).[34] By this time, the rebellion was long over, having collapsed after the defeat of the Royalist forces at Balvenie on 7 May. The following summer, Urquhart appeared before the Commissioners of the General Assembly, and was let off with a caution and an injunction that he confer with John Annand, minister of Inverness regarding his 'dangerous opinions'.[35] This clemency no doubt reflected the spirit of compromise which once more affected Scottish politics as a result of the arrival of Charles II to unite the Royalists and Covenanters against Cromwell.

Despite the defeat of the Scottish army at Dunbar on 3 September 1650, resistance to the Cromwellian regime continued to be strong in Scotland. Charles II was crowned at Scone on 1 January 1651, and in May of that year the Assembly rescinded its act discriminating against 'Malignants'. A new Scottish army, which by his own testimony (below, p. 61) included Urquhart among its number, had assembled at Stirling by the end of June; but the passage of the English enemy through Fife to Perth left the way clear for an invasion of England itself, and at the beginning of August the Scots were marching south. Amongst the baggage was, as we have seen, a collection of Urquhart's papers, not perhaps of the size he subsequently claimed but nevertheless containing, no doubt, genealogical materials and notes on his projection for the Universal Language. The disaster at Worcester produced the final crisis from which Urquhart's financial affairs never recovered; but it was also the occasion for a burst of literary productivity which for the first time gave him some claim to be regarded as an important writer. From what he was able to salvage he produced, initially, the *ΠΑΝΤΟΧΡΟΝΟΧΑΝΟΝ; or, a Peculiar Promptuary of Time*, a genealogical account of the family of Urquhart from Adam and Eve to Sir Thomas himself, which was published by Richard Baddeley in the early part of 1652. This almost entirely spurious pedigree, which reads like an exaggerated parody of the fictitious genealogies of the Scottish royal house still enjoying a certain currency in the mid-seventeenth century,[36] is asserted by Urquhart's persona, one 'G.P.' to be merely a preface to a more elaborate work which will document the assertions here made; this is a promising device to which Urquhart returned in both *The Jewel* and *Logopandecteision*.

All three works, for all their encyclopaedic subject matter and wide-ranging rhetoric, are in fact directed towards a single pair of objectives: securing the release of their author from the imprisonment which was the consequence of the defeat of the Royalists at Worcester, and reversing his financial fortunes. As the genealogical materials of *A Peculiar Promptuary* are reworked in *The Jewel*, so the linguistic and philosophical elements of this latter work are incorporated in the *Logopandecteision*, which was published in 1653, after Urquhart's return from Scotland about the beginning of the year. His financial difficulties remained as intractable as ever, and it was only after avoiding an attempt by Leslie of Findrassie to obtain his arrest as a prisoner of war that he was able to make his way back to England.[37] The bargain offered in *The Jewel*, and more explicitly in *Logopandecteision*, seems never to have been taken up, and the only financial benefit accruing to the author would appear to have been from the sale of the works themselves. Urquhart had, meanwhile, also been preparing a translation of his beloved Rabelais, and the first two books of this were published by Richard Baddeley in 1653. The continuator of this work, Pierre Motteux, states that it had been Urquhart's intention to translate all five books of *Gargantua* and *Pantagruel*, but that he only completed the third, which was found in manuscript after his death.[38] That he already knew the satires of Rabelais well is manifest from the character of much of the humour of *The Jewel*, and even from a few specific details; but the completion of so much work within a couple of years at Worcester would be a remarkable feat. It is impossible to tell how much of this material already existed before the battle. There must be a germ of truth in Urquhart's story of the partial loss of his papers at Worcester, but there is a distinct probability that some at least of his translation of Rabelais had been made before September 1651.

When he was eventually released from captivity it was, it would seem, to go abroad; this may or may not have been a condition of his freedom. There would have been little to attract him in Commonwealth Britain. From the existence of two letters written in Middelburg in Zeeland on 20 September 1655 (Appendix I, p. 46), and 1 July 1658, it would seem that he may have established himself in this Dutch town which had for so long maintained a Scottish trading community.[39] There is certainly no evidence that he ever returned to his homeland. Nor is there any independent corroboration of the eighteenth-century story that he died 'in a fit of excessive laughter' on hearing the news of the Restoration of Charles II. All that can be said is that the timing would appear to be about right, and that the anecdote bears the distinctive stamp of Urquhart's personality. On 4 May 1660, a notary public in Aberdeenshire saw his written consent to the sale to one Andrew Gerard of the lands of Wester Walkerhill, from which it may be deduced that he was still alive a little before that date.[40] Charles II was proclaimed king the following day, and returned to his kingdom on 29 May. At the beginning of August, Sir Thomas' brother, Sir Alexander, was petitioning the Council for a commission as hereditary Sheriff of Cromarty, as the eldest surviving son of the previous Sir Thomas Urquhart.[41] We can therefore be fairly certain that our author died within three months of hearing the news of the Restoration, which lends a degree of credibility to the story of the laughter-fit. Equally, of course, it could provide the occasion for a tale which corresponds so well with the character of its subject.

Sir Alexander Urquhart was not to enjoy the office of Sheriff. He had to face an almost immediate challenge from John Urquhart of Craigfintry, who had, as we have seen, been styling himself 'of Cromarty' for several years. He now petitioned Parliament for recognition as Sheriff, and an act to this effect was passed on 20 March 1661.[42] Sir Alexander seems to have acknowledged the justice of this claim, for he made no objection to the accession of his cousin, and the process of decline which had begun a quarter of a century before was complete.

The literary legacy of Sir Thomas Urquhart was, happily, greater than his material one. As a translator he has deservedly been acclaimed, for his version of Rabelais bears the mark of a man altogether in sympathy with the fantastic imagination and keen satirical wit of the French original. His own original compositions have been appreciated less, for they lack the accessibility of the Rabelais and make a number of complex demands on a modern audience. Yet they repay careful reading, and there is much to enjoy in the apparently haphazard construction of *The Jewel*. Generically unclassifiable, it represents Urquhart's later original works at their most vivid, and it contains most of his best writing. By coming to terms with *The Jewel*, therefore, we can also begin to understand this fantastic, quixotic, perverse man.

II

In his *Epigrams: Divine and Moral*, Urquhart frequently returns to the theme of Fortune, always confidently asserting that man's duty is to remain stoically unaffected by its worst blows:

> Let's take in patience sicknesse, banishments,
> Paine, losse of goods, death and enforced strife,
> For none of those are so much punishments
> As tributes which we pay unto this life,

From the whole tract whereof we cannot borrow
One dram of joy that is not mix'd with sorrow.[43]

The unwitting irony is that his three major original works provide clear proof that when some of the hardships mentioned in the first two lines did occur, Sir Thomas proved constitutionally incapable of maintaining the lofty vision he had recommended in earlier, less troubled times. *A Peculiar Promptuary of Time*, *The Jewel*, and *Logopandecteision* are all essentially passionate complaints addressed to Cromwell's Government, protesting that a man of Urquhart's genius should not be prevented from achieving the many great schemes he has in mind through having to worry about imprisonment, the annexation of his estates and the malice of Presbyterian fanatics. They make this point in different ways; they do so with an imaginative ingenuity and a power over words which make all three worthy of serious literary analysis; but in essence they all proclaim that Thomas Urquhart, Knight found the tenets of Thomas Urquhart, epigrammatist, too passive to bear.

As we have seen, these works were composed, for the most part, within a very compressed time scale, generated by the desperation of Urquhart's position in the aftermath of Worcester. Imprisoned as a victim of civil war, having lost (apparently) a large number of literary manuscripts which he valued highly, his estates lost because of his father's mismanagement and the apparent vindictiveness of his creditors, huge debts still hanging over his head, Urquhart chose the weapon he handled best — words — to bring his claims to the attention of his captors. In the process, he created a strange new mode blending panegyric and complaint, history and romance. Some of the rhetorical features of these independent works can be found also in Urquhart's translations from Rabelais, where his linguistic virtuosity causes him to be more adventurous verbally than Rabelais himself: this major work has still to be fully discussed despite studies as varied as those of Roe and Brown.[44] Our primary concern, however, is with this rhetorical mode as it is developed in *The Jewel* and the earlier original writings, for it is the *Epigrams* and *The Trissotetras* which cast the most interesting light upon the development of Urquhart's literary methods and the achievement of his three central works.

The *Epigrams* have been unfairly dealt with by most previous critics. The wrong criterion has been used to judge them. As Willcock rightly reminds us, in the seventeenth century an epigram was not necessarily intended to be witty, merely to convey a single thought in a fashion brief enough to be suitable for inscriptions.[45] Further, the basis for assessment has almost always been the published, highminded epigrams, not the less austere ones which remain in manuscript and are generally of a higher standard.[46] But even if we make these allowances, it must be admitted that the *Epigrams* disappoint. Their sentiments are usually banal and their metre frequently faulty. Prose was to be Urquhart's natural medium, and one in which, oddly, his ear for rhythm was to prove as reliable as it had been suspect in his verse. Already we can hear this in the long Ciceronian periods of the Dedication to *Epigrams: Divine and Moral,* where also there sounds for the first time that sublimely unselfconscious note of patrician self-esteem which will characterize *The Jewel* and the other two original works of the post-Worcester period. Who but Urquhart could interrupt the consistent note of dedicatory humility to state that the Marquis of Hamilton had principally been chosen because only the most exalted of patrons was suited to these, the 'sublimest' of poems? Already Urquhart suggests that he can become his own finest panegyrist.

The Trissotetras moves further in the direction of *The Jewel.* The vibrantly self-confident tone is maintained, and a new device which was to become a hallmark of Urquhart's autoeulogistic style makes its first appearance. Of the three short introductions to this eccentric treatise, which expresses trigonometrical formulae logarithmically,[47] the last is an extended eulogy on Urquhart himself. Although this is subscribed 'J.A.', the style and ideas are recognizably Urquhart's own.[48] 'J.A.', is the predecessor of 'G.P.' the presenter of *A Peculiar Promptuary of Time,* and of 'Christianus Presbyteromastix', who purports to be the editor of Urquhart's work on the Universal Language and author of *The Jewel.* Secondly, as in the later works his expansive style and his love of new words coined from foreign roots (especially Greek) make the prose extremely complex. When we add to this the abstruseness of his mathematical method, it becomes clear that only the most dedicated of students would have been able to follow his arguments. Although Urquhart does provide a glossary, some of its explanations are every bit as obscure as the terms they seek to interpret:

> Oppobasal, is said of those moods which have a catheteuretick concordance in their datas of the same cathetopposite angles, and the same bases. (*Works*, p. 141)

Yet, just as he excuses the highflown rhetoric of *The Jewel* for not being nearly highflown enough, so he praises the nearly impenetrable *Trissotetras* for its simplicity. Everything, he notes happily, has been explained 'with all possible brevity and clarity', so that any student 'in seven weeks at most … may attaine to more knowledge therein then otherwise he could do for his heart in the space of a twelve-moneth'.

A more important parallel between *The Trissotetras* and the post-Worcester tracts, however, is that all four present to the public a project which, it is claimed, will advance knowledge immeasurably. In *The Trissotetras* this is logarithmical trig-onometry, in *A Peculiar Promptuary of Time* the genealogy of the Urquharts, and in *The Jewel* and *Logopandecteision* the Universal Language. The 'trissotetrail' scheme is evaluated primarily in academic terms, but it is also stated to be of greater worth than 'millions of gold and severall rich territories'. It is also to be viewed only as a modest beginning, because Urquhart hopes to undertake further 'laborious employments' in the service of sympathetic mathematicians. As we shall see, these two arguments (monetary value and offered continuation) will be advanced in the post-Worcester tracts, where circumstances dictate that the tone and application are changed. Now, the value of his discoveries becomes an argument for returning his money and lands, and the further researches (or indeed the remainder of incomplete current research) will only be pursued if and when he is returned to his proper place in the Scottish hierarchy. The note of belligerence and blackmail is new, but the basic rhetorical pattern is already present in the earlier mathematical tract.

Composed in its present form shortly before *The Jewel*, *A Peculiar Promptuary of Time* seems to modern eyes extraordinary in every way, for in it, with a great display of detail, Urquhart traces the development of his line as far back as Adam. The relationship between high nobility and the possession of a distinguished lineage was, of course, an orthodoxy at this period, and one which is supported by many earlier writers including the poet Henryson:

> It is contrair the lawis of nature
> A gentill man to be degenerate,
> Nocht folowing of his progeniture
> The worthy reule and the lordly estate . . .[49]

The address 'To the Reader', composed by the shadowy 'G.P.' who writes in Urquhart's own grandiloquent style, clearly indicates that the purpose of this treatise is to magnify Sir Thomas with a view to establishing *his* greatness and gaining the freedom of one with so many impeccable ancestors:

> . . . it is humbly desired, and, as I believe, from the hearts of all that are acquainted with him, that the greatest State in the world stain not their glory by being the Atropos to cut the thred of that which Saturne's sith hath not been able to mow in the progress of all former ages, especially in the person of him whose inward abilities are like to produce effects conducible to the State of as long continuance for the future. (*Works*, p. 152)

And it is true that the genealogical credentials presented are of the highest, although more likely to impress rulers with a hierarchical view of society than the government of Cromwell. Urquhart takes his line through Adam and Seth to Japhet, who (in keeping with medieval interpretations of the Biblical account) receives as his patrimony the whole of Europe. The first actually to bear the name of Urquhart is Esormon, Prince of Achaia who was born, according to the *Promptuary*, in 2139 B.C. Throughout the whole remarkable process, as Willcock wryly remarks, 'the habits of the Urquharts to form alliances and friendships with persons afterwards famous in sacred and secular history is very marked'.[50] Thus Phrenedon Urquhart is a leading member of the house of Abraham, and Pamprosodos Urquhart marries the Egyptian princess (by the name of Termuth!) who found Moses in the bulrushes. In later years the family is claimed to have ruled Ireland — an obvious parallel with the Irish sojourn of the house of Canmore according to the traditional Scottish genealogies — and to have been a major force in Scottish history. Lutork Urquhart is captain-general to Fergus I, the mythic King of the Scots, and one William Urquhart proves the saviour of Robert the Bruce. In the ninth century or thereabouts, the fanciful names (Vistoso, Marsidalio, Hedomenos and so on) give way to more familiar forms: Carolo Urquhart (the godson of Charlemagne!) has a son Endymion, while the Urquhart knighted by Malcolm Canmore is actually called Sir Jasper.

Ludicrous as much of this is, it cannot simply be dismissed as the witterings of a deranged mind, although in *The Jewel* Urquhart does quote approvingly the Senecan maxim (which he attributes incorrectly to Aristotle) that *Nullum magnum ingenium sine mixtura dementiae* (there can be no great wit without some element of craziness). While it would appear that Urquhart used authentic family records for the latter part of his genealogy, perhaps from the early fourteenth century onwards,[51] and much can be explained by reference to the Scottish tradition of mythical history, there remains a substantial element which he could hardly have expected the most uncritical of audiences to accept unquestioningly. The eulogistic gambit which Urquhart plays here, elevating his own position by reference (through a persona) to his noble ancestry, is compounded by a process of exaggeration which is another feature of his mature style. It is likely that Willcock was correct in reminding us of the comic genealogy of Pantagruel which Rabelais includes in Book II, and which Urquhart very probably knew at the time he was composing the *Promptuary*.[52] The element of hyperbole is common to both, and suggests that we are to be impressed as much by the elaborate inventiveness with which Sir Thomas carries off his outrageous genealogizing as we are by the nobility of his progenitors.

We find also a development of the techniques used in *The Trissotetras*. He has become practised in the art of panegyrical rhetoric (directed mainly at himself and those who help him), while the needs of the time help to hone the scathing invective which demeans his enemies. He is also creating a persona who is at once to be admired for his great gifts and pitied for his impotence in the face of a peculiarly malevolent Fortune. The reader, therefore, is intended rationally to hold him in awe, emotionally to sympathize with him. Urquhart knew as well as anyone that the first skill of persuasive rhetoric is to win over the audience. Having done this, he presents his valuable scheme much as he had done in *The Tressotetras*. But this time, the promises to extend it are much more detailed. He will widen the scope of his work, doing the same thing for all illustrious families descended from the Urquharts. Place-names derived from Urquhart will also be studied and — most astounding of all — he will prove from Arabic, Greek and Latin sources that the present genealogy is founded on proofs as sound as those of Euclid. All these marvellous plans will, of course, only be brought to fruition if his freedom is granted and his lands restored. Thus emerges the element of threat which was to take on a more intricate form in the work which appeared later in the same year.

This was *The Jewel*, a work which in its apparent formlessness, its movement from one mode to another, its exuberent wordiness and its seemingly contradictory comments on literary method resolutely defies any attempt at generic classification.[53] The analysis which follows does not attempt to impose too confining an intellectual pattern on the book, but it does seek to establish the overall plan, relating that to the author's proclaimed intentions.

To do this, it is necessary to begin with the major 'contradictions' which the narrator introduces concerning the manner of his writing. Towards the end of a work which has been characterized by verbal inventiveness and rhetorical complexity, he laments that he could have 'enlarged this discourse with a choicer variety of phrase and made it overflow the field of the reader's understanding with an inundation of greater eloquence'. Or, as Charles Whibley puts it, 'the conclusion of the *Exquisite Jewel*, the most complicated rhapsody in English prose, is nothing else than an apology for its simple reticence'.[54] As Urquhart was too well versed in rhetorical theory to be unaware of his own stylistic mode, this must on one level be viewed as a conventional 'modesty topos' (*excusatio*).[55] But it serves two further purposes. It establishes that, in fact, he *can* be even more of a virtuoso than he has already proved, and it draws attention to the importance of his message, this time in the context of the decorum which is appropriate to his theme. He has properly chosen as high a style for this theme as is consistent with conveying it clearly: he has denied his rhetorical skill while doubly displaying it.[56]

In the discussion so far, it is assumed that Sir Thomas Urquhart is indeed the author of *The Jewel*, which leads naturally on to the second 'contradiction'; for with great regularity the narrative voice denies this, speaking of Sir Thomas in the third person. Most obviously, he claims on p. 53 that he has incorporated two-and-a-quarter sheets of Sir Thomas' own papers, rescued from Worcester, into a work which is otherwise his own. Hence the title: Sir Thomas' contribution is the 'gold' or the jewel, his own the 'dunghill'.[57] He confirms this claimed position on p. 188, referring to Urquhart as the man 'whose writings I in this tractate intermix with my own'.

There can be no doubt that this claim is false. The style of the entire work is obviously Urquhart's; the form and obsessional ideas too close to *A Peculiar Promptuary of Time* and *Logopandectei- sion* for anyone seriously to suppose that he was not the author. Then why pretend? On a practical level, it permits him to disown the petition if, perchance, its hierarchical and still essentially Royalist views did not have the desired effect on Cromwell, Fleetwood and Overton.[58] Such an argument might have saved him but it would have been specious, for in the last paragraph of 'The Epistle Liminary' Urquhart, citing Virgil and Scaliger, tacitly admits that the persona of 'Christianus Presbyteromastix' (a name chosen for its strong, even offensive anti-Presbyterian nuances) is a pose employed to make his arguments as forceful as possible. It allows him to praise himself more flamboyantly than ever; it creates a persona entirely (and not surprisingly) sympathetic to his case; and it places all this within a tradition earlier espoused by writers of the highest merit. Once more the contradiction is apparent only; once more its solution suggests an author well versed in the skills of persuasive dialectic and an audience capable of appreciating such rhetorical play.

Yet it is the third 'contradiction' which is, at least initially, the most puzzling. On the one hand, Urquhart confesses that he had to compose at speed, vying with the printer as to who could work more quickly. He 'admits' to writing without due thought and even claims this as a strength, showing that 'extemporanneaness in some kinde of subjects may very probably be more successful then premeditation'. When discussing the fortunes of Scots in foreign countries, he admits that he is only listing them as they occur to his fallible memory (p. 178), a haphazard approach which had earlier been strongly suggested by a passage concerning the Earl of Argyll:

> ... as his judgment increased and that he ripened in knowledge, declining from that neoterick faith and waning in his love to Presbytery as he waxed in the experience of the world, of a strict Puritan that he was at first he became afterwards the most obstinate and rigid Papist that ever was upon the earth. He was a lord, I know. Nay more, he was an earle! I, that he was and one of the first of them. Ho now! Pescods on it! Crawford, Lodi Lindsay puts me in minde of him. It was the old Earl of Argile, this Marquis of Argile's father! That was he. That was the man ... (p. 98).

All this supposes a formlessness, a lack of artistic care which fits in incongruously with the rhetorical subtlety which we have seen to be a characteristic of Urquhart's work. On the other hand, there is his claim in *Logopandecteision* that he composed 'no treatises, whether in prose or verse, without some considerable deliberation'. And if everything is indeed so haphazard, why does he refer to a 'compositive' (synthetic) mode of argument, in which the reasoning is 'methodically deduced'? Why are the infallible principles established as early as p. 81 applied so rigorously to his own case on pp. 202–4? All this, surely, assumes the very care and forethought which elsewhere he has summarily denied.

Urquhart's actual approach is a mixture of the two. The following quotation, which comes at the end of a particularly disorderly list, gives in miniature the key to the larger method:

> ... in this heterogenean miscellany we have proceeded from the body to the purse. (p. 171)

That is, while individual elements may have been thrown together, the governing pattern has been carefully thought out. Like Geoffrey of Vinsauf's responsible artist in the *Poetria Nova*, Urquhart has taken care that 'the mind's hand shapes the entire house before the body's hand builds it'.[59] The various lines of argument and narrative, however eccentrically phrased or counterpointed, are all ultimately part of a powerful plea on behalf of Urquhart himself. The method is broadly 'compositive', in that the extended personal petition is explicitly made only at the end, and on grounds deduced from the earlier argument. Most critics have been blind to this controlling plan, which will be the subject of the analysis which follows.

Meanwhile, it might well be asked: 'Why take such care in designing the house, if you are going to make a virtue out of casually laying the individual bricks?' Surely Urquhart's case would have been more effectively advanced if the same orderly intellect had been brought to bear upon details, and indeed upon some aspects of the 'oeconomie'? It must be admitted that some parts of *The Jewel* are undeniably disappointing and formless. Urquhart clearly wrote the work under great pressure. Whether or not his story of matching the typesetter's pace is literally true, the book was certainly written in haste and in circumstances which can hardly be regarded as favourable. By emphasizing spontaneity of composition, he not only excused himself from the tedious arrangement of details (something which had never been his strong point!), but he strengthened the sympathetic bonds between reader and narrator. One cannot help warming to this poor, time-threatened creature who sometimes transmits to us the frustrations of the writing experience. Both the premeditation of the larger plan and the apparently unprepared presentation of some of its constituent parts are thus made allies in Urquhart's process of persuasion. But it is possible to take the point a stage further. We may even suspect Urquhart of taking pains at times to *simulate* the spontaneity which he claims. The passage about the Earl of Argyll cited above is a case in point. We surely recognize that Urquhart remembers from the outset the identity of his subject, and the pretence of forgetfulness is part of a deliberately-crafted rhetorical conceit, the effect of which is to highlight the revelation of Argyll's villainy and to build a climax within the paragraph. There could be no clearer example of the artifice which underlies Urquhart's elaborate mask of amateurish informality.

Even those critics (and they are in the majority) who regard

The Jewel as an entertaining but haphazard muddle accept that it has two thoroughly developed high-points: the discussion of the Universal Language and the tale of the Admirable Crichton. These are indeed the most important episodes, but it should be recognized that they actually form part of a careful, if complex, overall pattern. Within that scheme their functions are different, but their ultimate intention is the same.

The Language *is* 'the jewel'. According to the narrator's fiction, it is the part which Urquhart himself composed, which was preserved in the destruction of its author's manuscripts after Worcester. As it is used in *The Jewel*, and with more elaborate argument in *Logopandecteision*, its function is essentially practical: it is the bait which is meant to tempt the Government into treating the knight more favourably than any of his fellow-prisoners, a ploy which, as we have seen, Urquhart actually attempted to carry off. There is some reason to suppose that Urquhart's outline of his Universal Language did exist before his captivity and the composition of *The Jewel*. In his work, the outline description is framed by the narrator's pleas on behalf of its creator. Not once within the description of the Language does Urquhart refer to his own case; but he only achieves this by omitting sections 38–49. The lacuna is indicated by the numbering of the paragraphs in *The Jewel*, and the missing portion appears the following year in the complete version published in *Logopandecteision*.[60] It is in this omitted part that Urquhart praises his achievements abroad and refers specifically to the vindictiveness of his Scottish creditors, a subject which receives much expanded treatment in the later work. This 'digression' (as he calls it) does not refer to Worcester or to any subsequent events; it is therefore probable that the introduction to the Language *had* been composed prior to that event and *was* part of his rescued papers.[61] The decision to omit paragraphs 38–49 is not fortuitous: it is occasioned by Urquhart's choice of a mode in which he ostensibly lets another eulogize and cavil on his behalf, not needing to do so himself.

The fragmentary nature of the description of the Universal Langauge is essential to its rhetorical effect. Being only 'the preface he [Urquhart] intended to premise before the grammar and lexicon', it is entirely useless without the main body of the Language. The narrator's introduction makes it clear that only

Urquhart could complete a work of such magnitude. His concluding comments after the *Universal Language* (pp. 80–87) has been presented in outline provide both philosophical and mercenary reasons for capitalizing on the scheme 'for the advantage of this nation'. To do so would show a proper understanding of justice; it would also indicate concurrence with the idea that knowledge should be valued above wealth. That is on the higher level. But by a clever, if sophistic, twist of logic, the latter argument is also used to prove that the creator of knowledge (in this case Sir Thomas) should be rewarded by the return of all his wealth (in this case his lands, rents and reparation for his lost manuscripts). In addition, students who have learned this language will complete their studies two years earlier then they do now, a saving which the narrator conservatively estimates at £10,000. The rhetorical strategy of presenting the 'fragmentary' outline as a sort of trailer, advertizing the virtues of the Universal Language without yet revealing its secrets, is alluded to explicitly by Urquhart in *Logopandecteision*:

> Thus, seeing matters of the greatest worth may be undervalued by such as are destitute of understanding, who would reap any benefit by what is good, till it be appreciated should be charie of its prestitution; let this therefore suffice, why to this preface or introduction I have not as yet subjoyned the Grammar and Lexicon. But why it is I would extoll the worth thereof without the jeopardy of vaine-glory, the reason is clear and evident; being necessitated ... to merchandise it for the redintegrating of an ancient family, it needeth not be thought strange that in some measure I descend to the fashion of the shop-keepers, who to scrue up the buyer to the higher price will tell them no better can be had for mony, 'tis the choicest ware in England, and if any can match it, he shall have it for nought. So in matter of this literatorie chaffer, I have determined not to be too rash in the prestitution thereof, least it should be vilified, yet went on in my laudatives to procure the greater longing, that an ardent desire might stir up an emacity to the furtherance of my proposed end. (*Works*, p. 332)

In founding his hopes of recovery of his family's fortunes upon the creation of a Universal Language, Urquhart was responding to a notable vogue among contemporary scholars. Motivated by the desire both to develop a medium of international communication which could offset the decline of Latin in the face of the vernacular languages and to evolve a form of expression which would be a perfect reflection of the structure of the world, avoiding the inconsistency and arbitrariness of natural languages, seventeenth century logicians and others had set themselves the task of creating such a Universal Language.[62] Although there was much interest in the concept on the Continent, it seems that England was the centre of this activity. It was Francis Bacon who, at the beginning of the century, first articulated the need for a single system of characters into which all languages could be transposed, and attempts were made to devise a Universal Character by Francis Lodwick (*A Common writing*, 1647) and Cave Beck (*The universal character*, 1657).[63] But it was quickly realized that serious philosophical advantages could derive only from a systematically created language with 'rules certain and easie', for 'the truer description of things' and 'to admit easie and quick entrance to the things themselves'.[64] It was the possibility of such a logical and cognitive tool which interested Descartes in the project for a Universal Language, and that interest extended as far as Descartes' correspondent Mersenne, whose *Harmonie universelle* (1636) contained a discussion of the subject, Tomaso Campanella, Comenius, and Athanasius Kircher.[65]

In England, men such as Francis Lodwick and Samuel Hartlib were working in the field during the 1640s, and in touch with developments on the Continent. Lodwick's *Ground-Work for the Framing of a New Perfect Language* appeared in 1652 (the same year as *The Jewel!*), while later essays in the same genre were to be produced by George Dalgarno, an Aberdonian working in Oxford, and by John Wilkins.[66] It is hardly likely that Urquhart was unaware of all this current interest in the subject which he made the centrepiece of *The Jewel*; indeed, it would seem that it was its very currency which made it a potentially useful bargaining counter.

How serious was its 'inventor', then, in putting forward his scheme? The intellectual basis which he offers certainly falls within the mainstream of philosophical speculation on Universal Language, notwithstanding Urquhart's boast that his proposal 'never hitherto hath been so much as thought upon by any'. The integration of language and nature which is fundamental to Urquhart's argument was the essence of all such seventeenth century schemes, and he agrees with contemporary writers in emphasizing the assistance which an entirely regular, logical linguistic framework would be to the memory. The link between logical structure and the operation of the memory in learning the language is made by Urquhart in a striking metaphor:

> ... for better understanding whereof with all its dependant boughs, sprigs and ramelets I have before my lexicon set down the division thereof, making use of another allegory, into so many cities which are subdivided into streets, they againe into lanes, those into houses, these into stories whereof each room standeth for a word; and all these so methodically, that who observeth my precepts thereanent shall at the first hearing of a word know to what city it belongeth and consequently not be ignorant of some general signification thereof, till, after a most exact prying into all its letters, finding the street, lane, house, story and room thereby denotated, he punctually hit upon the very proper thing it represents in its most specifical signification. (p. 73)

This claim differs from the aspirations of Urquhart's fellow language planners only in the concreteness with which it appears to have been worked out, and the completeness of the logical system which it purports to have embodied in language.

But this brings us to the heart of the problem which arises from Urquhart's outline of his language. Wonderfully ordered and philosophically admirable as the scheme is, it is difficult to believe that its proposer had, as he claims, actually developed it beyond the outline stage, or even that he could have done so if the Government had risen to his bait. Every word in this system sufficient for expressing 'all the things in this world, both in themselves, actions, ways of doing, situations, pendicles, relations, connexions, pathetick interpositions and all other appurtenances to a perfect elocution' is derived from one of 250 'prime radices', and contains within it not just its essential semantic value but information to tell us

> what part of speech it is; or if a noun, unto what
> predicament or class it is to be reduced, whether it be the
> signe of a real or notional thing or somewhat concerning
> mechanick trades in their tooles or tearmes; or if real,
> whether natural or artificial, complete or incomplete. . . .
> (p. 73)

Not only does it do all this within 'seven syllables at most', but if it is a noun or a verb it may begin either with a vowel or a consonant 'as to the peruser shall seem most expedient', it will have at least ten synonyms, and it will be equally meaningful backwards or forwards. Nor is the accidence of the Language any less remarkable. It has, according to its inventor, eleven cases, four numbers, eleven genders, seven modes, four voices, and twelve parts of speech. Was Urquhart serious? Had he actually worked out the system, as he claims, or was he either a disingenuous charlatan or a deluded crank? Or is the whole project a spoof, revealing 'at least partly satirical intent'?[67] And if the latter, at whom was the satire directed?

The answer perhaps lies in the rhetorical mode which dominates the whole of *The Jewel*, and indeed all of Urquhart's works. Hyperbole is the key to understanding, here as elsewhere. The man who claimed to have written 1100 epigrams in thirteen weeks, who traced his ancestry through 153 generations from Adam, who would extol the deeds of James Crichton in terms which cannot be accepted other than as the most outrageous exaggeration, whose translations of Rabelais go far beyond their original in hyperbolic flights, who adopts verbal and syntactical excess as a stylistic stock-in-trade, has invented the perfect language, one which outdoes all its rivals on every imaginable criterion. The terms in which it is described consistently manifest this preoccupation with the superiority of Urquhart's language:

> . . . in the cases of all the declinable parts of speech it
> surpasseth all other languages whatsoever — for whilst
> others have but five or six at most, it hath ten besides the
> nominative (p. 74)

> ... in this language the verbs and participles have four
> voices, although it was never heard that ever any other
> language had above three. (p. 74)

> ... as for the yeer of God, the moneth of that yeer, week of
> the moneth, day of that week, partition of the day, hour of
> that partition, quarter and half quarter of the hour, a
> word of one syllable in this language will express it all to
> the full. (p. 76)

It is surely not to be expected that we will swallow all this as
literally true. It is part of a hyperbolic rhetoric which is pro-
gressively developed throughout the sixty-three advantages
which Urquhart claims for his invention, ranging from the
highest aspirations of Platonic philosophy to such trivia as 'a
wonderful facility . . . in making of anagrams' and the
identification through his name in the language of every link in a
soldier's chain of command. The ploy demands, of course, that
the actual details of the scheme should remain a mystery, to be
revealed only when Urquhart has struck his bargain with the
government. Urquhart has grasped, better than many serious
proposers of the Perfect Language, the linguistic implications of
the philosophical notion, and he pursues them ruthlessly to their
logical conclusion. A man who could invent such a system would
indeed be worthy of his country's gratitude, and neither *The
Jewel* or *Logopandecteision* allows any doubt that Urquhart is the
man. Any ridicule which may accrue to the principle of the
Universal Language as a result of Urquhart's hyperbolic
description is secondary to the game which he is playing: to
invent such an 'invention', one might conclude, itself reveals the
inventor's inestimable worth. Well might the narrator remark
that

> to contrive a language of this perfection will be thought
> by the primest wits of this age a work of a great
> understanding. (p. 80)

That Urquhart had not actually done so is insignificant beside
the elegantly judged outrageousness of his claims; for they too
are 'a work of a great understanding'.

If this deals with the Language, what of the form and
purposes of the rest of the work? Although it escapes any precise

26

generic classification, its strongest links are certainly with classical epideictic oratory and panegyrical biography. The ornate style is usually chosen for this mode, and the preferred stylistic devices of repetition, periphrasis, comparison, digression and prosopopeia all appear with regularity in *The Jewel*. Ultimately didactic in intention, it is concerned with praise and blame, often comparing 'the subject of the oration . . . to paragons of the past'.[68] The most memorable of these in *The Jewel* is, of course, Crichton; but before discussing his role it will be helpful to examine the wider patterns of praise and blame.

Both opening and conclusion celebrate the worth of Sir Thomas, but they do so in a manner which highlights five particular sources of his glory. In the 'Epistle Liminary', his *nobility* is stressed first. As Sir Thomas Urqhart of Cromarty, he represents a lineage of such dignity that it becomes almost inconceivable that his liberty and inheritances have been taken away from him. This has happened because he has refused to conform to the ideas of *religion* then being pursued in the name of 'presbyterial government'. *Politically*, he prefers, even embodies, the older system rather than the new, apparently spiritual and democratic ways poineered by Knox. He is a man of *military* might and of *learning*, having composed these papers which will be 'the cream, the marrow and the most especial part of the book'. These values are again stressed at the end, just before the elaborate 'modesty topos' and the petition. In evaluating his case, the Government is asked to consider his *military* position as prisoner of war and his claims, as creator of the Universal Language, to have advanced *learning*. His *noble* birth is highlighted, while his position at a time of *religious* uncertainty and *political* infighting is defined as one free from 'hypocrisie, covetousness and tergiversation'.

The major appeal, therefore, is, as in almost all pieces of classical epideictic oratory after Aristotle, to the subject's virtue. The form is circular, with the same five major grounds for praise appearing at the end as at the beginning. The initial claim to a 'compositive' procedure is justified, for each of the latter statements is specifically related to one of the axioms set out near the beginning. And of course, in the interim each of the lines of eulogy has been carefully developed by a process involving praise, blame and comparison.

Five major set pieces, extremely varied in form, establish the positive side of the case. The genealogy, taken over in detail from *A Peculiar Promptuary of Time*, immediately establishes, for those who have eyes to see, that here is a man of noble family;[69] one whose lot since the Creation of the world has been to mix with and counsel the greatest in many lands. Any crimes committed against him are rendered more odious by the standing of his ancestors.

He is also a man of military prowess, never having been forced to flee in battle before Worcester. As such, he has a further line of powerful Scottish 'ancestors'. The long lists of successful Scottish soldiers are not solely an attempt to restore Scotland's national pride. The narrator has warned us that this 'treatise . . . imparts beyond what is primarily expressed in it', and from that point of view their courage is a reflection of Urquhart's own.[70] Similarly, the varied lists of academics, scientists and men of letters act as a mirror for that omnicompetent thinker and writer, Sir Thomas Urquhart himself.

If the genealogy and the lists are means of praising Urquhart's nobility and learning, his religious attitudes — perhaps the principal cause of his present situation — are also considered in a set piece, as direct as the others have been indirect:

> Nor shall we need to think it strange that in the world there are so many several religions, if we consider that the divers temperaments of our bodies alter our inclinations, from whose disparity arise repugnant laws which long obedience makes it seem a sacriledge to violate. In my opinion truly there is nothing more natural than veriety etc. (p. 160)

An attack on the narrow-mindedness of the fanatical Covenanters follows; but the conclusion returns to a less bitter, more *laissez-faire* outlook, enabling Urquhart to oppose his true enemies while, to a degree, seeking to placate Cromwell.

His known political views — the need to strengthen the alliance with England, particularly through a union of Parliaments and a reform of both legal systems — are also made clear, this time through lengthy quotations from the speeches of Francis Bacon.[71] The narrator applauds and adds judicious comments, all of which would doubtless have pleased the ambitious revolutionary government to which they were actually being addressed.

Through genealogy; military and academic lists; a direct plea from the narrator; and the quoted oratory of Bacon, the positive sides of Urquhart's position are variously promoted. Each is, in its own way, a set piece, although the academic list in particular shows that tendency to formlessness and digressive tediousness for which the narrator has previously apologized. The rhetoric of 'blame', however, runs like a *leitmotiv* throughout the work, becoming more intensely personal as Urquhart's own case comes more regularly to the centre of the stage. The focus is unrelievedly on the Presbyterians, and from the outset Urquhart's wide range of vocabulary bombards them mercilessly. The main charge is that they have besmirched Scotland's reputation by preventing today's would-be heroes from matching the standards attained by their predecessors. Towards the end of the treatise, however, these hypothetical, oppressed, unfulfilled, thwarted heroes have become largely identified with Sir Thomas himself, and their antagonists with his known enemies. The three ungrateful preachers, for example, have their feet very firmly set in Cromarty, and their viciousness has apparently been directed solely at its puzzled, benevolent laird.

The five levels of judgement remain. The Presbyterians are accused of disdaining inherited titles, trying to demand unfair rents from landholders, and generally denying to the nobility any part in the new scheme of things. No new martial leaders of any note have emerged, not because of a new-found cowardice rampant in Scotland but because presbyterian self-interest has turned the glorious international warfare of yesteryear into petty civil wars. When creating his lists of scientific and literary men, the narrator frequently breaks off to indicate how few if any are Presbyterians; while the limitatons of that creed on freedom of thought are also highlighted. Politically, their parochialism and pettiness are consciously set against Bacon's open-minded statesmanship. Above all, their religion is bitterly attacked as a means by which untalented, selfish men may scratch their way towards temporal power. Presbyterian greed is discussed not only because it is the antithesis of Christianity's highest ideal — charity — but because it suits Urquhart's personal cause to do so. The narrator draws on his considerable resources of vocabulary to strengthen this condemnation:

> those *quomodocunquizing* cluster-fists and rapacious varlets have given of late such cannibal-like proofs by their inhumanity and obdurate carriage towards some whose shos' strings they are not worthy to unty; that were it not that a more able pen then mine will assuredly not faile to jerke them on all sides, in case, by their better demeanor for the future, they endeavor not to wipe off the blot wherewith their native country, by their sordid avarice and miserable baseness, hath been so foully stained, I would at this very instant blaze them out in their names and surnames, notwithstanding the vizard of Presbyterian zeal wherewith they marke themselves, that like so many wolves, foxes or Athenian Timons, they might in all time coming be debarred the benefit of any honest conversation. (p. 55)

If the praises of Urquhart (and hence of Scotland) are methodically and powerfully advanced, the forces threatening to frustrate him (it) are vilified as comprehensively, and with even more verbal inventiveness. The 'allegoric' method[72] enables his case to be equated with that of Scotland generally and his achievements to be prefigured through comparison with earlier redoubtable Scotsmen. Some he is clearly superior to. In intellect, if not necessarily in native wit, he surpasses Francis Sinclair, for whom 'astronomy might have signified something to eat', while his lack of ruthless political ambition places him abóve William Alexander, Earl of Stirling. Others, like Alexander Ross or Napier of Merchiston, may surpass him in particular qualities but lack others which form the treatise's definition of the perfect Scottish nobleman.

And this brings us to Crichton, for in him are presented to the utmost degree those five qualities singled out for eulogy. He is the perfect gentleman and courtier; a superb scholar; the invincible man of arms; the debater on all varieties of religion but follower of none; the believer in hierarchical government who nonetheless stands apart from political involvement. His story may well be based on historical truth,[73] but it is un-doubtedly adapted and romanticized so that these character-

istics stand out. Structurally, it is the high point of the narrator's
'Vindication' of Scotland and Urquhart; being given the degree
of detailed consideration fitting for such a purpose. It occupies
almost a quarter of the whole work, and is carefully positioned so
as to dominate its centre; it is endowed with Urquhart's finest,
most poetic prose. But it also suggests a parallel with the
discussion of the Language which precedes it. Freeing Urquhart
from his many enemies will produce not only a breakthrough in
philosophy; it will also, hypothetically, permit our hero to
develop into another Crichton, conferring on the court of
Cromwell all the glory achieved by the latter for Mantua.

The Jewel, then, is in all these ways a carefully planned piece
of eulogistic rhetoric. The circular argumentative structure, the
clever use of a supposedly sympathetic narrative persona, the
consistent application of the rhetoric of praise and blame to a
limited number of themes, the correlation throughout between
Urquhart's fate and Scotland's, and the extended analyses of the
Universal Language (demonstrating what Urquhart can do)
and Crichton's character (illustrating what Urquhart can be),
each has its part to play in the intended glorification of the
Knight of Cromarty. A year later he would be using in
Logopandecteision a somewhat different form and a more
desperately personal approach. But for the majority of his
readers, no doubt, *The Jewel* will remain his most complex and
most satisfying 'rhapsody in praise of self'.

III

The development of Urquhart's rhetorical techniques which we
have been examining is paralleled by another, in vocabulary
and style. Nothing could be more straightforward than the
diction and stylistic patterning of his early *Epigrams*:

> Let never want of money vexe your braine,
> Seeing all contentment is in th'only mind;
> To the which mony doth no more pertaine
> Then to the hierarchies of angel-kind:
>> Thus gold being earthly, and the mind sublime,
>> T'abase your spirit is a sort of crime. (*Works*, p. 38)

The rhetorical skill of such pieces lies in the balanced restraint which is most evident in the opposition of 'gold' and 'mind' in the penultimate line, and in the neatness of the final couplet. While the thought never rises much above the banal, the *Epigrams* are at their best notable for this simple elegance. They contrast, in this respect, with the dedicatory letter to the Marquis of Hamilton which precedes the collection, which provides an early example of the intricacy of Urquhart's prose syntax:

> And what others, bot being able to reach into, have therefore admired in the Legend of the Worthies hath, since the yeeres of discretion, bin the constant object of your dailie exercise, and complyed with your very most neglected cogitations; which glorious and rare endowments, out-reaching the extent of vulgar goodnesse, and seeing the more wonderfull that it is not long since by your birth you did grace the world with the honour of your presence, doe possesse the faculties of my soul with a stedfast resolution so unfainedly to acknowledge the absolute right your Lordship hath over me and the inclinations of my mind that, as I cannot impart that portion of the fruits thereof to any which by a prior disposition is not already yours, so may not I, though the matter be but small, without breach of duty devote this Dedication to another. (*Works*, p. 4)

The decorum of dedicatory letters no doubt governs the complex structure and elevated diction here, but Urquhart appears throughout his prose writings to be most at home in this vein and he seldom abandons the Latinate periodic sentence which dominates this early letter and which rises to a peak of rhetorical display in the eulogistic arias of *The Jewel*.

Nowhere is the high style more consistently exemplified than in the account of the life and death of Crichton, in which whole paragraphs are made up of such rolling periods marked by complex metaphors and elaborate parenthetical statements. The balance which in its simple form was characteristic of the *Epigrams* now appears in a more complex guise among strings of images and subordinate clauses, as at the end of one of Urquhart's most outrageous sentences, describing audience reactions to Crichton's one-man performance at the court of Mantua:

> ... one of my lady dutchess' chief maids of honour, by the vehemencie of the shock of those incomprehensible raptures, burst forth into a laughter to the rupture of a veine in her body; and another young lady, by the irresistible violence of the pleasure unawares infused, where the tender receptibilitie of her too too tickled fancie was least able to hold out, so unprovidedly was surprised that, with no less impetuositie of ridibundal passion then as hath been told occasioned a fracture in the other young ladie's modestie, she, not being able longer to support the well-beloved burthen of so excessive delight and intransing joys of such mercurial exhilarations, through the ineffable extasie of an overmastered apprehension fell back in a swoon without the appearance of any other life into her then what by the most refined wits of theological speculators is conceived to be exerced by the purest parts of the separated entelechies of blessed saints in their sublimest conversations with the celestial hierarchies. This accident procured the incoming of an apothecarie with restoratives as the other did that of a surgeon with consolidative medicaments. (p. 117)

This passage, which comes at the end of a sentence which is actually three times as long as the portion just quoted, carefully interweaves the circumstances of the two young women who are overcome by Crichton's thespian talents, a balance which is reinforced by the introduction of the apothecary and the surgeon. But other features of Urquhart's techniques are equally evident: each noun seems to bring with it an even more striking adjective, every main clause is punctuated with adverbial phrase or participial construction, and the hyperbolic statement of the second young lady's swoon is embodied in a splendid theological comparison with 'the separated entelechies of blessed saints'. Against all this elaborate exaggeration there is the informal phrase 'too too tickled fancie', which neatly lightens the tone and reminds us of the real nature of the occasion upon which so much rhetorical effort is being lavished. In truth, the medium here *is* the message, for the outrageous rhetoric of

Urquhart's description is undoubtedly intended to mirror the outrageousness of the thespian display which is being ascribed to Crichton, which earns him the love of the young prince of Mantua's mistress, and which is thus the mainspring of the action as well as being a measure of the hero's virtues as a courtier.

Elsewhere, elaborate sentence structure is more modestly applied to more straightforward ends. Even the relatively functional prose of the introduction to the Universal Language, for example, illustrates some of the same features:

> Thus is it that, as according to the largeness of the plat of a building and compactedness of its walls, the workmaster contriveth his roofs, platforms, outjettings and other such like parts and portions of the whole; just so, conform to the extent and reach which a language in its flexions and compositions hath obtained at first, have the sprucest linguists hitherto bin pleased to make use of the words thereto belonging. (p. 66)

It is the management of such sentences which demonstrates the lucidity underlying Urquhart's more flamboyant passages; and it is striking that for all its complexity his prose seldom shows signs of any loss of control. The analogy between the builder and the linguistic craftsman is one which tells us a good deal about Urquhart's own approach to composition. The engineering of the sentence quoted above, turning on the fulcrum of 'just so' and balancing 'according to' and 'conform to' in order to develop the argument, reveals a strong sense of order, without which the more elaborate rhetoric of the set pieces would certanly crack and bring the whole syntactical structure down in ruins.

In diction, as in syntax, there are marked contrasts within *The Jewel*. The attention to detail with which Urquhart treats his subject matter frequently draws him into densely packed specialist vocabulary, as in parts of his exposition of the Universal Language, in his account of Crichton's dramatic performance, or in the combat which leads to his death. Coupled with this use of jargon is a more general characteristic of Urquhart's prose: in *The Jewel*, more than any other of his works, is manifested an almost obsessive fascination with learned coinages and foreign borrowings of all kinds. Almost every page of *The Jewel* affords examples of these traits, but again they are more concentrated (as one would expect) in those passages which are rhetorically most elaborate:

> ... [Crichton] did by their assistance so conglomerate, shuffle, mix and interlace the gestures, inclinations, actions and very tones of the speech of those fifteen several sorts of men whose carriages he did personate into an inestimable *ollapodrida* of immaterial morsels of divers kinds, suitable to the very ambrosian relish of the Heliconian nymphs, that in the peripetia of this drammatical exercitation, by the inchanted transportation of the eyes and eares of its spectabundal auditorie, one would have sworne that they all had looked with multiplying glasses ... (p. 116)

The variety of Urquhart's vocabulary is represented in full by this passage: the learned joke of 'spectabundal auditorie' (viewing hearers) is reinforced by the Latinate phrasing, the Spanish term *ollapodrida*[74] fits incongruously beside 'inestimable' and 'immaterial', while the rhetorical term 'peripetia' is naturally linked with the Latinism 'exercitation'. The juxtaposition of 'conglomerate' and 'shuffle', moreover, illustrates the way in which Urquhart frequently introduces a more colloquial word where it will have its most striking effect. The eclecticism of *The Jewel*'s style is as important as its fantastic exaggeration; no source of vocabulary is ignored in enhancing the 'copiousness' of Urquhart's language. We may have to wait until the details of the Universal Language have been published to acquire a perfect philosophical medium, but in the meantime the author does everything he can to develop the rhetorical possibilities of English.

And it must be emphasized that it is *English* in which *The Jewel* was written. Proud Scot though Urquhart was, there are few traces of his origins in his language, and throughout his works he proves how far English had supplanted Scots as the medium of serious writing in Scotland. Occasional Scotticisms have, however, slipped through, perhaps unnoticed by the printer: the legal term 'thereanent' occurs in the exposition of the logical structure of the Universal Language, and is soon followed by the distinctively north-eastern form 'moneth' for 'month', which seems to have been a regular feature of Urquhart's linguistic repertoire.[75] There seems, indeed, to be a relative concentration of Scottish terms at about this point, for 'blitery', which twice appears in variant spellings nearby, is very probably derived from the abusive Scots noun 'bluiter'.[76] But these isolated occurrences are hardly enough to give even this part of *The Jewel* anything like a Scottish flavour. Like most of his literary contemporaries, Urquhart had abandoned — largely, no doubt, in search of a wider audience, as is clear from the fact that all his works were published in London — the Scots literary tradition which had flourished into the reign of James VI.

The language of *The Jewel*, like all its other rhetorical features, is designed to put its author in a favourable light, to demonstrate his learning and his wit, and to heighten the oratorical effect of the ironically distanced eulogy of Sir Thomas Urquhart which is its controlling theme. The ease with which classical sources and medieval tags are alike worked into the argument, the learned coinages and borrowings, the elaborate and lucid syntax: all contribute to the force of Urquhart's prose style and embody the estimate of his worth which is explicitly argued by the narrator. The final, characteristic stroke is the hyperbolic exhaustiveness with which the narrator enumerates the rhetorical figures he *might* have used, had he not been content to let Sir Thomas' merits speak for themselves:

> All those figures and tropes besides what are not here mentioned (these synecdochically standing for all, to shun the tediousness of a too prolix enumeration) I could have adhibited to the embellishment of this tractate, had not the matter it self been more prevalent with me then the superficial formality of a quaint discourse. (p. 206)

Even here the parenthesis is introduced to draw our attention to the care with which the author has avoided prolixity, at the end of one of the most prolix passages in the whole work, and at the very moment of forswearing 'superficial formality'. The rhetoric which denies itself is the last, and almost the most daring, version of Urquhart's authorial vanishing trick; and like the Universal Language which can never be, it demonstrates better than any formal proof the fantastic wit and unbounded *amour*

36

propre of Sir Thomas Urquhart of Cromarty, knight, soldier, scholar, gentleman and Royalist, a man whose imagination was certainly too great for the age in which he lived.

1. *Calendar of State Papers: Domestic* (1651), p. 433.
2. Ibid., p. 446.
3. Ibid., p. 465.
4. *Calendar of State Papers: Domestic* (1651–2), p. 332; (1652–3), p. 33.
5. The etymology of 'quire' (from Lat. *quaternion*) implies four sheets, so that 116½ quires would amount to a minimum of 466 sheets; but by the seventeenth century it had also come to refer to a papermaker's measure of 24–25 sheets, which would give a figure close to 3,000 sheets in total.
6. *Fasti Aberdonensis* (Spalding Club, Aberdeen 1854), p. 457. Lunan himself had matriculated in 1611, ibid., p. 453.
7. See below, p. 164.
8. *Logopandecteision*, VI, 49, *Works* (Maitland Club, Edinburgh 1834), p. 402. All references to Urquhart's works other than *The Jewel* are drawn from this edition.
9. *Reg. Mag. Sig.* (1634–51), no. 534.
10. Cf. *Logopandecteision*, V, 28–53, *Works*, pp. 378–84.
11. Cf. *Reg. Mag. Sig.* (1634–51), nos. 543, 546, 566.
12. The case is discussed by John Willcock, *Sir Thomas Urquhart of Cromartie* (Edinburgh 1899), pp. 16–17; and Henrietta Tayler, *The History of the Family of Urquhart* (Aberdeen 1946), pp. 38–9. Cf. *Reg. Privy Council*, vi, 485–6.
13. *Reg. Mag. Sig.* (1634–51), no. 739.
14. *Reg. Privy Council*, vi, 414.
15. See Willcock, op. cit., pp. 15–16.
16. *Reg. Privy Council*, vi, 430.
17. *Works*, p. 336.
18. For a succinct exposition of these events and their background, see Gordon Donaldson, *Scotland: James V to James VII* (Edinburgh 1965), pp. 307–16.
19. James Gordon: *History of Scots Affairs* (Spalding Club, 3 vols., Aberdeen 1841), I, 61.
20. John Spalding: *Memorialls of the Trubles in Scotland and in England* (Spalding Club, 2 vols., Aberdeen 1850), I, 181.

21. Ibid., I, 182.

22. Ibid., I, 192.

23. See below, p. 172.

24. This manuscript was first noticed in *Scottish Journal of Topography* 1 (1847–8), 201–2, having recently been sold by the Earl of Hyndford. It was later in the possession of Professor Ferguson of the University of Glasgow, by whose permission it was seen by John Willcock, who describes it, op. cit., pp. 116–17. It was sold by Sotheby's on 17 November 1920, eventually passing into the collection of James S. Osborn, now housed in the Beinecke Library, Yale University.

25. The list is given by Willcock, op. cit., p. 116. In addition to those thus favoured, many other figures about the court are the recipients of individual epigrams. It is a curious feature of the MS. in its present state that the names of individuals have in most cases been obliterated.

26. *Works*, p. 172.

27. This remarkable engraving, then in the collection at Craigston Castle, was printed by Henrietta Tayler, op. cit.; the original is now in the National Library of Scotland.

28. Sir Thomas senior was described as 'umquhill' on 14 June 1642, *Annals of Banff*, ii, 418.

29. *Calendar of Proceedings of the Committee for Advance of Money 1642–56* (3 vols., London 1888), i, 381.

30. *Works*, pp. 55–8.

31. SRO, RS 5/19, ff. 423^r–424^v.

32. *APS*, vi, 37.

33. Willcock, op. cit., pp. 72–4.

34. NLS, Wodrow MSS, Quarto MS. II, ff. 66–7.

35. *General Assembly Commission Records*, ii, 243.

36. Buchanan's history was reprinted at Frankfurt in 1624 and at Amsterdam in 1643, while that of Hector Boece, by far the most fanciful account, was twice reprinted in Paris in 1574 and 1575 and formed the basis of parts of the *Respublica* published in Amsterdam in 1627.

37. *Logopandecteision*, V, 35, *Works*, p. 380.

38. The first two books were published as separate volumes in 1653; Motteux edited the third for his 1693 version, and added his own translation of Books IV and V the following year.

39. For the earlier history of the Scottish trading settlement at Middelburg, see M. P. Roseboom: *The Scottish Staple in the Netherlands*. (The Hague, 1910).

40. Reg. Sasines Aberdeen, SRO, RS 5/21, ff. 279^r–281^v.

41. *Calendar of State Papers: Domestic* (1660–1), p. 237.

42. *APS*, vii, 70–1.

43. *Works*, p. 49.

44. Cf. Huntington Brown: *Rabelais in English Literature* (Cambridge, Mass. 1933); F. C. Roe: *Sir Thomas Urquhart and Rabelais*, (Oxford, 1957).

45. Willcock, op. cit., p. 111.

46. The selection of moral epigrams which Urquhart made for publication clearly involved the elimination of everything trivial or risque, and the inevitable consequence is the moralistic stuffiness which pervades the printed collection.

47. See the analysis by Richard Boston in the introduction to his selections, *The Admirable Urquhart* (London, 1975). Urquhart expresses his debt to Napier of Merchiston in his introductory address 'To the Reader', *Works*, pp. 59–60.

48. Notably the argument that this mathematical treatise reveals Urquhart's skill as a poet and orator just as surely as 'his elaboured poems' show him a philosopher and mathematician. He argues for this interconnection in other works both explicitly and by the use of mathematical similes or exempla; cf. also his taste for 'cyphral' poems.

49. *The Poems of Robert Henryson*, Denton Fox (Ed.) (Oxford 1981), p. 132.

50. Willcock, op. cit., p. 132.

51. The earliest documentary evidence which supports Urquhart's genealogy is a charter of David II, dated 1358, in favour of Adam Urquhart, whose father was apparently named William: v. Tayler, op. cit., pp. 16–17.

52. Willcock, p. 144. Rabelaisian echoes in *The Jewel* indicate that Urquhart knew *Gargantua* and *Pantagruel* before 1652; cf. Brown, op. cit., pp. 119–20.

53. There are some superficial parallels between *The Jewel* and the Marquis of Worcester's *A Century of Inventions* (London, 1663), but the Marquis lacks Urquhart's rhetorical inventiveness and eccentric imagination.

54. Charles Whibley, *Studies in Frankness* (London, 1910), p. 254.

55. See E. R. Curtius, *European Literature and the Latin Middle Ages, trans.* W. R. Trask (New York, 1953), pp. 83–5.

56. For a full discussion of the Idea of Praise in the Renaissance and the rhetorical conventions behind it, see Oscar B. Hardison Jr, *The Enduring Monument* (Chapel Hill, 1962).

57. On the etymology of Urquhart's 'Greek' title, to which the author himself contributed a fascinating commentary while the book was still in the press, see below pp. 211–12, and 215.

58. See Willcock, op. cit., p. 96: 'His hopes and anticipations ... were not daunted by the fact that to do what he required would need several legislative changes, a reversal of proceedings in Scottish courts of law, and a substantial grant from the Treasury'.

59. *Poetria Nova of Geoffrey of Vinsauf*, trans.; Margaret F. Nims (Toronto, 1967), p. 17.

60. See below, pp. 211–12.

61. The alternative is to believe that Urquhart deliberately falsified his 'fragment' by creating the impression of an omission, already intending to make good the deleted section on a subsequent occasion. Even by the standards of Urquhart's elaborate fictions, this does not seem likely.

62. For an authoritative account of the background to Urquhart's linguistic views, see James Knowlson, *Universal Language Schemes in England and France 1600–1800* (Toronto, 1975).

63. Lodwick's work is printed, with a careful account of its context, in *The Works of Francis Lodwick*, Vivian Salmon (Ed.) (London, 1972).

64. Lodwick, *The Ground-work*, ibid., pp. 204–5.

65. See also Vivian Salmon, 'Language-Planning in Seventeenth-Century England: Its Context and Aims', *In Memory of J. R. Firth*, ed. C. E. Bazell *et. al.*, (London, 1966), pp. 370–97, reprinted in *The Study of Language in Seventeenth-Century England* (Amsterdam, 1979), pp. 129–56.

66. On Dalgarno, see Vivian Salmon, 'The Evolution of Dalgarno's *Ars signorum* (1661)', *Studies in Language and Literature in Honour of Margaret Schlauch* (Warsaw, 1966), pp. 153–71, and *The Study of Language*, pp. 157–75; and J. D. McClure, 'The "Universal Languages" of Thomas Urquhart and George Dalgarno', *Actes du 2ᵉ Colloque de Langue et de Litterature Ecossaises (Moyen Age et Renaissance)* ed. J.-J. Blanchot and C. Graf (Strasbourg, 1979), pp. 133–47.

67. Vivian Salmon (Ed.): *The Works of Francis Lodwick*, p. 28.

68. Hardison, op. cit., p. 31.

69. And for those who proved impervious to the subtle approach, Urquhart thoughtfully provides an advertisement for his earlier work (see below, p. 57).

70. It should be noted that the order in which these lists are presented is determined by the country in which the officers spent most of their military career. This provides the overall control argued for above.

71. Bacon did not only share Urquhart's political opinions; he also initiated, as we have seen, the seventeenth-century interest in the creation of a Universal Language.

72. Urquhart's work clearly stops short of formal allegory, yet there is a sense in which the misfortunes of the author are identified with the misfortunes of his country, both coming together in the disaster at Worcester.

73. See Patrick Tytler, *Life of the Admirable Crichton* (Edinburgh, 1823).

74. The term means literally 'a rotten pot', and was known in English as the name of a popular Spanish dish by the end of the sixteenth

century. Its metaphoric use is attested by Thomas Randolph in *The Muse's Looking-glass* (London, 1634), where it is a synonym for 'medley'.

75. It occurs also in Urquhart's letter to the Earl of Leven, dated from Middelburg on 20 September 1655 (see below, Appendix, p. 46).

76. See below, p. 220.

APPENDIX I

Unpublished Letters of Sir Thomas Urquhart

[See also the long letter from Urquhart to his cousin John Urquhart of Craigfintray, edited by C. H. Wilkinson as *A Challenge from Sir Thomas Urquhart* (Luttrell Reprints no. 4, Oxford, 1948).]

1. To Robert Farquhar of Mounie, 18 December 1648

Much honored freind, wnderstanding by Mr Thomas McKenzie þat you haue his band for four hundreth merks for his entrie to the lands off Ballacuth, quhich he thinkes too much being bot a compryser *wi*thout possessione, for a litle somme off money not haueing a purpose to enjoy the land; and besyds because not long since my wmq*uhi*ll f*ath*yr gott ane entre from the present heritor theroff; and being certainly informed be Mr Thomas þat you promeised him quhateuer ease off the sayd somme I wald giue him, you wald condiscend to it, I will request you to accept off tuo hundreth merks and to giue him his band off four hundreth for besyds diuerse o þ*er* respects in my absence off the Cuntrey he was at paines and charges in our affaires as my bro þ*er* Dunlugus knoues, so þat we suld deale courteously vith him. And so exspecting you will doo me this favour quhich in accompt salbe taken from yow by your

wery lowing frend
to doe you service

Cromerty þis Monday   Tho: Urquhart.
the 18th of Decemb. 1648

2. To Mr Robert Douglas, Moderator of the General Assembly

Richt reverend,

Least my being accessorie to the late unvarrantable undertaking at Invernes should make me be loked upon as one that hath not given satisfaction to the kirk with whom abow all I intend to keipe a good understanding, and altho I was unhappilie engadged þerin be reason of the high and exasperating provocationes of Sir James Fraser, governour þerof, which in some measure might have excused me, I having had then itself no evall designe aganst the church or state and at no tyme befor, not so much as in show, bene contrary to the proposed course of aithas as by the enclosed testificat from our presbitrie will be the bettir evidenced unto your reverence; and that at the very first intimation made by the state of ther dislike þerof I deperted the course offered my self to the generall livetennant, and accordingly obtaned his papir of abolition reseating me in the same integritie in matir of life and fortune that formerly I was in, there remaineing only now my immatriculation to the kirk; and doubting that my being estimated in qualitie abow a captane or livetennant mey procure the chargeing of me southwards which pro loco et tempore becaus of the many dormant captiones that for my father*is* debt ly undeservedly gapeing to ensnare me, I would willingly declyne and thairfor bege of your reverence the favour to grant me a reference to this our presbitrie of the Chanonry of Ross, with a prescription of the maner of the satisfaction 3ow would haue me to mak, who am

3our reverences
most humble & most affectionat
servant
Tho: Urquhart

Chanonrie of Ros, þe 14
November 1649.

*NLS, Wodrow MSS, Quarto MS. II,
ff. 66ʳ–67ʳ.*

3. *To Robert Farquhar of Mounie, 30 July 1653*

Sir,

I received your letter, and according to your desire therein shall doe what lyes in me for oftaking the sequestration, which the publicke affaires of this land togither with an inward grudge against our country in general hath hitherto retarded. You wrote to me that the laird of Innes clameth right to some of the quarter tiths of Cromartie, but for all the mischief Dundasse hath done I can shew tasks upon them. If you have got a charge from the Laird of Innes send me the copie thereof, and I shall doe my best to rack his title. I will forbeare to speak more till I see what further proceiding he makes because I am not very apt to beleeve that a man of his experience, and repute will in such a calamitous time medle with what concernes him not, to the prejudice of those whom he is bound by many ties to doe rather good then bad office to.

Sir,

I am

London, this Saterday
the 30th of Julie 1653

Your assured friend
to doe you service
Tho: Urquhart

*Beinecke Library, Gordonstoun
Papers, Box I.*

4. *To Mr John Macronald, Advocate, 29 December 1653*

Worthie friend,

Your letter after it [was] brought hither was long keept before it came to my hands, the change of governement having occasioned for awhile both a seazing on packets and stop in the posts. I am glad of your late returne to Edinburgh, and know that my adversaries took advantage of your absence, but I hope it shall not at last make much for them, for the depositions of the witnesses were utterly false, which I can prove when I see them. Let me intreat you, Master Macronald, to haue a special care of those papers of mine I left with you, that when I goe to Ed*inburgh*

I may have them either from yourself or someone else in your absence. I would gladly heare from Lesmirtie, to whom I several times have writen without any answer from him. I beseech you let me heare from you concerning Lethintie. The Laird of Belnagoune was buryed this day; he dyed three days agoe of a disease which held him twentie days, it being a kind of consumption.

London, this Thirsday   Your Loving and assured friend,
the 29 Dec. 1653.   Tho: Urquhart.

*SRO**

5. To Mr John Macronald, Advocate, 14 January 1654.

Worthie Sir,

This is now the fourth letter I have written to you since you came to Ed*inburgh*. If they have not come to your hands I can not help it; for the post gets them heer from me. In case the direction be not right upon the back advertise me by your nixt how it should be. Let me know whether you have got an answer from Mr Livingston or no, of the letter you intrusted to me. As for answer to Sir Robert Farquhars letter he shall have it the nixt week with a cosen of his owne, one Forbas, unto whom he hath written to that effect. I pray you write her to me *if* ther be a garison in Cromartie and *if* as it is reported heer my Lord Keanmore hath taken eleven of the English foot colours, and where that was [done]. I wrote to Doctor Ogston twice since I received any answer from him. Ther is nothing heer but revolutions which makes all particular businesses to be the more retarded. Not forgetting my recommendation to Mr Summer I remaine

London, this Saterday,   Your loving and assured friend
the 14th of Jan. 1653/4.   Tho: Urquhart.

*SRO**

* Transcribed from photostats in the Beinecke Library where the SRO reference is given as 'Report of 1806, p. 33, xxix, nos. 171–172'.

My lord, may it please your excellence,

That unto which at London I had purchased in behalf of Colonel Jhon Urquhart the subscriptions of so many noble and worthie men being rather a certificat of his descent then a borebrief, and by several letters which since my comming to Holland I have received from the Colonel, perceiving in him an exceeding great desire to have his borebrief dispatched and sent unto him in as ample and splendid a manner as may be, I have thought good to make bold to inclose heerin my letter to Sir James Balfour togither with the Colonel[s'] genealogie or Extraction insert within it, both which when your Excell*ence* hath been pleased to peruse my humble intreatie is your Excell*ence* would vouchsafe to move Sir James to dispatch the said pedigree or borebrief with all the exactness and hast that may be. As for the charge and expence thereof let me request your Excellencie to disburse it, and what ever it amount it, it shall upon the Recette of the note thereof be payed within three moneths after in what place and to whomsoever you shall be pleased to appoint to receive it. Your Excellence may be pleased to advise what seals togither with Sir James Balfours oune are fit to be appended to the parchment thereof. I shall with impatience attend your Excellencies answer which if I be not so happie as to get speedily, I will be forced to presume to importune your Excellencie at every occasion with copies of the same.

My Lord,

I am
Your excellences
Most humble and most affectionat

Midleburgh in Zealand,
servant,

This monday the 10/20 of Sept. 1655.
Tho: Urquhart.

SRO, GD 26/13/267.

A NOTE ON THE TEXT

This edition is based on the first (1652) edition of *The Jewel*. Except in cases of uncertainty or special interest the abbreviations of the original have been expanded without notice. Evident typographical errors have been silently emended; in a few cases of particular interest, difficult or unusual readings are discussed in the Commentary. Urquhart and his printer consistently mark the plurals of foreign words with ''s': in such cases, the apostrophe had been silently deleted. In all other respects punctuation has been modernized and a more regular paragraph division introduced. The original spelling has been maintained, but 'i' and 'j', 'u', 'v' and 'w' have been normalized.

In the 1652 edition, a number of 'Errata' are noted immediately after the Genealogy. The new readings have been introduced into the present edition, usually without comment. With the exception of the substitution of 'execute' for 'live' (see below, p. 105), these corrections are all of a minor nature.

The Discovery of
A most exquisite Jewel

ΕΚΣΚΥΒΑΛΑΥΡΟΝ[1]:
OR,
The Discovery of
A moſt exquiſite JEWEL,
more precious then Diamonds
inchaſed in Gold, the like whereof
was never ſeen in any age; found in the
kennel of *Worceſter*-ſtreets, the day
after the Fight, and ſix before the Autumnal Æquinox[2] *anno* 1651.

Serving in this place,

To frontal a VINDICATION
of the honour of *SCOTLAND*,
from that Infamy, whereinto the Rigid
Presbyterian party of that Nation,
out of their Covetouſneſs and
ambition, moſt diſſembled-
ly hath involved it.

Diſtichon ad Librum ſequitur, quo tres ter adæquant
Muſarum numerum, caſus, & articuli.[3]

voc. *nom.* 1 *abl.* 2 *abl.* *dat.*
O thou'rt a Book in truth with love to many,
3 *abl.* 4 *abl.* *acc.* *gen.*
Done by and for the free'ſt-ſpoke *Scot* of any.

Efficiens & finis ſunt ſibi invicem cauſæ.[4]

LONDON, Printed by *Ja: Cottrel*; and are to
be ſold by *Rich. Baddely*, at the Middle-
Temple-gate. 1652.

[THE 1652 EDITION OF *THE JEWEL*]

Title page. The title page of the 1652 edition of *The Jewel* is reproduced opposite. The area enclosed by the surrounding single rule is 130 × 74 mm.

Formula. 8vo: A⁸, a⁸, B–T⁸, ****²; [$1–4 (–A1, a4, L3) signed]. Pp. [1–32], 1–284, [1–8] (some mis-pagination in quire D).

Contents. A1 title (verso blank); A2ʳ–a4ʳ The Epistle Liminary, signed Christianus Presbyteromastix; a4ᵛ–a5ᵛ The names of the chiefs of the name of Urquhart, and of their primitive fathers . . . [begins with 1 Adam, and ends 153 Sir Thomas, printed in double columns]; a6ʳ–a7ʳ The names of the mothers of the chiefs . . . [begins with 1 Eva, and ends 146 Christian, in double columns]; a7ᵛ [errata]; a8 [blank]; B1–T8 text; on T8ᵛ, 'FINIS.'; ****1–2 [errata 3 lines, follows on address beginning: "it having been told to me that the title word of this book is absurd. . . ." etc. Contents of ****1–2 from *Bibl. Aberdonensis* entry].

References. Wing U134; J. F. K. Johnstone and A. W. Robertson, *Bibliographia Aberdonensis*, vol. 2, p. 362. (Sir Thomas Urquhart is accepted as author by these sources, the British Museum Catalogue and the National Union Catalogue).

Copies. National Library of Scotland Ry.IV.h.51 (imperfect: wanting the two leaves signed ****); H.32.f.37 (imperfect: wanting a8, the two leaves signed ****; quire L misbound between M and N); L.C.1457 (imperfect: wanting a8, the two leaves signed ****; cropped); BCL.A3111 (imperfect: wanting T8, the two leaves signed ****).

Other locations. British Library; Bodleian; Dulwich College; Glasgow University Library (according to *Bibl. Aberdonensis* this copy has the two leaves signed ****); Folger Shakespeare Library (according to the *Catalog of printed books* this copy is known to want the two leaves signed ****); Newberry Library; Harvard; Yale; Princeton; Henry E. Huntington Library; William Andrews Clark Memorial Library.

Kennel: *gutter* (See facing title page, line 8).

THE EPISTLE LIMINARY

The scope of this treatise is, for the weal of the publick in the propagation of learning and vertue throughout the whole Isle of Great Britain, in all humility to intreat the honorable Parliament of this Commonwealth, with consent of the Councel of State thereof, to grant to Sir Thomas Urquhart of Cromarty his former liberty and the enjoyment of his own inheritance, with all the immunities and priviledges thereto belonging. The reasons of this demand in an unusual, though compositive, way are so methodically deduced that their recapitulation here, how curt soever I could make it, would afford but little more compendiousness to the reader, unless all were to be summed up in this: that seeing the obtaining of his desires would be conducible to the whole land and prejudicial to no good member in it, he should therefore be favoured with the benefit of the grant thereof and refusal of nothing appertaining to it.

By reason of his being a Scotish man, a great deal therein is spoken in favor of that country and many pregnant arguments inferred for the incorporating of both nations into one, with an indissolubility of union for the future in an identity of priviledges, laws and customs. As by the praising of many the coetaneans and compatriots of his no-less-deserving predecessors, Scotland is much honored; so, to vindicate the reputation thereof from any late scandal, it is fitly represented how the miscariage of a few should not occasion an universal imputation. The unjust usurpation of the clergy, the Judaical practices of some merchants and abused simplicity of the gentry have in the mindes of forraigners engraven a discredible opinion of that nation which will never be wiped off under a Presbyterial government, for where ever it bears sway, etc. Here I must stop, for should I give way to my pen to decipher the enormities of that rule, I would, by outbulking the book with this epistle,

Liminary: *preliminary*   Compositive: *synthetic*   Coetaneans: *contemporaries*

make the porch greater then the lodging, enter into a digression longer then the purpose and outstrip the period with the parenthesis. Therefore out of that inclination which prompts me to conceal the faults of those in whom there may be any hope of a cordial penitency for having committed them, I will not at this time lanch forth into the prodigious depth of Presbyterian plots nor rip up the sores of their ecclesiastical tyranny till their implacable obduredness and unreclaimability of nature give open testimonies of their standing to their first erroneous principles and not acknowledging a subordination to a secular authority.

For the present then, it shall suffice that I bestow upon them a gentle admonition to refrain from that ambitious designe of spiritual soveraignty; or, to use the phrase of their patron Knox,[5] that I warn them with the first sound of the trumpet to give the civil magistrate his due. But if after this Diansounding they, instead of apparelling their consciences with the garment of righteousness, come forth to the field of publick affaires with their rusty armor of iniquity; then let them not blame me if, for the love of my country whose honour they have defaced and the best inhabitants whereof they have born down with oppression, I refuse not the employment of taking up banner against them and giving them a home charge with clareens under the conduct of reason and common sense, their old and inveterate enemies. Now seeing that in this introitory discourse, to avoid the excursive pomp of a too large ranging at random, I am limited to some few pages; should I employ them all to attend the Presbyter's greatness, it would argue in me great inconsideracy in preferring him to his betters. Therefore till I have the leisure to bestow a whole sheet by it self upon honest Sir John,[6] who in that kind of liberality towards the fornicator and malignant was the nonpareil of the world, that therein, as in a habit of repentance, he may be exposed to the publike view of the honest men of Scotland whom he hath so much injured, I must confine my self now to so much bounds (without more) as barely may suffice to excuse the superficial erratas both of pen and press.

This treatise, like the words of 'mass', 'dinner', 'supper' and such like, which besides the things by them signified do conno-

Diansounding: *trumpet call*   Clareens: *shrill trumpets*   Introitory: *introductory*

tate the times of morning, noon, night or any other tide or season, importing beyond what is primarily expressed in it (a certain space of time, within which unto the world should be made obvious its final promulgation), and that being but a fortnight, lest a longer delay, by not giving timely information to the state might prove very prejudicial (if not totally destructive) to the aforesaid Sir Thomas Urquhart in whose house, as he is informed by letters from thence, there is at this present an English garison,[7] and whose lands are so over-run and exhausted by these publike pressures that since he hath been a prisoner of war, which is now half a yeer, he hath not received the value of one farthing of his own means; and having designed for the press at first but five sheets, viz. the three first and some two about the latter end, I deemed the aforesaid time of two weeks of extent sufficient for encompassing a work of so short a breath. But by chance two diurnals having been brought to me, in one whereof was contained the relation of the irrational proceedings of the Presbytery of Aberdeen against Sir Alexander Irvin of Drum[8] together with his just appeal from their tyrannical jurisdiction to Colonel Overton, the then only competent judge that was there; and in the other a petition or grievance of the commons of Scotland[9] against the merciless and cruel task-masters that the Presbyterian zeal had set above them these many yeers past; wherein, whether that petition was suppositious or no, there was not any thing the truth whereof might not be testified by thousands of honest people in Scotland and ten times more of their roguery then in it is specified; and besides all that, there being nothing in the mouthes almost of all this country more common then the words of the 'perfidious Scot', the 'treacherous Scot', the 'false brother', the 'covetous Scot' and 'knot of knaves' and other suchlike indignities fixed upon the whole nation for the baseness of some — I resolved on a sudden (for the undeceiving of honest men and the imbuing of their minds with a better opinion of Scotish spirits) to insert the martial and literary endowments of some natives of that soyle, though much eclipsed by their coclimatary wasps of a Presbyterian crue.

Diurnals: *journals*   Coclimatary: *of the same region*   Wasps: *malignants*
Crue: *sty*

51

Thus my task increasing, and not being able to inlarge my time for the cause aforesaid, I was necessitated to husband it the better, to over-triple my diligence and do the work by proportion of above three dayes in the space of one; wherefore laying aside al other businesses and cooping my self up daily for some hours together betwixt the case and the printing press, I usually afforded the setter copy[10] at the rate of above a whole printed sheet in the day, which (although by reason of the smallness of a pica letter and close couching thereof, it did amount to three full sheets of my writing) the aforesaid setter nevertheless, so nimble a workman he was, would in the space of 24 hours make dispatch of the whole and be ready for another sheet. He and I striving thus who should compose fastest, he with his hand and I with my brain; and his uncasing of the letters and placing them in the composing instrument, standing for my conception; and his plenishing of the gally and imposing of the form, encountering with the supposed equivalue of my writing, we would almost every foot so jump together in this joynt expedition and so nearly overtake other in our intended course, that I was oftentimes (to keep him doing) glad to tear off parcels of ten or twelve lines apeece and give him them till more were ready; unto which he would so suddenly put an order that almost still before the ink of the writen letters was dry their representatives were, out of their respective boxes, ranked in the composing-stick; by means of which great haste, I, writing but upon the loose sheets of cording quires, which (as I minced and tore them), looking like pieces of waste paper troublesome to get rallyed after such dispersive scattredness, I had not the leisure to read what I had written till it came to a proof and sometimes to a full revise: so that, by vertue of this unanimous contest and joint emulation betwixt the theoretick and practical part, which of us should overhye other in celerity, we in the space of fourteen working-daies compleated this whole book, such as it is, from the first notion of the brain till the last motion of the press; and that without any other help on my side either of quick or dead, for books I had none nor possibly would I have made use of any, although I could have commanded them, then what (by the

Cording quires: *the two outside quires of the ream*   Rallyed: *collected, reassembled*
Overhye: *overtake through speed*

favour of God) my own judgment and fancy did suggest unto me; save so much as, by way of information, a servant of mine would now and then bring to me from some reduced officer of the primitive parliament, touching the proper names of some Scotish warriors abroad, which I was very apt to forget.

I speak not this to excuse gross faults, if there be any, nor yet to praise my owne acuteness, though there were none, but to shew that extemporaneanness in some kinde of subjects may very probably be more successeful then premeditation; and that a too punctually digested method and over-nicely selected phrase, savouring of affectation, diminish oftentimes very much of the grace that otherwayes would attend a natural ingenuity. If the State of England be pleased with this book I care neither for Zoil nor Momus;[11] but if otherwaies, then shall it displease me whose resolution from its first contrivance was willingly to submit it to their judicious censure.

It is intituled *Εκσκυβαλαυρον* because of those few sheets of Sir Thomas Urquhart's papers which were found in the kennel of Worcester streets; they being the cream, the marrow and most especial part of the book; and albeit they extend not in bulk to above two sheets and a quarter of that small letter as it lieth in an octavo size, yet that synecdochically the whole should be designed by it lacketh not its precedent: for logick sometimes is called *Dialectica* although it be but a part of logick; and that discipline which treats of the dimensions of continuate quantity named geometry, albeit how to measure the earth be fully instructed by geodesie, one of the smallest parts of that divine science. That which is properly France is not the hundreth part of the kingdom of that name. Moscovy, Fez and Morocco, though empires, have their denominations from cities of the same name; so have the Kingdoms of Leon, Toledo, Murcia, Granada, Valencia and Naples with the Isles of Mayorca, Minorca, Sardinia, Malta and Rhodes and so forth through other territories.

It mentioneth Sir Thomas Urquhart in the third person, which seldom is done by any other author in a treatise of his own penning, although Virgil said, *"Ille ego qui quondam"*;[12] and

Kennel: *gutter*   Synecdochically: *whereby a more comprehensive term is used for a less comprehensive or vice versa*   Geodesie: *land surveying*

Scaliger the younger, "*Ego sum magnus ille Josephus*".[13]
Nevertheless to satisfie the reader's curiosity and all honest men
of the Isle of Britain, rather then to write Anonymos, I will
subscribe my self,

CHRISTIANUS PRESBYTEROMASTIX[14]

The names of the chiefs[15] of the name of Urquhart and of their primitive fathers, as by authentick records and traditions they were from time to time, through the various generations of that family successively conveyed till the present yeer 1652

1	Adam 1	32	Arthmios	63	Epsephicos	94	Prosenes
2	Seth	33	Hypsegoras	64	Eutropos	95	Sosomenos
3	Enos	34	Autarces	65	Coryphaeus	96	Philalethes
4	Cainan	35	Evages	66	Etoimos	97	Thaleros
5	Mahalaleel	36	Atarbes	67	Spudaeos	98	Polyaenos
6	Jared	37	Pamprosodos	68	Eumestor	99	Cratesimachos
7	Enoch	38	Gethon	69	Griphon	100	Eunaemon
8	Methusalah	39	Holocleros	70	Emmenes	101	Diasemos
9	Lamech	40	Molin	71	Pathomachon	102	Saphenus
10	Noah	41	Epitimon	72	Anepsios	103	Bramoso
11	Japhet	42	Hypotyphos	73	Auloprepes	104	Celanas
12	Javan 1	43	Melobolon	74	Corosylos	105	Vistoso
13	Penuel	44	Propetes	75	Daetalon	106	Polido
14	Tycheros 1	45	Euplocamos	76	Beltistos	107	Lustroso
15	Pasiteles	46	Philophon	77	Horaeos	108	Chrestander
16	ESORMON	47	Syngenes	78	Orthophron	109	Spectabundo
17	Cratynter	48	Polyphrades	79	Apsicoros	110	Philodulos
18	Thrasymedes	49	Cainotomos	80	Philaplus	111	Paladino
19	Evippos	50	Rodrigo	81	Megaletor	112	Comicello
20	Cleotinus	51	Dicarches	82	Nomostor	113	Regisato
21	Litoboros	52	Exagastos	83	Astioremon	114	Arguto
22	Apodemos	53	Denapon	84	Phronematias	115	Nicarchos
23	Bathybulos	54	Artistes	85	Lutork	116	Marsidalio
24	Phrenedon	55	Thymoleon	86	Machemos	117	Hedumenos
25	Zameles	56	Eustochos	87	Stichopaeo	118	Agenor
26	Choronomos	57	Bianor	88	Epalomenos	119	Diaprepon
27	Leptologon	58	Thryllumenos	89	Tycheros 2	120	Stragayo
28	Aglaestos	59	Mellessen	90	Apechon	121	Zeron
29	Megalonus	60	Alypos	91	Enacmes	122	Polyteles
30	Evemeros	61	Anochlos	92	Javan 2	123	Vocompos
31	Callophron	62	Homognios	93	Lematias	124	Carolo

125 Endymion	133 Sir Adam	140 David	147 Alexander 1
126 Sebastian	134 Edward	141 Francis	148 Thomas 1
127 Lawrence	135 Richard	142 William 1	149 Alexander 2
128 Olipher	136 Sir Philip	143 Adam 3	150 Walter
129 Quintin	137 Robert	144 John	151 Henry
130 Goodwin	138 George	145 Sir William 2	152 Sir Thomas 2
131 Frederick	139 James	146 William 3	153 Sir Thomas 3
132 Sir Jaspar			

The names of the mothers of the chiefs of the name of Urquhart, as also of the mothers of their primitive fathers. The authority for the truth thereof being derived from the same authentick records and tradition on which is grounded the above-written genealogie of their male collaterals.

1 Eva	26 Calaglais	51 Clarabella	76 Barosa
2 Shifka	27 Theoglena	52 Eromena	77 Epimona
3 Mahla	28 Pammerissa	53 Zocallis	78 Diosa
4 Bilha	29 Floridula	54 Lepida	79 Bonita
5 Timnah	30 Chrysocomis	55 Nicolia	80 Aretusa
6 Aholima	31 Arrenopas	56 Proteusa	81 Bendita
7 Zilpa	32 Tharsalia	57 Gozosa	82 Regalletta
8 Noema	33 Maia	58 Venusta	83 Isumena
9 Ada	34 Roma	59 Prosectica	84 Antaxia
10 Titea	35 Termuth	60 Delotera	85 Bergola
11 Debora	36 Vegeta	61 Tracara	86 Viracia
12 Neginothi	37 Callimeris	62 Pothina	87 Dynastis
13 Hottir	38 Panthea	63 Cordata	88 Dalga
14 Orpah	39 Gonima	64 Aretias	89 Eutocusa
15 Axa	40 Ganymena	65 Musurga	90 Corriba
16 Narfesia	41 Thespesia	66 Romalia	91 Praecelsa
17 Goshenni	42 Hypermnestra	67 Orthoiusa	92 Plausidica
18 Briageta	43 Horatia	68 Recatada	93 Donosa
19 Andronia	44 Philumena	69 Chariestera	94 Solicaelia
20 Pusena	45 Neopis	70 Rexenora	95 Bontadosa
21 Emphaneola	46 Thymelica	71 Philerga	96 Calliparia
22 Bonaria	47 Ephamilla	72 Thomyris	97 Creleuca
23 Peninah	48 Porrima	73 Varonilla	98 Pancala
24 Asymbleta	49 Lampedo	74 Stranella	99 Dominella
25 Carissa	50 Teleclyta	75 Aequanima	100 Mundula

101 Pamphais	113 Lampusa	125 Dorothy	136 Rosalind
102 Philtrusa	114 Vistosa	126 Lawretta	137 Lillias
103 Meliglena	115 Hermosina	127 Genivieve	138 Brigid
104 Philetium	116 Bramata	128 Marjory	139 Agnes
105 Tersa	117 Zaglopis	129 Jane	140 Susanna
106 Dulcicora	118 Androlema	130 Anne	141 Catherine
107 Gethosyna	119 Trastevole	131 Magdalen	142 Helen
108 Collabella	120 Suaviloqua	132 Girsel	143 Beatrice
109 Eucnema	121 Francoline	133 Mary	144 Elizabeth
110 Tortolina	122 Matilda	134 Sophia	145 Elizabeth
111 Ripulita	123 Allegra	135 Eleonore	146 Christian
112 Urbana	124 Winnifred		

Let such as would know more hereof be pleased to have recourse to the book treating of the genealogy of that family, intituled *Παντοχρονόχανον*[16] which together with this is to be sold by one and the same stationer.

He should obtain all his desires,
Who offers more then he requires.

No sooner had the total rout of the regal party at Worcester given way to the taking of that city and surrendring up of all the prisoners to the custody of the marshal-general and his deputies, but the liberty, customary at such occasions to be connived at in favours of a victorious army, imboldened some of the new-levied forces of the adjacent counties to confirm their conquest by the spoil of the captives. For the better atchievement of which designe, not reckoning those great many others that in all the other corners of the town were ferreting every room for plunder, a string or two of exquisite snaps and clean shavers, if ever there were any, rushing into Master Spilsbury's house[17] (who is a very honest man and hath an exceeding good woman to his wife) broke into an upper chamber, where, finding besides scarlet cloaks, buff suits, arms of all sorts and other such rich chaffer, at such an exigent escheatable to the prevalent soldier, seven large portmantles ful of precious commodity; in three whereof, after a most exact search for gold, silver, apparel, linen or any whatever adornments of the body or pocket-implements as was seized upon in the other four, not hitting on any thing but mauscripts in folio to the quantity of sixscore and eight quires and a half, divided into six hundred fourty and two quinternions and upwards, the quinternion consisting of five sheets and the quire of five and twenty, besides some writings of suits in law and bonds, in both worth above three thousand pounds English, they in a trice carried all whatever els was in the room away save those papers, which they then threw down on the floor as unfit for their use. Yet immediately thereafter, when upon carts the aforesaid baggage was put to be transported to the country, and

Snaps: *swindlers*   Shavers: *plunderers*   Chaffer: *merchandise*
Exigent: *critical occasion*   Escheatable: *liable to confiscation*
Quinternions: *gatherings of five sheets*

that by the example of many hundreds of both horse and foot whom they had loaded with spoil, they were assaulted with the temptation of a new booty, they, apprehending how useful the paper might be unto them, went back for it and bore it straight away; which done, to every one of those their camarads whom they met with in the streets, they gave as much thereof for packeting up of raisins, figs, dates, almonds, caraway and other such like dry confections and other ware as was requisite; who, doing the same themselves, did together with others kindle pipes of tobacco with a great part thereof and threw out all the remainder upon the streets save so much as they deemed necessary for inferiour employments and posteriour uses.

Of those dispersedly-rejected bundles of paper, some were gathered up by grocers, druggists, chandlers, pie-makers or such as stood in need of any cartapaciatory utensil and put in present service to the utter undoing of all the writing thereof both in its matter and order. One quinternion nevertheless, two days after the fight on the Friday morning, together with two other loose sheets more, by vertue of a drizelling rain which had made it stick fast to the ground, where there was a heap of seven and twenty dead men lying upon one another, was by the command of one Master Braughton[18] taken up by a servant of his; who, after he had, in the best manner he could, cleansed it from the mire and mud of the kennel, did forthwith present it to the perusal of his master in whose hands it no sooner came, but — instantly perceiving by the periodical couching of the discourse, marginal figures and breaks here and there according to the variety of the subject, that the whole purpose was destinated for the press and by the author put into a garb befitting either the stationer or printer's acceptance, yet because it seemed imperfect and to have relation to subsequent tractates — he made all the enquiry he could for trial whether there were any more such quintenons or no; by means whereof he got full information that above three thousand sheets of the like paper, written after that fashion and with the same hand, were utterly lost and imbezzeled after the manner aforesaid; and was so fully assured of the misfortune, that to gather up spilt water, comprehend the windes within his fist and recover those papers

Cartapaciatory: *enclosing* (in paper)

again, he thought would be a work of one and the same labour and facility. Therefore because he despaired of attaining to any more, he the more carefully endeavoured to preserve what he had made purchase of; and this he did very heedfully in the country for three months together and afterwards in the city of London; where at last, I getting notice thereof, thought good in regard of the great moan made for the loss of Sir Thomas Urquhart's manuscripts, to try at the said Sir Thomas whether these seven sheets were any of his papers or no. Whereupon, after communication with him, it was found that they were but a parcel of the Preface he intended to premise before the grammar and lexicon of an universal language; the whole Preface consisting of two quires of paper, the grammar of three and the lexicon of seven; the other five score and sixteen quires and a half, treating of metaphysical, mathematical, moral, mythological, epigrammatical, dialectical and chronological matters in a way never hitherto trod upon by any; being brought by the said Sir Thomas into England for two reasons: first, lest they should have been altogether lost at Sterlin;[19] and next, to have them printed at London with the best conveniencie that might stand with indemnity of the author, whom, when I had asked if his fancie could serve him to make up these papers again, especially in so far as concerned the new language, his answer was that if he wanted not encouragement, with the favour of a little time he could do much therein; but unless he were sure to possess his own with freedom it would be impossible for him to accomplish a task of so great moment and laboriousness. This modest reply, grounded upon so much reason, hath emboldened me to subjoyn hereto what was couched in those papers which were found by Master Braughton; to the end the reader may perceive whether the performance of so great a work as is mentioned there be not worth the enjoyment of his predecessors' inheritance, although he had not had a lawful title thereunto by his birthright and lineal succession, which he hath.

The Title of those found Papers was thus:
An introduction to The Universal Language; wherein whatever is uttred in other languages hath signification in it, whilst it affordeth expressions both for copiousness, variety and conciseness in all manner of subjects, which no language else is able to

reach unto: most fit for such as would with ease attaine to a most expedite facility of expressing themselves in all the learned sciences, faculties, arts, disciplines, mechanick trades and all other discourses whatsoever, whether serious or recreative.

The matter of the Preface begun after this manner
as it was divided into several Articles.

1. Words are the signes of things, it being to signifie that they were instituted at first; nor can they be, as such, directed to any other end whether they be articulate or inarticulate.

2. All things are either real or rational and the real either natural or artificial.

3. There ought to be a proportion betwixt the signe and thing signified. Therefore should all things, whether real or rational, have their proper words assigned unto them.

4. Man is called a microcosme because he may by his conceptions and words containe within him the representatives of what in the whole world is comprehended.

5. Seeing there is in nature such affinity 'twixt words and things as there ought to be in whatever is ordained for one another, that language is to be accounted most conform to nature which with greatest variety expresseth all manner of things.

6. As all things of a single, compleat being by Aristotle into ten classes were divided, so may the words whereby those things are to be signified be set apart in their several store-houses.

7. Arts, sciences, mechanick trades, notional faculties and whatever is excogitable by man have their own method, by vertue whereof the learned of these latter times have orderly digested them. Yet hath none hitherto considered of a mark whereby words of the same faculty, art, trade or science should be dignosced from those of another by the very sound of the word at the first hearing.

8. A tree will be known by its leaves, a stone by its grit, a flower by the smel, meats by the taste, musick by the ear, colours by the eye, the several natures of things with their properties and essential qualities by the intellect; and accordingly as the things are in themselves diversified, the judicious and learned man,

Excogitable: *capable of being thought out*   Dignosced: *distinguished*

after he hath conceived them aright, sequestreth them in the several cels of his understanding, each in their definite and respective places.

9. But in matter of the words whereby those things are expressed, no language every hitherto framed hath observed any order relating to the thing signified by them; for if the words be ranked in their alphabetical series, the things represented by them will fall to be in several predicaments; and if the things themselves be categorically classed, the word whereby they are made known will not be tyed to any alphabetical rule.

10. This is an imperfection incident to all the languages that ever yet have been known; by reason whereof, foraign tongues are said to be hard to learn and, when obtained, easily forgot.

11. The effigies of Jupiter in the likeness of a bull should be liker to that of Io metamorphosed into a cow then to the statue of Bucephalus which was a horse; and the picture of Alcibiades ought to have more resemblance with that of Coriolanus being both handsome men, then with the image of Thersites[20] who was of a deformed feature. Just so should things semblable in nature be represented by words of a like composure; and as the true, intelligible species do present unto our minds the similitude of things as they are in the object, even so ought the word expressive of our conceptions so to agree or vary in their contexture as the things themselves, which are conceived by them, do in their natures.

12. Besides this imperfection in all languages, there is yet another — that no language upon the face of the earth hath a perfect alphabet, one lacking those letters which another hath, none having all, and all of them *in cumulo* lacking some. But that which makes the defect so much the greater is that these same few consonants and vowels commonly made use of are never by two nations pronounced after the same fashion; the French A with the English being the Greek *Hτα*; and the Italian B with the Spanish, the Hebrew Vau.

13. This is that which maketh those of one dominion so unskilful in the idiome of another and, after many yeers abode in a strange land, despaire from attaining at any time to the perfect accent of the language thereof, because, as the waters of that

Sequestreth: *separates*   In cumulo: *in total*

stream cannot be wholesome whose source is corrupted nor the superstructure sure whereof the ground-work is ruinous, so doth the various manners of pronouncing one and the same alphabet in several nations produce this great and most lamentable obstruction in the discipline of languages.

14. The G of the Latin word *legit* is after four several manners pronounced by the English, French, Spanish and Dutch. The Ch likewise is differently pronounced by divers nations, some uttering it after the fashion of the Hebrew Shin, as the French do in the words *chasteau, chascun, chastier, chatel*; or like the Greek Kappa, as in the Italian words *chiedere, chiazzare, chinatura*; or as in Italy are sounded the words *ciascheduno, ciarlatano*, for so do the Spanish and English pronounce it, as in the words *achaque, leche, chamber, chance*. Other nations of a guttural flexibility pronounce it after the fashion of the Greek *X*. Nor need we to labor for examples in other letters, for there is scarce any hitherto received, either consonant or vowel, which in some one and other, taking in all nations, is not pronounced after three or four several fashions.

15. As the alphabets are imperfect, some having but 19 letters, others 22 and some 24 (few exceeding that number) so do the words composed of those letters in the several languages come far short of the number of things which, to have the reputation of a perfect tongue, ought to be expressed by them.

16. For supply of this deficiencie each language borrows from another; nor is the perfectest amongst them, without being beholden to another, in all things enuncible, bastant to afford instruction. Many astronomical and medicinal terms have the Greeks borrowed from the Arabians, for which they by exchange have from the Grecians received payment of many words naturalized in their physical, logical and metaphysical treatises. As for the Latin, it oweth all its scientifick dictions to the Greek and Arabick; yet did the Roman Conquest give adoption to many Latin words in both these languages, especially in matters of military discipline and prudential law.

17. And as for all other languages as yet spoke, though to some of them be ascribed the title of original tongues, I may safely avouch there is none of them which, of it self alone, is able to

Bastant: *sufficient*

afford the smattring of an elocution fit for indoctrinating of us in the precepts and maximes of moral and intellectual vertues.

18. But, which is more, and that which most of all evinceth the sterility of all the languages that since the deluge have been spoke, though all of them quintescenced in one capable of the perfections of each, yet that one so befitted and accommodated for compendiousness and variety of phrase should not be able, amidst so great wealth, to afford without circumlocution the proper and convenient representation of a thing, yea of many thousands of things whereof each should be expressed with one single word alone.

19. Some languages have copiousness of discourse which are barren in composition: such is the Latine. Others are compendious in expression which hardly have any flection at all:[21] of this kinde are the Dutch, the English and Irish.

20. Greek hath the agglutinative faculty[22] of incorporating words, yet runneth not so glib in poesie as doth the Latine, though far more abundant. The Hebrew likewise, with its auxiliary dialects of Arabick, Caldean, Syriack, Aethiopian and Samaritan, compoundeth prettily and hath some store of words, yet falleth short by many stages of the Greek.

21. The French, Spanish and Italians are but dialects of the Latine,[23] as the English is of the Saxon tongue, though with this difference that the mixture of Latine with the Gaulish, Moresco and Gotish tongues make up the three first languages; but the meer qualification of the Saxon with the old British frameth not the English to the full, for that, by its promiscuous and ubiquitary borrowing, it consisteth almost of all languages; which I speak not in dispraise thereof, although I may with confidence aver, that were all the four aforesaid languages stript of what is not originally their own, we should not be able with them all in any part of the world to purchase so much as our breakfast in a market.

22. Now to return from these to the learned languages, we much acknowledge it to be very strange why, after thousands of yeers continual practice in the polishing of them by men of approved faculties, there is neither in them nor any other tongue

Quintescenced: *purified to the highest degree*   Flection: *inflexion*
Agglutinative: *facility of combining roots into compounds*

65

hitherto found out, one single word expressive of the vice opposite either to temperance or chastity in the defect, though many rigid monks, even nowadays, be guilty of the one as Diogenes of old was of the other.[24]

23. But that which makes this disease the more incurable is, that when an exuberant spirit would to any high researched conceit adapt a peculiar word of his own coyning, he is branded with incivility, if he apologize not for his boldness with a *"Quod ita dixerim parcant Ciceronianae manes, ignoscat Demosthenis genius"*[25] and other such phrases, acknowledging his fault of making use of words never uttered by others or at least by such as were most renowned for eloquence.

24. Though learning sustain great prejudice by this restraint of liberty to endenizon new citizens in the commonwealth of languages, yet do I conceive the reason thereof to proceed from this: that it is thought a less incongruity to express a thing by circumlocution then by appropriating a single word thereto to transgress the bounds of the language; as in architecture it is esteemed an errour of less consequence to make a circuitory passage from one room to another then, by the extravagancie of an irregular sallie, to frame projectures disproportionable to the found of the house.

25. Thus is it that, as according to the largeness of the plat of a building and compactedness of its walls, the work-master contriveth his roofs, platforms, outjettings and other such like parts and portions of the whole; just so, conform to the extent and reach which a language in its flexions and compositions hath obtained at first, have the sprucest linguists hitherto bin pleased to make use of the words thereto belonging.

26. The 'bonification' and 'virtuification' of Lully, Scotus's 'hexeity' and 'albedineity' of Suarez[26] are words exploded by those that affect the purity of the Latine diction. Yet if such were demanded, what other no less concise expression would comport with the neatness of that language? Their answer would be *"altum silentium"*; so easie a matter it is for many to finde fault with what they are not able to mend.

Endenizon: *naturalize*   Sallie: *projection*   Found: *foundation*
Plat: *surface*   Outjettings: *projections*   Hexeity: *thisness, individuality*
Albedineity: *whiteness*   Altum silentium: *'A great silence'*

27. Nevertheless why for representing to our understandings the essence of accidents, the fluency of the form as it is *in fieri*, the faculty of the agent and habit that facilitates it with many thousands of other such expressions, the tearms are not so genuine as of the members of a man's body or utensils of his house? The reason is, because the first inventers of languages, who contrived them for necessity, were not so profoundly versed in philosophical quiddities as those that succeeded after them; whose literature increasing, procured their excursion beyond the representatives of the common objects imagined by their forefathers.

28. I have known some to have built houses for necessity, having no other aime before their eyes but barely to dwell in them, who nevertheless in a very short space were so enriched, that after they had taken pleasure to polish and adorn what formerly they had but rudely squared, their moveables so multiplyed upon them, that they would have wished they had made them of a larger extent.

29. Even so, though these languages may be refined by some quaint derivatives and witty compositions; like the striking forth of new lights and doors, outjetting of kernels, erecting of prickets, barbicans and such like various structures upon one and the same foundation; yet being limited to a certain basis beyond which the versed in them must not pass, they cannot roam at such random as otherwise they might, had their language been of a larger scope at first.

30. Thus, albeit Latine be far better polished now then it was in the days of Ennius and Livius Andronicus,[27] yet had the Latinists at first been such philosophers as afterward they were, it would have attained to a great deale of more perfection then it is at for the present.

31. What I have delivered in freedome of the learned languages, I would not have wrested to a sinister sense, as if I meant any thing to their disparagement; for truly I think the time well bestowed which boyes in their tender yeers employ towards the learning of them in a subordination to the excellent things that in them are couched.

In fieri: in becoming   Quiddities: *subtleties*   Kernels: *battlements*
Prickets: *pinnacles*   Barbicans: *double towers erected over gate or bridge*

32. But ingenuously I must acknowledge my averseness of opinion from those who are so superstitiously addicted to these languages, that they account it learning enough to speak them, although they knew nothing else; which is an error worthy rebuke, seeing *philosophia sunt res, non verba*[28] and that whatever the signes be, the things by them signified ought still to be of greater worth.

33. For it boots not so much by what kinds of tokens any matter be brought into our minde, as that the things made known unto us by such representatives be of some considerable value; not much unlike the Innes-a-court-gentlemen at London[29] who, usually repairing to their commons at the blowing of a horne, are better pleased with such a signe, so the fare be good, then if they were warned to courser cates by the sound of a bell or trumpet.

34. Another reason prompteth me thereto, which is this: that in this frozen climate of ours there is hardly any that is not possessed with the opinion that not only the three fore-named languages but a great many other, whom they call originals — whereof they reckon ten or eleven in Europe and some fifty-eight more (or thereabouts) in other nations — were at the confusion of Babel,[30] immediately from God by a miracle infused into men; being induced to believe this, not so much for that they had not perused the interpretation of the rabbies on that text (declaring the misunderstanding whereunto the builders were involved by diversity of speech to have proceeded from nothing else but their various and discrepant pronunciation of one and the same language), as that they deemed languages to be of an invention so sublime, that naturally the wit of man was not able to reach their composure.

35. Some believe this so pertinaciously, that they esteem all men infidels that are of another faith; whilst in the mean while I may confidently assever that the assertors of such a tenet do thereby extreamly dishonor God who, doing whatever is done by nature (as the actions of an ambassador as an ambassador are reputed to be those of the soveraign that sent him) would not have the power he hath given to nature to be disclaimed by any or any thing said by us in derogation thereof.

Common: *collegiate meal*   Cates: *victuals*   Rabbies: *rabbis*

68

36. Should we deny our obedience to the just decree of an inferior judge because he from whom his authority is derived did not pronounce the sentence? Subordinate magistrates have their power even in great matters; which to decline, by saying they have no authority, should make the averrer fall within the compass of a breach of the statute called *scandalum magnatum*.[31]

37. There are of those with us, that wear gowns and beards longer then ever did Aristotle and Aesculapius,[32] who, when they see an eclipse of the sun or moon or a comet in the aire, straight would delude the commons with an opinion that those things are immediately from God for the sins of the people, as if no natural cause could be produced for such like apparitions.

[Here is the number of twelve articles wanting][33]

50. For which cause they are much to blame that think it impossible for any man naturally to frame a language of greater perfection then Greek, Hebrew or Latine.

51. For who, in stead of affording the true cause of a thing, unnecessarily runs to miracles, tacitely acknowledgeth that God naturally cannot do it; wherein he committeth blasphemy, as that souldier may be accounted guilty of contumacie and disobedience who, rejecting the orders wherewith an inferiour officer is authorized to command him, absolutely refuseth compearance unless the general himself come in person to require it of him.

52. As there is a possibility such a language may be, so doe I think it very requisite such a language were, both for affording of conciseness and abundance of expression.

53. Such as extol those languages most are enforced sometimes to say that *Laborant penuria verborum*[34] and thereunto immediately subjoyn this reason, *Quia plures sunt res quam verba*.[35]

54. That is soon said and *ad pauca respicientes facile enuntiant*.[36] But here I ask them how they come to know that there are more things then words, taking things (as in this sence they ought to be taken) for things universal; because there is no word spoken which to the conceit of man is not able to represent more individuals then one, be it sun, moon, Phoenix or what you will,

Compearance: *to present himself*

even amongst verbs and syncategorematical signes which do onely suppone for the modalities of things. Therefore is each word the sign of an universal thing; 'Peter' signifying either this Peter or that Peter and any whatever name, surname or title being communicable to one and many.

55. Thus though both words and thoughts as they are signs be universal, yet do I believe that those who did attribute less universality to words then things knew not definitely the full number of words, taking words for any articulate pronunciation.

56. Nay, I will go further: there is no alphabet in the world, be the calculator never so well skill'd in arithmetick, by vertue whereof the exact number of words may be known, because that number must comprehend all the combinations that letters can have with one another; and this cannot be done if any letter be wanting, and consequently by no alphabet as yet framed wherein, as I have already said in the twelfth article, there is a deficiencie of many letters.

57. The universal alphabet therefore must be first conceived before the exactness of that computation can be attained unto.

58. Then is it, when, having couched an alphabet materiative of all the words the mouth of man with its whole implements is able to pronounce, and bringing all these words within the systeme of a language which, by reason of its logopandocie may deservedly be intituled 'The Universal Tongue', that nothing will better merit the labour of a grammatical arithmetician then, after due enumeration, *hinc inde*, to appariate the words of the universal language with the things of the universe.

59. The analogie therein 'twixt the signe and thing signified holding the more exactly, that as, according to Aristotle, there can be no more worlds but one,[37] because all the matter whereof worlds can be composed is in this; so can there be no universal language but this I am about to divulge unto the world because all the words enuncible are in it contained.

60. If any officious critick will run to the omnipotencie of God for framing more worlds, according to the common saying,

Syncategorematical: *whereby a word can only be used in conjunction with another word or words*   Suppone for: *represent*   Materiative: *providing the matter of*
Logopandocie: *readiness to admit of words of all kinds*
Hinc inde: from different directions   Appariate: *match*

70

'Nothing is impossible to God that implies not a contra-diction',[38] so he must have recourse to the same omnipotent power for furnishing of man with other speech-tools then his tongue, throat, roof of the mouth, lips and teeth before the contexture of another universal language can be warped.

61. That I should hit upon the invention of that, for the furtherance of philosophy and other disciplines and arts, which never hitherto hath been so much as thought upon by any, and that in a matter of so great extent as the expressing of all the things in the world, both in themselves, actions, ways of doing, situations, pendicles, relations, connexions, pathetick inter-positions and all other appurtenances to a perfect elocution without being beholding to any language in the world; insomuch as one word will hardly be believed by our fidimplicitary gown-men who, satisfied with their prdecessors' contrivances and taking all things literally, without examina-tion, blaterate, to the nauseating even of vulgar ears, those exotick proverbs,[39] 'There is no new thing under the sun', '*Nihil dictum quod non dictum prius*' and 'Beware of philosophers' — authoridating this on Paul, the first on Solomon and the other on Terence.

62. But, poor souls, they understand not that in the passage of Solomon is meant, that there is no innovation in the essence of natural things; all transmutations on the same matter being into formes which, as they differ from some, so have an essential uniformity with others pre-existent in the same kind.

63. And when it was said by Paul, "Beware of philosophers", he meant such sophisters as themselves who, under the vizzard of I know not what, corrupt the chanels of the truth and pervert all philosophy and learning.

64. As for the sayings of Terence, whether Scipio couched them or himself, they ought to be inferred rather as testimonies of neat Latine then for asserting of infallible verities.

65. If there hath been no new thing under the sun according to the adulterate sense of those pristinary lobcocks, how comes the invention of syllogisms to be attributed to Aristotle, that of the

Warped: *devised*   Pendicles: *things pertaining*
Fidimplicitary: *putting implicit faith in others' teachings*   Blaterate: *babble*
Vizzard: *mask, disguise*   Lobcocks: *country bumpkins*

71

sphere to Archimedes and logarithms to Neper? It was not Swart then and Gertudenburg that found out gunpowder and the art of printing,[40] for these two men lived after the decease of Solomon.

66. Had there been canon in Solomon's dayes, Rehoboam by all appearance would have made use of them[41] for the recovery of his inheritance; nor had some mention of artillery been omitted in the books of the Macchabees.

67. Pancerola's Treatise, *De Novis Adimpertis*,[42] although Polydor Virgil were totally forgot, would be, had there been no new thing since Solomon penn'd *Ecclesiastes*, but as a discourse of Platonick reminiscences and calling to minde some formerly-lost fancies.

68. Truly I am so far from being of the opinion of those archaeomanetick coxcombs, that I really think there will alwayes be new inventions where there are excellent spirits.

69. For as I ascribe unto my self the invention of the trissotetrail trigonometry for facility of calculation by representatives of letters and syllables, the proving of the equipollencie and opposition both of plaine and modal enunciations by rules of geometry, the unfolding of the chiefest part of philosophy by a continuated geographical allegory; and above a hundred other several books on different subjects, the conceit of so much as one whereof never entered into the braines of any before my self (although many of them have been lost at Worcester fight) so am I confident that others after me may fall upon some straine of another kind, never before that dreamed upon by those of foregoing ages.

70. Now to the end the reader may be more enamored of the language wherein I am to publish a grammer and lexicon, I will here set down some few qualities and advantages peculiar to it self and which no language else, although all other concurred with it, is able to reach unto.

71. First, there is not a word utterable by the mouth of man which, in this language, hath not a peculiar signification by it self, so that the allegation of *Bliteri* by the Summulists will be of small validity.[43]

Archaeomanetick: *antiquarian*   Trissotetrail: *running on threes or fours*
Equipollencie: *equivalence between propositions (logic)*
Bliteri: *foolish or outrageous speech. (See Commentary p. 220)*

72. Secondly, such as will harken to my instructions, if some strange word be proposed to them, whereof there are many thousands of millions, deviseable by the wit of man, which never hitherto by any breathing have been uttered, shall be able (although he know not the ultimate signification thereof) to declare what part of speech it is; or if a noune, unto what predicament or class it is to be reduced, whether it be the signe of a real or notional thing or somewhat concerning mechanick trades in their tooles or tearmes; or if real, whether natural or artificial, compleat or incompleat; for words here do suppone for the things which they signifie, as when we see my Lord General's picture,[44] we say, "There is my Lord General".

73. Thirdly, this world of words hath but two hundred and fifty prime radices upon which all the rest are branched; for better understanding whereof with all its dependant boughs, sprigs and ramelets, I have before my lexicon set down the division thereof, making use of another allegory, into so many cities which are subdivided into streets, they againe into lanes, those into houses, these into stories whereof each room standeth for a word; and all these so methodically, that who observeth my precepts thereanent shall at the first hearing of a word know to what city it belongeth and consequently not be ignorant of some general signification thereof, till, after a most exact prying into all its letters, finding the street, lane, house, story and room thereby denotated, he punctually hit upon the very proper thing it represents in its most specifical signification.

74. Fourthly, by vertue of adjectitious syllabicals annexible to nouns and verbs there will arise of several words, what compound, what derivative, belonging in this language to one noune or to one verb alone, a greater number then doth pertaine to all the parts of speech in the most copious language in the world besides.

75. Fifthly, so great energy to every meanest constitutive part of a word in this language is appropriated, that one word thereof, though but of seven syllables at most, shal comprehend that which no language else in the world is able to express in fewer then four-score and fifteen several words — and that not only a

Predicament: *category*   Radices: *roots*   Ramelets: *small branches*

73

word here and there for masterie's sake but several millions of such, which, to any initiated in the rudiments of my grammer, shall be easie to frame.

76. Sixthly, in the cases of all the declinable parts of speech it surpasseth all other languages whatsoever — for, whilst others have but five or six at most, it hath ten besides the nominative.

77. Seventhly, there is none of the learned languages but hath store of nouns defective of some case or other; but in this language there is no heteroclite in any declinable word nor redundancie or deficiency of cases.

78. Eighthly, every word capable of number is better provided therewith in this language then by any other, for in stead of two or three numbers, which others have, this affordeth you four: to wit, the singular, dual, plural and redual.[45]

79. Ninthly, it is not in this as other languages wherein some words lack one number and some another, for here each casitive or personal part of speech is endued with all the numbers.

80. Tenthly, in this tongue there are eleven genders wherein likewise it exceedeth all other languages.

81. Eleventhly, verbs, mongrels, participles and hybrids have all of them ten tenses besides the present, which number no language else is able to attaine to.

82. Twelfthly, though there be many conjugable words in other languages defective of tenses yet doth this tongue allow of no such anomaly but granteth all to each.

83. Thirteenthly, in lieu of six moods, which other languages have at most, this one enjoyeth seven in its conjugable words.

84. Fourteenthly, verbs here or other conjugable parts of speech admit of no want of moodes as doe other languages.

85. Fifteenthly, in this language the verbs and participles have four voices, although it was never heard that ever any other language had above three.

86. Sixteenthly, no other tongue hath above eight or nine parts of speech but this hath twelve.

87. Seventeenthly, for variety of diction in each part of speech it surmounteth all the languages in the world.

88. Eighteenthly, each noun thereof or verb may begin or end

Heteroclite: *irregularity*   Redual: *double dual*
Mongrels: *words formed of elements from different languages*

with a vowel or consonant, as to the peruser shall seem most expedient.

89. Nineteenthly, every word of this language, declinable or indeclinable, hath at least ten several *synonymas*.

90. Twentiethly, each of these *synonymas* in some circumstance of the signification differeth from the rest.

91. One and twentiethly, every faculty, science, art, trade or discipline requiring many words for expression of the knowledge thereof hath each its respective root from whence all the words thereto belonging are derived.

92. Two and twentiethly, in this language the opposite members of a division have usually the same letters in the words which signifie them; the initial and final letter being all one with a transmutation only in the middle ones.

93. Three and twentiethly, every word in this language signifieth as well backward as forward; and how ever you invert the letters, still shall you fall upon significant words, whereby a wonderful facility is obtained in making of anagrams.

94. Four and twentiethly, there is no language in the world but for every word thereof it will afford you another of the same signification of equal syllables with it and beginning or ending, or both, with vowels or consonants as it doth.

95. Five and twentiethly, by vertue hereof there is no hexameter, elegiack, saphick, asclepiad, iambick or any other kind of Latine or Greek verse, but I will afford you another in this language of the same sort without a syllable more or less in the one then the other, spondae answering to spondae, dactil to dactil, caesure to caesure, and each foot to other with all uniformity imaginable.

96. Six and twentiethly, as it trotteth easily with metrical feet, so at the end of the career of each line hath it the dexterity, after the maner of our English and other vernaculary tongues, to stop with the closure of a rime; in the framing whereof, the well-versed in that language shall have so little labour, that for every word therein he shall be able to furnish at least five hundred several monosyllables of the same termination with it.

97. Seven and twentiethly, in translating verses of any vernaculary tongue, such as Italian, French, Spanish, Slavonian,

Asclepiad: *verse consisting of a spondae, two (or three) choriambi and an iambus*

75

Dutch, Irish, English or whatever it be, it affords you words of the same signification, syllable for syllable, and in the closure of each line a ryme as in the original.

98. Eight and twentiethly, by this language and the letters thereof, we may do such admirable feats in numbers, that no cyfering can reach its compendiousness; for whereas the ordinary way of numbring by thousands of thousands of thousands of thousands doth but confuse the hearer's understanding (to remedy which I devised even by cyfering it self a far more exact maner of numeration, as in the treatise of arithmetick, which I have ready for the press, is evidently apparent), this language affordeth so concise words for numbering, that the number for setting down, whereof would require in vulgar arithmetick more figures in a row then there might be grains of sand containable from the center of the earth to the highest heavens, is in it expressed by two letters.

99. Nine and twentiethly, what rational logarithms do by writing, this language doth by heart and by adding of letters shall multiply numbers, which is a most exquisite secret.

100. Thirtiethly, the digits are expressed by vowels and the consonants stand for all the results of the Cephalisme from ten to eighty-one inclusively,[46] whereby many pretty arithmetical tricks are performed.

101. One and thirtiethly, in the denomination of the fixed stars it affordeth the most significant way imaginary; for by the single word alone which represents the star, you shall know the magnitude together with the longitude and latitude, both in degrees and minutes, of the star that is expressed by it.

102. Two and thirtiethly, by one word in this language we shall understand what degree or what minute of the degree of a signe in the zodiake, the sun or moon or any other planet is in.

103. Three and thirtiethly, as for the yeer of God, the moneth of that yeer, week of the moneth, day of that week, partition of the day, hour of that partition, quarter and half quarter of the hour, a word of one syllable in this language will express it all to the full.

104. Four and thirtiethly, in this language also, words

Cephalisme: *a multiplication table.* (*See Commentary p. 220*)

expressive of herbs represent unto us with what degree of cold, moisture, heat or driness they are qualified; together with some other property distinguishing them from other herbs.

105. Five and thirtiethly, in matter of colours, we shall learn by words in this language the proportion of light, shadow or darkness commixed in them.

106. Six and thirtiethly, in the composition of syllables by vowels and consonants, it affordeth the aptest words that can be imagined for expressing how many vowels and consonants any syllable is compounded of and how placed in priority and situation to one another; which secret in this language is exceeding necessary for understanding the vigour of derivatives in their variety of signification.

107. Seven and thirtiethly, for attaining to that dexterity which Mithridates, King of Pontus, was said to have[47] in calling all his souldiers of an army of threescore thousand men by their names and surnames, this language will be so convenient, that if a general, according to the rules thereof, will give new names to his souldiers, whether horse, foot or dragoons, as the French use to do to their infantry by their *noms de guerre*; he shall be able, at the first hearing of the word that represents the name of a souldier, to know of what brigade, regiment, troop, company, squadron or division he is and whether he be of the cavalry or of the foot, a single souldier or an officer, or belonging to the artillery or baggage; which device in my opinion is not unuseful for those great captains that would endear themselves in the favour of the souldiery.

108. Eight and thirtiethly, in the contexture of nouns, pronouns and preposital articles united together, it administreth many wonderful varieties of laconick expressions as in the grammar thereof shall more at large be made known unto you.

109. Nine and thirtiethly, every word in this language is significative of a number; because, as words may be increased by addition of letters and syllables, so of numbers is there a progress *in infinitum*.

110. Fourtiethly, in this language every number, how great soever, may be expressed by one single word.

Noms de guerre: names adopted in war   *In infinitum: infinitely*

111. One and fourtiethly, as every number essentially differeth from another, so shall the words expressive of several numbers be from one another distinguished.

112. Two and fourtiethly, no language but this hath in its words the whole number of letters, that is ten vowels and five and twenty consonants, by which means there is no word escapes the latitude thereof.

113. Three and fourtiethly, as its interjections are more numerous, so are they more emphatical in their respective expression of passions then that part of speech is in any other language whatsoever.

114. Four and fourtiethly, the more syllables there be in any one word of this language, the manyer several significations it hath, with which propriety no other language is endowed.

115. Five and fourtiethly, all the several genders in this language are as well competent to verbs as nouns; by vertue whereof, at the first uttering of a verb in the active voice, you shall know whether it be a god, a goddess, a man, a woman, a beast or any thing inanimate (and so thorow the other five genders) that doth the action; which excellencie is altogether peculiar unto this language.

116. Six and fourtiethly, in this language there is an art out of every word, of what kinde of speech soever it be, to frame a verb; whereby, for expressing all manner of actions, a great facility is attained unto.

117. Seven and fourtiethly, to all manner of verbs and many syncategorematical words is allowed in this language a flexion by cases, unknown to other tongues, thereby to represent unto our understandings more compendious expressions then is possible to afford by any other means.

118. Eight and fortiethly, of all languages this is the most compendious in complement and consequently fittest for courtiers and ladies.

119. Nine and fourtiethly, for writing of missives, letters of state and all other manner of epistles, whether serious or otherways, it affordeth the compactest stile of any language in the world and therefore, of all other, the most requisite to be learned by statesmen and merchants.

120. Fiftiethly, no language in matter of prayer and ejaculations to Almighty God is able, for conciseness of expression, to

compare with it and therefore, of all other, the most fit for the use of churchmen and spirits inclined to devotion.

121. One and fiftiethly, this language hath a modification of the tense, whether present, preterite or future, of so curious invention for couching much matter in few words, that no other language ever had the like.

122. Two and fiftiethly, there is not a proper name in any country of the world for which this language affords not a peculiar word without being beholding to any other.

123. Three and fiftiethly, in many thousands of words belonging to this language there is not a letter which hath not a peculiar signification by it self.

124. Four and fiftiethly, the polysyllables of this language do all of them signifie by their monosyllables, which no word in any other language doth, *ex instituto*, but the compound ones; for, though the syllabical parts of *ex lex* separately signifie as in the compound, yet those of '*homo*' do it not, nor yet those of '*dote*' or '*domus*', as in the whole; and so it is in all other languages except the same; for there are in the Italian and Latine tongues words of ten, eleven or twelve syllables whereof not one syllable by it self doth signifie any thing at all in that language of what it doth in the whole, as '*adolescenturiatissimamente*', '*Honorificicabilitudinitatibus*', etc.

125. Five and fiftiethly, all the languages in the world will be beholding to this and this to none.

126. Six and fiftiethly, there is yet another wonder in this language which, although a little touched by the by in the fifty eighth article of this preface, I will mention yet once more, and it is this: that though this language have advantage of all other, it is impossible any other in time coming surpass it, because, as I have already said, it comprehendeth, first, all words expressible; and then, in matter of the obliquity of cases and tenses, the contrivance of indeclinable parts and right disposure of vowels and consonants for distinguishing of various significations within the latitude of letters, cannot be afforded a way so expedient.

127. Seven and fiftiethly, the greatest wonder of all is that of all the languages in the world it is the easiest to learn, a boy of ten

Ex instituto: according to law   *Ex lex: according to law*

yeers old being able to attaine to the knowledge thereof in three moneths space, because there are in it many facilitations for the memory which no other language hath but it self.

128. Eight and fiftiethly, sooner shall one reach the understanding of things to be signified by the words of this language then by those of any other, for that as logarithms in comparison of absolute numbers so do the words thereof in their initials respectively vary according to the nature of the things which they signifie.

129. Nine and fiftiethly, for pithiness of proverbs, oracles and sentences no language can parallel with it.

130. Sixtiethly, in axioms, maximes and aphorismes it is excellent above all other languages.

131. One and sixtiethly, for definitions, divisions and distinctions no language is so apt.

132. Two and sixtiethly, for the affirmation, negation and infinitation of propositions, it hath proprieties unknown to any other language, most necessary for knowledge.

133. Three and sixtiethly, in matter of enthymems, syllogisms and all manner of illative ratiocination, it is the most compendious in the world.

134. Besides these sixty and three advantages above all other languages, I might have couched thrice as many more of no less consideration then the aforesaid, but that these same will suffice to sharpen the longing of the generous reader after the intrinsecal and most researched secrets of the new grammer and lexicon which I am to evulge.

To contrive a language of this perfection will be thought by the primest wits of this age a work of a great undertaking and that the promover of so excellent an invention should not lack for any encouragement tending to the accomplishment of a task of such maine concernment. If any say there are too many languages already, and that, by their multiplicity and confusion, the

Infinitation: *one of the forms of immediate inference in which one term (usually the predicate of the original proposition) is made negative*   Proprieties: *peculiarities*
Enthymems: *arguments based on merely probable grounds*
Illative: *introducing or stating an inference*   Intrinsecal: *intimate*
Promover: *promoter*

knowledge of things having been much retarded, this fabrick of a new one may be well forborn because it would but intangle the minde with more impestrements, where there was too much difficulty before; I answer that this maketh not one more but, in a manner, comprehendeth all in it; whereby it facilitates and doth not obstruct, for by making Greek, Latin and all the other learned languages the more expressive, it furthers the progress of all arts and sciences, to the attaining whereof the uttering of our conceptions in due and significant tearms hath, by some of the most literate men in former ages, been esteemed so exceeding requisite that, for attributing a kind of necessity thereunto, they are till this houre called by the name of Nominal Philosophers.[48] It being thus very apparent to any well affected to literature, that the performance of such a designe would be of a great expediency for scholars; equity it self seemeth to plead that unto him by whom a benefit redounds to many, is competent by many a proportionable retribution. Yet, seeing nothing ought to be charged on the publick but upon considerations of great weight, I will premise some few infallible principles, that upon them the world may see how demonstratively are grounded the author's most reasonable demands.

1. Each good thing is desirable because goodnesse is the object of the will.

2. Every thing that ought to be desired is really good because a well-directed will is not deceived with appearances.

3. The better a thing be, the more it is to be desired because there is a proportion betwixt the object and the faculty.

4. The mind is better then the body because by it we are the image of God.

5. The goods of the minde are better then those of the body because they give embellishment to the nobler part.

6. The goods of either minde or body are better then wealth because wealth is but subservient to either, and the end is more noble then the means which are ordained for it.

7. Learning is the good of the minde because it beautifieth it.

8. This new language is an invention full of learning because the knowledge of all arts and disciplines is much advanced by it.

9. A discovery is the revealment of some good thing which

Forborn: *done without*   Impestrements: *encumbrances*

formerly was either concealed or not at all known; for, in a discovery, two things are requisite — first, that it be good; secondly, that it be revealed.

10. Who discovereth a secret of money should have the fifth or third part thereof because there is an Act of Parliament for it.[49]

11. If there be any discovery in learning, the act ought to extend to it because the state is endowed with a soul as well as a body.

12. This new found out invention is a discovery of learning because the two *requisitas* of a discovery, together with the description of learning, are competent thereto.

13. Who discovereth most of the best good deserveth the best recompense because merit and reward are analogical in a proportion of the greater reward to the greater merit.

14. Though mony be not proportionable to learning, yet seeing the learned man may have need of money, he should not lack it; if not as a full recompence at least as a donative or largess should it be given unto him in testimony of his worth and the respect of others toward him, and withal to encourage him the more to eminent undertakings; for were it otherwise, the more deserving a man were, the worse he would be used, there being nothing so unreasonable as to refuse a little to any that stands in need thereof because a great deal more is due unto him; as if, in time of famine, there being no more but one peny-loaf to give unto a prince, he should be made to starve for the want of it because of his deserving better fare: for 'that which comprehends the more, comprehendeth the less'.

15. In matter of recompence for good things proceeding from the minde which, in the midst of flames, cannot be conquered and by vertue whereof a gallant man is alwayes free and invincible in his better part, we ought altogether to prescind and abstract from the conditions of the native country and person of the deserver, whether that be fertil or barren, or this at liberty or in durance; for these being things *quae non fecimus ipsi*,[50] we ought to say, "*Vix ea nostra voco*";[51] and therefore, seeing punishment and reward should attend the performance of nothing else but what did lye in our power to do or not to do, and that the specifying of good or bad actions dependeth upon the qualification of the intention, no man should be either punished

Prescind: *remove at once*

or rewarded for being either a Scotish man or a prisoner or both, if no other reason concur therewith; because the country of our birth and state of our person, as being oftentimes the effects of a good or bad fortune, are not alwayes in our power to command.

16. If by means of the aforesaid discovery may be effectuated the saving of great charges to the subjects of the land, a pecunial or praedial recompense will in so far be very answerable to the nature of that service; because, in matter of merit and the reward proportionable thereunto, money is with money and things vendible no less homogeneal then honor with vertue.

17. The state no doubt will deal proportionably with their prisoners of war without prosopolepsie or any respect to one more then another and that by a geometrical equity because it is just.

18. The state assuredly will grant the same freedom to one prisoner, *caeteris paribus*, which they do to another and upon the same terms, those of a like condition not being unequally faulty because they will not be unjust.

19. If any one prisoner of a like condition and quality, at the least, *in caeteris*, with another that hath obtained his liberty, represent to the publick somewhat conducible thereunto, which the other is not versed in, common equity requireth that he have a compensation sutable to that additional endowment; for, *si ab inaequalibus inaequalia demas, quae restant sunt aequalia*,[52] and the Act for Discoveries maintaines the truth thereof.[53]

20. Though it be commonly maintained amongst the Protestants, that we cannot supererogate towards Almighty God (albeit those of the Romish faith be of another opinion) for that God cannot be unjust, how severely soever he inflict his afflictions, and that all the favors he conferreth on mankind are of his meer grace, not our deserving; yet, that a subject may be capable of supererogation towards any sublunary state or soveraignty, is not only agreeable with all the religions of the world but also a maine principle of humane society and ground unalterable of politick government: for who transgresse not the limits of those good subjects whose actions, thoughts and words

Praedial: *in reference to acts of plunder*   Vendible: *saleable*
Prosopolepsie: *partiality*   Caeteris paribus: *other things being equal*
In caeteris: among others   Supererogate: *pay over and above*

shew at all times faithfulness, loyalty and obedience to the soveraign power under which they live, are universally esteemed by so doing to discharge their duty so to the full, that in reason no more can be required of them. If therefore it happen, besides this general bond of fidelity whereunto all the natives and inhabitants of a country are by their birth and protection inviolably ingaged, that any one more obliging then others performe some singular good office unto which he was not formerly tyed by the strictness of his allegiance, there is no doubt but that the publick, whom nature exempteth not from thankfulness more then private persons, should and will acknowledge such an action, exceeding the reach of his fellow-patriots and co-habitants, to be meritorious and therefore worthy of recompense; upon which consideration, according to the people's diversity of carriage in the well or ill demeaning of themselves, are built the two maine pillars of reward and punishment without which the strongest commonwealth on earth is not able to subsist long from falling to pieces. That it is so, I appeal to Scipio[54] who, with the approbation of all that lived since his dayes, exclaimed against Rome in these words, "*O ingratam patriam!*" as likewise to those many great statesmen and philosophers who from age to age twitted the Athenians with ingratitude for the ostracizing of Aristides;[55] for, if humane frailties were not incident to princes, states and incorporations as well as unto individuals in their single and private callings and particular deportments, there would never be any need of protestations, declarations or defensive war against the tyranny, usurpations and oppressions of misrule. Hence do I think that in a well pollished state, reward will not be wanting to him that merits it for his good service because punishment by the law attends the offender and *contrariorum eadem est ratio*.[56]

21. It is acknowledged by the laws and customs of this island, that the subjects thereof have a right of propriety to their goods, notwithstanding the titles of dominion and supremacy remaining in the persons of others above them; and that if for erecting a castle, fort, church, hospital, colledge, hall, magazine or any other kind of edifice tending to publike use, the state should be pleased to incroach upon the land of any private person — who doubteth but that such a man, of how mean soever a condition he be, will in justice be heard to give up and require the full

value of his land, that a compensation suitable to the worth thereof may be allowed to him, founding the equity of so just a retribution upon Ahab's case in Naboth's vineyard?[57] Now the soul and body of man being more a man's own, they being the constitutive parts whereof physically he is composed, then are the goods of fortune which totally are accidental to him; it follows clearly that a man hath a full right of propriety to the goods of his own mind, and consequently such goods being better (as hath been evidenced by the sixth axiome) then any external means, what can be more manifest than that he who is endowed with them, so careful a course being taken for the satisfaction of any in matter of outward wealth, may (at the best rate he can) capitulate for their disposal with what persons he thinks most concerned in the benefits and utility by them accrescing; because it is an argument *a minore ad maius* and therefore *a fortiori*.

22. If such a one nevertheless voluntarily accepts of a lesser recompence then by his deserving he may claim right unto, he is not unjustly dealt with; *quia volenti non fit injuria*[58] and *pactum hominis tollit conditionem legis.*[59]

These specious axiomes, definitions and uncontroulable maximes thus premised, I must make bold, in behalf of the author, to deduce from thence the equity of his desires in demanding that the same inheritance which for these several hundreds of yeers, through a great many progenitors, hath by his ancestors without the interruption of any other been possest, be now fully devolved on him with the same priviledges and immunities in all things as they enjoyed it. But, the better to make appear his ingenuity in this his suit and modestie in requiring no more, it is expedient to declare what it is he offereth unto the state for obliging them to vouchsafe him the grant of no less. May the reader therefore be pleased to understand, that it is the discovery of a secret in learning which, besides the great contentment it cannot chuse but yeeld to ingenious spirits, will

Capitulate: *bargain, treat*   Accrescing: *continuously growing*
A minore ad maius: from the lesser to the greater   *A fortiori: more strongly*
Uncontroulable: *incontrovertible*

afford a huge benefit to students of all sorts by the abridgement of their studies, in making them learn more in three yeers with the help thereof, then, without it, in the space of five. This saving of two yeers' charges to scholars in such a vast dominion as this is, although I speak nothing of the sparing of so much time which, to a methodical wit of any pregnancie, is a menage of an inestimable value, cannot be appreciated, how parsimonious soever they be in their diet and apparel, at less then ten thousand pounds English a yeer.

That this is a secret, it is clear by this, that never any since the laying of the foundations of the earth did so much as divulge a syllable thereof, which undoubtedly they would have done had they had any knowledge therein. And that none now living, be it spoken without disparagement of any, either knoweth it or knoweth how to go about it save the aforesaid author alone who is willing to forfeit all he demands, although by birth-right it be his own already and worth neer upon a thousand pounds sterlin a yeer, if without his help any breathing (notwithstanding the instructions may possibly be had by his lost papers, and by what in the preceding articles hath been in this little tractate promulgated) shall, within half a yeer after the date hereof, give any apparent testimony to the world that he hath any insight in this invention.

Which, that it is good and desirable, is evident by the first and second axiomes; and that it is a discovery and a discovery of learning by the ninth and twelfth; that the discovery of a matter of less moment then it deserveth great sums of money is manifest by the tenth and thirteenth; and that a retribution of great value should attend the disclosure of so prime a secret by the eleventh and fourteenth; that the knowledge of this invention is of more worth then either strength or wealth is proved by the fifth and sixth; and that it is more to be desired then any thing that is at the disposure of fortune by the third and fourth; that it doth promove reason, illuminate the judgement, further and improve literature by polishing and imbellishing the inward abilities of man and faculties of his minde is clear by the seventh and eighth.

Thus much of the invention or thing invented; which (as the fruit is to be accounted of less worth then the tree which yeerly

Promove: *promote*

produceth the like; cistern-water that daily diminisheth then that of a fountain, which is inexhaustible; and a hay-mow then the meadow[60] on which it grew) being, as in reason it ought to be, estimated at a rate much inferiour to the inventer from whose brains have already issued offsprings every whit as considerable with parturiencie for greater births if a malevolent time disobstetricate not their enixibility, it followeth of necessity that he should reap the benefit that is due for the invention with hopes of a higher remuneration for what of the like nature remaineth as yet unsatisfied. And although his being a Scot and a prisoner of war may perhaps in the opinion of some eclipse the splendor of so great an expectation, yet that it should not is most perspicuously evinced by the fifteenth axiome.

That he is a Scot he denieth not; but that he thereby meriteth to be either praised or dispraised is utterly to be disavowed, because it lay not in his power to appoint localities for his mother's residence at the time of his nativity or to enact any thing before he had a being himself.

True it is, that nothing is more usual in speech then to blame all for the fault of the greater part and to twit a whole country with that vice to which most of its inhabitants are inclined. Hence have we these sayings: the Spaniards are proud; the French inconstant; the Italians lecherous; the Cretians lyers; the Sicilians false; the Asiaticks effeminate; the Crovats cruel; the Dutch temulencious; the Polonians quarrelsome; the Saxons mutinous and so forth thorow other territories, nurseries of enormities of another kinde; although nothing be more certain then that there are some Spaniards as humble; French as constant; Italians chaste; Cretians true; Sicilians ingenuous; Asiaticks warlike; Crovates merciful; Dutch sober; Polonians peaceable and some Saxons as loyal as any in the world besides. By which account, all forreigners (for such are all the inhabitants on the earth in relation to those that are not their compatriots), yeelding to the *most* and *some* of each stranger-land in its respective vice and vertue; it may safely be avouched, that there is under the sun no national fault nor national deserving whereby

Hay-mow: *stack of hay*   Parturiencie: *the condition of bringing forth*
Disobstetricate: *hinder, retard (of birth)*
Enixibility: *possibility of being brought forth*   Temulencious: *drunken*

all merit to be punished or all rewarded because the badness of most in each destroys the universality of vertue, and the good inclination of some in all cuts off the generality of vice.

But to come neerer home: seeing Scotland was never loaded with so much disreputation for covetousness and hypocrisie as it is at this present, and that the knight for whom this treatise is intended, hath, as a patriot, some interest in the good name thereof; it is not amiss, that, for the love of him and all honest Scots, I glance a little at the occasion, if not the cause, of so heavie an imputation, especially that country having been aspersed therewith long before it had sustained the loss of any battel wherein the several miscarriages looked rather like the effect of what formerly had procured the said reproach then any way as the causes thereof; for where covetousness is predominant, fidelity, fortitude and vigilancie must needs discamp if Mammona[61] give the word; the concomitancie of vices, seeing *contrariorum eadem est ratio*, being a sequele from that infallible tenet in the morals, the concatenation of vertues.

How this covetousness under the mask of religion took such deep root in that land was one way occasioned by some ministers who, to augment their stipends and cram their bags full of money, thought fit to possess the mindes of the people with a strong opinion of their sanctity and implicite obedience to their injunctions; to which effect, most rigidly Israelitizing it in their synagogical Sanhedrins[62] and officiously bragging in their pulpits, even when Scotland, by divers notorious calamities of both sword, plague and famine, was brought very lowe; that no nation, for being likest to the Jews of any other, was so glorious as it; they, with a pharisaical superciliosity, would always rebuke the non-Covenanters and sectaries as publicans and sinners, unfit for the purity of their conversation, unless, by the malignancie or over-mastering power of a cross-winde, they should be forced to cale the hypocritical bunt, let fall the topgallant of their counterfeit devotion and, tackling about, to sail a quite contrary course, as many of them have already done, the better at last to cast anchor in the harbour of Profit which is the butt they aimed at and sole period of all their dissimulations.

Sanhedrins: *supreme councils*   Cale: *lower*   Bunt: *swelling sail*
Topgallant: *sails above the topsail*   Butt: *mark (archery)*

For I have known some, even of the most rigid zealots, who, rather then to forgo their present emoluments, by continual receiving and never erogating; by never sowing and always reaping; and by making the sterility of all men prove fruitful to them and their fertility barren to all, would wish presbytery were of as empty a sound as its homaeoteleft, blitery; and the Covenant which asserts it no less exploded from all ecclesiastical societies then Plautus' exolet phrases have been from the eloquent orations of Ciceron.[63]

But this affecting only a part of the tribe of Levi,[64] now the remainder of new Palestine, as the kirkomanetick philarchaists would have it called, comes to be upbraided with the same opprobry of covetousness is that which I am so heartily sorry for, that to wipe off its obloquy, I would undertake a pilgrimage to old Judea, visit the ruines of Jerusalem and trace the foot-steps of Zedekiah's fellow captives[65] to the gates of Babylon.

Yet did this so great an inconvenience proceed meerly from an incogitancy in not taking heed to what is prescribed by prudence, the directress of all vertues, and consequently of that which moderates the actions of giving and receiving, although it be *nobilius dare quam accipere*,[66] the non-vitiosity whereof by her injunctions dependeth on the judicious observing of all the circumstances mentioned in this mnemoneutick hexameter[67] — *quis, quid, ubi, quibus auxiliis, cur, quomodo, quando*, whose last particle, by the untimely taking of a just debt and unseasonable receiving of what at another time might have been lawfully required, being too carelessly regarded by the state and milice of that country, gave occasion to this contumely, the staine whereof remaineth still notwithstanding the loss in money, besides other prejudices sustained since, of ten times more then they got.

I heard once a Maronite Jew,[68] to vindicate the reputation of the family and village of the Iscariots in which he pretended to have some interest, very seriously relate that, according to the opinion of Rabbi Esra, the thirty peeces of silver delivered to

Erogating: *paying out*   Homaeoteleft: *word having similar ending*
Exolet: *obsolete*   Kirkomanetick: *adhering fanatically to the church*
Philarchaists: *lovers of the ancient, antiquaries*   Non-vitiosity: *virtue*
Mnemoneutick: *memory-aiding*

Judas was but the sum which, long before that, when Christ went up from Galilee to celebrate the Feast of Tabernacles at Jerusalem, Malchus the servant of Caiaphas had borrowed from him whilst he had charge of his master's bag, with assurance punctually to repay it him again at the subsequent term of the passover, as the fashion was then amongst the inhabitants of Judea. But although it were so, which we are not bound to give ear to because it is plainly set down in the fifth verse of the two and twentieth chapter of the Evangile according to Saint Luke, that the high priests made a covenant with Judas, yet should he not have received the mony in the very nick of the time that his master was to be apprehended.

This I rather believe for that I likewise heard a minister say, that he offends God who stretcheth forth his hand to take in the payment of any debt, how just so ever it be, upon a Sunday; and that though a purse full of gold were offered unto himself whilst he is a preaching in the pulpit, he would refuse it.

These collateral instances I introduce not for application but illustration sake; not for comparison but explication of the congruent adapting of necessary puntilios for the framing of a vertuous action.

Another thing there is that fixeth a grievous scandal upon that nation in matter of *philargyrie* or love of money and it is this: there hath been in London and repairing to it for these many yeers together, a knot of Scotish bankers,[69] collybists or coinecoursers, of traffickers in merchandise to and againe and of men of other professions who by hook and crook, *fas et nefas*, slight and might, all being as fish their net could catch, having feathered their nests to some purpose, look so idolatrously upon their Dagon of wealth[70] and so closely, like the earth's dull center, hug all unto themselves, that for no respect of vertue, honor, kinred, patriotism or whatever else, be it never so recommendable, will they depart from so much as one single peny, whose emission doth not, without any hazard of loss, in a very short time superlucrate beyond all conscience an additionall increase to the heap of that stock which they so much adore; which churlish and tenacious humor hath made many

Collybists: *usurers*   Coursers: *exchangers*   *Fas et nefas: right and wrong*
Superlucrate: *make an additional profit*

that were not acquainted with any else of that country to imagine all their compatriots infected with the same leprosie of a wretched peevishness whereof those *quomodocunquizing* cluster-fists and rapacious varlets have given of late such cannibal-like proofs by their inhumanity and obdurate carriage towards some whose shoos' strings they are not worthy to unty; that were it not that a more able pen then mine will assuredly not faile to jerk them on all sides, in case, by their better demeanor for the future, they endeavor not to wipe off the blot wherewith their native country, by their sordid avarice and miserable baseness, hath been so foully stained, I would at this very instant blaze them out in their names and surnames, notwithstanding the vizard of Presbyterian zeal wherewith they maske themselves, that like so many wolves, foxes or Athenian Timons,[71] they might in all time coming be debarred the benefit of any honest conversation.

Thus is it perceptible how usual it is, from the irregularity of a few to conclude an universal defection, and that the whole is faulty because a part is not right; there being in it a fallacy of induction, as if because this, that and the other are both greedy and dissembling, that therefore all other their countrymen are such, which will no wayes follow, if any one of these others be free from those vices; for that one particular negative, by the rules of contradictory opposites, will destroy an universal affirmative; and of such there are many thousands in that nation who are neither greedy nor dissemblers.

And so would all the rest, if a joint and unanimous course were taken to have their noblemen free from baseness; their churchmen from avarice; their merchants from deceit; their gentlemen from pusillanimity; their lawyers from prevarication; their tradesmen from idleness; their farmers from lying; their young men from pride; their old men from morosity; their rich from hard heartednes; their poor from theeving; their great ones from faction; their meaner sort from implicit sectatorship; the magistrates from injustice; the clients from litigiousness and all of them from dishonesty and disrespect of learning; which, though but negatives of vertue and at best but the *ultimum non esse*

Quomodocunquizing: making money in every possible way   Clusterfists: *niggards*
Sectatorship: *belonging to a sect*   *Ultimum non esse: the very worst case*

of vice, would nevertheless go near to restore the good fame of that country to its pristine integrity; the report whereof was raised to so high a pitch of old, that in a book in the last edition of a pretty bulk, written in the Latine tongue by one Dempster,[72] there is mention made, what for armes and arts, of at least five thousand illustrious men of Scotland, the last liver whereof dyed above fifty yeers ago.

Nor did their succession so far degenerate from the race of so worthy progenitors, but that even of late, although before the intestine garboyles of this island, several of them have for their fidelity, valor and gallantry[73] been exceedingly renowned over all France, Spaine, the Venetian territories, Pole, Moscovy, the Low-countryes, Swedland, Hungary, Germany, Denmark and other states and kingdoms, as may appear by General Ruddurford; my Lord General Sir James Spence of Wormiston, afterwards by the Swedish king created Earl of Orcholm; Sir Patrick Ruven, Governor of Ulme, general of an army of High-Germans and afterwards Earl of Forth and Branford; Sir Alexander Leslie, governor of the cities along the Baltick coast, field-marshal over the army in Westphalia and afterwards intituled *Scoticani foederis supremus dux*;[74] General James King, afterwards made Lord Ythen; Colonel David Leslie, commander of a regiment of horse over the Dutch and afterwards in these our domestick wars advanced to be lieutenant-general of both horse and foot; Major General Thomas Kar; Sir David Drummond, general major and Governor of Statin in Pomer; Sir George Douglas, colonel and afterwards employed in embassies betwixt the soveraigns of Britain and Swedland; Colonel George Lindsay, Earl of Craford; Colonel Lord Forbas; Colonel Lord Sancomb; Colonel Lodovick Leslie and in the late troubles at home Governor of Berwick and Tinmouth-sheels; Colonel Sir James Ramsey, Governor of Hanaw; Colonel Alexander Ramsey, Governor of Craszenach and quartermaster-general to the Duke of Wymar; Colonel William Bailif, afterwards in these our intestin broyls promoved to the charge of lieutenant-general; another Colonel Ramsey besides any of the former two, whose name I cannot hit upon; Sir James Lumsden, colonel in Germany and afterwards Governor of

Garboyles: *disturbances*

Newcastle and general major in the Scotish wars; Sir George Cunningham; Sir John Ruven; Sir John Hamilton; Sir John Meldrum; Sir Arthur Forbas; Sir Frederick Hamilton; Sir James Hamilton; Sir Francis Ruven; Sir John Innes; Sir William Balantine and several other knights, all colonels of horse or foot in the Swedish wars.

As likewise by Colonel Alexander Hamilton, agnamed dear Sandy, who afterwards in Scotland was made general of the artillery for that in some measure he had exerced the same charge in Dutchland under the command of Marquis James Hamilton, whose generalship over six thousand English in the Swedish service I had almost forgot; by Colonel Robert Cunningham; Colonel Robert Monro of Fowls; Colonel Obstol Monro; Colonel Hector Monro; Colonel Robert Monro, lately general major in Ireland, who wrote a book in folio, intituled *Monroe's Expedition*;[75] Colonel Assen Monro; Colonel James Seaton and Colonel James Seaton;[76] Colonel John Kinindmond; Colonel John Urquhart, who is a valiant souldier, expert commander and learned scholar; Colonel James Spence; Colonel Hugh Hamilton; Colonel Francis Sinclair; Colonel John Leslie of Wardes; Colonel John Leslie, agnamed the omnipotent, afterwards made major-general; Colonel Robert Lumsden; Colonel Robert Leslie; Colonel William Gun, who afterwards in the yeer 1639 was knighted by King CHARLES for his service done at the Bridge of Dee neer Aberdeen against the Earl of Montross,[77] by whom he was beaten; Colonel George Colen; Colonel Crichtoun; Colonel Liddel; Colonel Armestrong; Colonel John Gordon; Colonel James Cochburne; Colonel Thomas Thomson; Colonel Thomas Kinindmond; Colonel James Johnston; Colonel Edward Johnston; Colonel William Kinindmond; Colonel George Leslie; Colonel Robert Stuart; Colonel Alexander Forbas, agnamed the Bauld; Colonel William Cunningham; another Colonel Alexander Forbas; Colonel Alexander Leslie; Colonel Alexander Cunningham; Colonel Finess Forbas; Colonel David Edintoun; Colonel Sandilands; Colonel Walter Leckie and divers other Scotish colonels, what of horse and foot, many whereof within a short space thereafter attained to be general persons under the

Agnamed: *nicknamed*

93

command of Gustavus the Caesaromastix[78] who confided so much in the valour, loyalty and discretion of the Scotish nation, and they reciprocally in the gallantry, affection and magnanimity of him, that immediately after the battel at Leipisch,[79] in one place and at one time he had six and thirty Scotish colonels about him whereof some did command a whole brigad of horse, some a brigad composed of two regiments, half horse half foot, and others a brigade made up of foot only without horse; some againe had the command of a regiment of horse only without foot, some a regiment of horse alone without more and others of a regiment of dragoons; the half of the names of which colonels are not here inserted, though they were men of notable prowesse and in martial atchievements of most exquisite dexterity; whose regiments were commonly distinguished by the diversity of nations of which they were severally composed, many regiments of English, Scots, Danes, Sweds, Fins, Liflanders, Laplanders, High-Dutch and other nations, serving in that confederate war of Germany under the command of Scotish colonels.

And besides these above-mentioned colonels, when any of the foresaid number either dyed of himself, was killed in the fields, required a pass for other countryes or otherwise disposing of himself, did voluntarily demit his charge (another usually of the same nation succeeding in his place), other as many moe Scotish colonels, for any thing I know, as I have here set down, did serve in the same Swedish wars under the conduct of the Duke of Wymar, Gustavus Horne, Baneer and Torsisson,[80] without reckoning amongst them or any of the above-recited officers the number of more then threescore of the Scotish nation that were governors of cities, townes, citadels, forts and castles in the respective conquered provinces of the Dutch Empire.

Denmark in my opinion cannot goodly forget the magnanimous exploits of Sir Donald Mackie, Lord Reay, first colonel there and afterwards commander of a brigade under the Swedish standard; not yet of the colonels of the name of Monro and Henderson in the service of that king; as likewise of the Colonel Lord Spynay and others; besides ten governors at least, all Scots, intrusted with the charge of the most especial strengths and holds of importance that were within the confines of the Danish authority; although no mention were made of exempt Mowat living in Birren[81] in whose judgment and fidelity such

94

trust is reposed, that he is as it were Vice-King of Norway; what obligation the State of France doth owe to the old Lord Colvil, colonel of horse; the two Colonel Hepburnes, Sir John Hepburn by name, and Colonel Heburn of Wachton and Colonel Lord James Douglas, the last three whereof were *mareschaux de camp* and, had they survived the respective day wherein they successively dyed in the bed of honor, would undoubtedly very shortly after have been all of them made Mareschals of France, one of the highest preferments belonging to the milice of that nation, is not unknown to those that are acquainted with the French affaires; and truly as for Sir John Heburn (albeit no mention was made of him in the list of Scots officers in the Swedish service) he had under Gustavus the charge of a brigad of foot, and so gallantly behaved himself at the battel of Leipisch, that unto him, in so far as praise is due to man, was attributed the honour of the day.

Sir Andrew Gray, Sir John Seatoun, Sir John Fulerton, the Earl of Irvin, Sir Patrick Morray, Colonel Erskin, Colonel Andrew Linsay, Colonel Mowat, Colonel Morison, Colonel Thomas Hume, Colonel John Forbas, Colonel Liviston, Colonel John Leslie besides a great many other Scots of their charge, condition and quality, were all colonels under the pay of Lewis the Thirteenth of France.[82] Some of those also, though not listed in the former roll, had, before they engaged themselves in the French employment, standing regiments under the command of the Swedish king.

The interest of France, Swedland and Denmark not being able to bound the valour of the Scotish nation within the limits of their territories, the several expeditions into Hungary, Dalmatia and Croatia against the Turks; into Transylvania against Bethleem Gabor; to Italy against the Venetians and in Germany against Count Mansfield and the confederate princes can testifie the many martial exploits of Colonel Sir John Henderson, Colonel William Johnston (who shortly thereafter did excellent service to this King of Portugal and is a man of an upright minde and a most undaunted courage), Colonel Lithco, Colonel Wedderburne, Colonel Bruce and of many other

Mareschaux de camp: field marshals   Milice: *militia*

colonels of that country whose names I know not; but above all the two eminent ones, Colonel Leslie and Colonel Gordon;[83] the first whereof is made an hereditary Marquess of the Empire and colonel-general of the whole infantry of all the imperial forces; and the other gratified with the priviledge of the Golden Key as a cognizance of his being raised to the dignity of High Chamberlain of the Emperour's court; which splendid and illustrious places of so sublime honour and pre-eminence were deservedly conferred on them for such extraordinary great services done by them for the weal and grandeur of the Caesarean majesty, as did by far surpass the performance of any to the Austrian family, now living in this age.

But lest the emperour should brag too much of the gallantry of those Scots above others of that nation, his cousin the King of Spaine is able to outvie him in the person of the ever-renowned Earl of Bodwel[84] whose unparallel'd valour, so frequently tried in Scotland, France, Germany, the Low-Countries, Spain, Italy and other parts, in a very short time began to be so redoubtable, that at last he became a terrour to all the most desperate duellists and bravos of Europe and a queller of the fury of the proudest champions of his age; for all the innumerable combats which he fought against both Turks and Christians, both on horse and foot, closed always with the death or subjection of the adversary of whatever degree or condition soever he might be, that was so bold as to cope with and encounter him in that kinde of hostility; the Gasconads of France, Rodomontads of Spain, Fanfaronads of Italy[85] and bragadochio brags of all other countries could no more astonish his invincible heart then would the cheeping of a mouse a bear robbed of her whelps. That warlike and strong Mahometan who dared, like another Goliath, and appealled the stoutest and most valiant of the Christian faith to enter the lists with him and fight in the defence of their religion, was, after many hundreds of galliant Christians had been foyled by him, thrown dead to the ground by the vigour and dexterity of his hand. He would very often in the presence of ladies whose intimate favourite he was, to give some proof of the undantedness of his courage, by the meer activity of his body with the help of a single sword, set upon a lyon in his greatest fierceness and kill him dead upon the place. For running, vaulting, jumping, throwing of the barr and other suchlike feats of nimbleness, strength and agility, he was the only paragon of the world and unmatched by any.

Whilst in Madrid, Genua, Milan, Venice, Florence, Naples, Paris, Bruxelles, Vienna and other great and magnificent cities, for the defence of the honour and reputation of the ladies whom he affected, he had in such measure incurred the hatred and indignation of some great and potent princes, that, to affront him, they had sent numbers of Spadassins and Acuchilladores[86] to surprise him at their best advantage; he would often times, all alone, buckle with ten or twelve of them and lay such load and so thick and threefold upon them, that he would quickly make them for their safeties betake themselves to their heels with a vengeance at their back; by which meanes he gave such evidence of his greatness of resolution, strenuitie of person, excellency in conduct and incomparable magnanimity of spirit, that, being comfortable to his friends, formidable to his foes and admirable to all, such as formerly had been his cruellest enemies and most deeply had plotted and projected his ruine, were at last content out of a remorse of conscience to acknowledge the ascendent of his worth above theirs and to sue, in all humility, to be reconciled to him. To this demand of theirs, out of his wonted generosity which was never wanting, when either goodness or mercie required the making use thereof, having fully condescended, he past the whole remainder of his days in great security and with all ease desirable in the city of Naples, where, in a vigorous old age, environed with his friends and enjoying the benefit of all his senses till the last hour, he dyed in full peace and quietness; and there I leave him. For should I undertake condignly to set down all the martial atchievements and acts of prowess performed by him in turnaments, duels, battels, skirmishes and fortuite encounters against Scots, French, Dutch, Polonians, Hungarians, Spaniards, Italians and others, were it not that there are above ten thousand as yet living who, as eye witnesses, can verifie the truth of what I have related of him, the history thereof to succeeding ages would seem so incredible, that they would but look upon it at best but as on a Romance stuft with deeds of chivalrie like those of Amades de Gaule, Esplandian and Don Sylves de la Selve.[87]

Fortuite: *chance*

Next to the renowned Count Bodwel in the service of that great Don Philippe, tetrarch of the world, upon whose subjects the sun never sets, are to be recorded, besides a great many other colonels of Scotland, those valorous and worthy Scots, Colonel William Sempil, Colonel Boyd and Colonel Lodovick Lindsay, Earl of Crawford. There is yet another Scotish colonel that served this King of Spain whose name is upon my tongue's end and yet I cannot hit upon it. He was not a souldier bred, yet for many yeers together bore charge in Flanders under the command of Spinola.[88] In his youth-hood he was so strong and stiff a Presbyterian, that he was the onely man in Scotland made choice of and relied upon for the establishment and upholding of that government, as the arch-prop and main pillar thereof; but as his judgment increased and that he ripened in knowledge, declining from that neoterick faith and waining in his love to Presbytery as he waxed in experience of the world, of a strict Puritan that he was at first, he became afterwards the most obstinate and rigid Papist that ever was upon the earth. It is strange my memory should so faile me, that I cannot remember his title. He was a lord, I know. Nay more, he was an earle! I, that he was, and one of the first of them. Ho now! Pescods on it! Crawford, Lodi Lindsay puts me in minde of him. It was the old Earl of Argile,[89] this Marquis of Argile's father! That was he. That was the man, etc.

Now, as steel is best resisted and overcome by steel, and that the Scots, like Ismael,[90] whose hand was against every man and every man's hand against him, have been of late so ingaged in all the wars of Christendome, espousing in a manner the interest of all the princes thereof; that, what battel soever at any time these forty yeers past hath been struck within the continent of Europe, all the Scots that fought in that field were never overthrown and totally routed, for if some of them were captives and taken prisoners, others of that nation were victorious and givers of quarter; valour and mercy on the one side with misfortune and subjection upon the other side, meeting one another in the persons of compatriots on both sides; so the gold and treasure of the Indias, not being able to purchase all the affections of

Tetrarch: *ruler of a fourth part*   Neoterick: *recent*

Scotland to the furtherance of Castilian designes, there have been of late several Scotish colonels under the command of the Prince of Orange[91] in opposition of the Spagniard: viz, Colonel Edmond, who took the valiant Count de Buccoy twice prisoner in the field; Sir Henry Balfour; Sir David Balfour; Colonel Brog, who took a Spanish general in the field upon the head of his army; Sir Francis Henderson; Colonel Scot; Earl of Bacliugh; Colonel Sir James Livistoun, now Earl of Calander and lately in these our tourmoyles at home lieutenant-general of both horse and foot; besides a great many other worthy colonels amongst which I will only commemorate one, named Colonel Douglas, who to the States of Holland was often times serviceable in discharging the office and duty of general engineer; whereof they are now so sensible, that, to have him alive againe and of that vigour and freshness in both body and spirit wherewith he was endowed in the day he was killed on, they would give thrice his weight in gold; and well they might, for some few weeks before the fight wherein he was slaine, he presented to them twelve articles and heads of such wonderful feats for the use of the wars both by sea and land, to be performed by him, flowing from the remotest springs of mathematical secrets and those of natural philosophy, that none of this age saw nor any of our forefathers ever heard the like, save what, out of Cicero, Livy, Plutarch and other old Greek and Latin writers, we have couched of the admirable inventions made use of by Archimedes in defence of the city of Syracusa[92] against the continual assaults of the Romane forces, both by sea and land, under the conduct of Marcellus. To speak really, I think there hath not been any in this age of the Scotish nation, save Neper and Crichtoun, who, for abilities of the minde in matter of practical inventions useful for men of industry, merit to be compared with him; and yet of these two, notwithstanding their precellency in learning, I would be altogether silent because I made account to mention no other Scotish men here but such as have been famous for souldiery and brought up at the schoole of Mars, were it not that, besides their profoundness in literature, they were inriched with military qualifications beyond expression.

As for Neper, otherwayes designed Lord Marchiston, he is for his logarithmical device so compleatly praised in that Preface of the author's[93] which ushers a trigonometrical book of his,

99

intituled *The Trissotetras*, that to add any more thereunto would but obscure with an empty sound the clearness of what is already said; therefore I will allow him no share in this discourse but in so far as concerneth an almost incomprehensible device which, being in the mouths of the most of Scotland and yet unknown to any that ever was in the world but himself, deserveth very well to be taken notice of in this place, and it is this: he had the skill, as is commonly reported, to frame an engine for invention not much unlike that of Archita's Dove,[94] which, by vertue of some secret springs, inward resorts, with other implements and materials fit for the purpose inclosed within the bowels thereof, had the power, if proportionable in bulk to the action required of it (for he could have made it of all sizes) to clear a field of four miles circumference of all the living creatures exceeding a foot of hight that should be found thereon, how neer soever they might be to one another; by which means he made it appear that he was able with the help of this machine alone to kill thirty thousand Turkes without the hazard of one Christian. Of this it is said that, upon a wager, he gave proof upon a large plaine in Scotland to the destruction of a great many herds of cattel and flocks of sheep, whereof some were distant from other half a mile on all sides and some a whole mile. To continue the thred of the story as I have it, I must not forget that, when he was most earnestly desired by an old acquaintance and professed friend of his, even about the time of his contracting that disease whereof he dyed, he would be pleased for the honour of his family and his own everlasting memory to posterity to reveal unto him the manner of the contrivance of so ingenious a mystery; subjoining thereto, for the better persuading of him, that it were a thousand pities that so excellent an invention should be buryed with him in the grave and that after his decease nothing should be known thereof, his answer was: that for the ruine and overthrow of man there were too many devices already framed, which, if he could make to be fewer, he would with all his might endeavour to do; and that therefore, seeing the malice and rancor rooted in the heart of mankind will not suffer them to diminish; by any new conceit of his the number of them should never be increased. Divinely spoken, truly.

To speak a little now of his compatriot Crichtoun,[95] I hope will not offend the ingenuous reader who may know, by what is already displayed, that it cannot be heterogeneal from the proposed purpose to make report of that magnanimous act atchieved by him at the Duke of Mantua's court[96] to the honour not only of his own but to the eternal renown also of the whole Isle of Britain; the manner whereof was thus.

A certain Italian gentleman of a mighty, able, strong, nimble and vigorous body; by nature fierce, cruell, warlike and audacious, and in the gladiatory art so superlatively expert and dextrous, that all the most skilful teachers of escrime and fencing-masters of Italy (which in matter of choice professors in that faculty needed never as yet to yeild to any nation in the world) were by him beaten to their good behaviour and, by blows and thrusts given in, which they could not avoid, enforced to acknowledge him their over comer. Bethinking himself how, after so great a conquest of reputation, he might by such means be very suddenly enriched, he projected a course of exchanging the blunt to sharp and the foiles into tucks; and in this resolution, providing a purse full of gold worth neer upon four hundred pounds English money, traveled alongst the most especial and considerable parts of Spaine, France, the Low Countryes, Germany, Pole, Hungary, Greece, Italy and other places, where ever there was greatest probability of encountring with the eagerest and most atrocious duellists; and immediately after his arrival to any city or town that gave apparent likelihood of some one or other champion that would enter the lists and cope with him, he boldly challenged them with sound of trumpet in the chief marketplace, to adventure an equal sum of money against that of his, to be disputed at the sword's point who should have both. There failed not several brave men, almost of all nations, who accepting of his cartels, were not afraid to hazard both their person and coine against him; but, till he midled with this Crichtoun, so maine was the ascendent he had above all his antagonists, and so unlucky the fate of such as offered to scuffle with him, that all his opposing combatants of what state or dominion soever they were, who had not lost both their life and gold, were glad for the preservation of their person, though

Heterogeneal: *diverse, apart*   Escrime: *fencing*   Tucks: *rapiers*
Atrocious: *fierce*   Cartels: *written challenges*

sometimes with a great expence of blood, to leave both their reputation and mony behind them.

At last, returning homewards to his own country, loaded with honor and wealth or rather the spoile of the reputation of those forraigners whom the Italians call *Tramontani*,[97] he by the way after his accustomed manner of abording other places, repaired to the city of Mantua, where the Duke, according to the courtesie usually bestowed on him by other princes, vouchsafed him a protection and savegard for his person. He, as formerly he was wont to do, by beat of drum, sound of trumpet and several printed papers disclosing his designe, battered on all the chief gates, posts and pillars of the town, gave all men to understand that his purpose was to challenge at the single rapier any whosever of that city or country that durst be so bold as to fight with him, provided he would deposite a bag of five hundred Spanish pistols over against another of the same value which himself should lay down; upon this condition, that the enjoyment of both should be the conqueror's due.

His challenge was not long unanswered, for it happened at the same time that three of the most notable cutters in the world, and so highly cryed up for valour that all the bravos of the land were content to give way to their domineering, how insolent soever they should prove because of their former constantly-obtained victories in the field, were all three together at the court of Mantua; who, hearing of such a harvest of five hundred pistols to be reaped, as they expected very soon and with ease, had almost contested amongst themselves for the priority of the first encounterer but that one of my lord duke's courtiers moved them to cast lots for who should be first, second and third in case none of the former two should prove victorious. Without more adoe, he whose chance it was to answer the cartel with the first defiance, presented himself within the barriers or place appointed for the fight, where, his adversary attending him, as soon as the trumpet sounded a charge, they jointly fel to work; and, because I am not now to amplifie the particulars of a combat, although the dispute was very hot for a while, yet, whose fortune it was to be the first of the three in the field had the disaster to be the first of the three that was foyled; for at last, with

Abording: *approaching*   Barriers: *lists*

102

a thrust in the throat he was killed dead upon the ground. This nevertheless not a whit dismayed the other two, for the nixt day he that was second in the roll gave his appearance after the same manner as the first had done but with no better success, for he likewise was laid flat dead upon the place by means of a thrust he received in the heart. The last of the three, finding that he was as sure of being engaged in the fight as if he had been the first in order, pluckt up his heart, knit his spirits together and, on the day after the death of the second, most couragiously entering the lists, demeaned himself for a while with great activity and skill; but at last, his luck being the same with those that preceded him, by a thrust in the belly he within four and twenty hours after gave up the ghost.

These, you may imagine, were lamentable spectacles to the Duke and citie of Mantua who, casting down their faces for shame, knew not what course to take for reparation of their honour. The conquering duellist, proud of a victory so highly tending to both his honour and profit, for the space of a whole fortnight or two weeks together marched daily along the streets of Mantua without any opposition or controulment like another Romulus or Marcellus in triumph;[98] which, the never-too-much-to-be-admired Crichtoun perceiving, to wipe off the imputation of cowardise lying upon the court of Mantua to which he had but even then arrived (although formerly he had been a domestick thereof), he could neither eat nor drink till he had first sent a challenge to the conqueror, appelling him to repair with his best sword in his hand by nine of the clock in the morning of the next day in presence of the whole court and, in the same place where he had killed the other three, to fight with him upon this quarrel, that in the court of Mantua there were as valiant men as he; and, for his better encouragement to the desired undertaking, he assured him that to the aforesaid five hundred pistols he would adjoyn a thousand more, wishing him to do the like, that the victor, upon the point of his sword might carry away the richer booty.

The challenge with all its conditions is no sooner accepted of, the time and place mutually condescended upon kept accordingly and the fifteen hundred pistols *hinc inde* deposited, but of

Appelling: *challenging*

103

the two rapiers of equal weight, length and goodness, each taking one in presence of the duke, dutchess, with all the noblemen, ladies, magnificos and all the choicest of both men, women and maids of that citie, as soon as the signal for the duel was given by the shot of a great piece of ordnance of threescore and four pound ball, the two combatants with a lion-like animosity made their approach to one another, and, being within distance, the valiant Crichtoun, to make his adversary spend his fury the sooner, betook himself to the defensive part; wherein for a long time he shewed such excellent dexterity in warding the other's blows, slighting his falsifyings, in breaking measure and often by the agility of his body avoiding his thrusts, that he seemed but to play whilst the other was in earnest. The sweetness of Crichtoun's countenance in the hotest of the assault, like a glance of lightning on the hearts of the spectators, brought all the Italian ladies on a sudden to be enamoured of him; whilst the sternness of the other's aspect, he looking like an enraged bear, would have struck terrour into wolves and affrighted an English mastiff. Though they were both in their linens, to wit, shirts and drawers, without any other apparel, and in all outward conveniencies equally adjusted, the Italian, with redoubling his stroaks, foamed at the mouth with a cholerick heart and fetched a pantling breath. The Scot, in sustaining his charge, kept himself in a pleasant temper without passion and made void his designes. He alters his wards from tierce to quart; he primes and seconds it, now high now lowe, and casts his body like another Prothee[99] into all the shapes he can to spie an open on his adversary and lay hold of an advantage but all in vain; for the invincible Crichtoun, whom no cunning was able to surprise, contrepostures his respective wards and, with an incredible nimbleness of both hand and foot, evades his intent and frustrates the invasion. Now is it that the never before conquered Italian, finding himself a little faint, enters into a consideration that he may be overmatched; whereupon, a sad apprehension of danger seizing upon all his spirits, he would gladly have his life bestowed on him as a gift, but that, having never been

Pantling: *panting*   Tierce: *third of the eight parries in fencing*
Quart: *fourth of the eight parries in fencing*
Primes: *first of the eight parries in fencing*
Seconds: *second of the eight parries in fencing*   Contrepostures: *counters*

accustomed to yeeld, he knows not how to beg it. Matchless Crichtoun, seeing it now high time to put a gallant catastrophe to that so long dubious combat, animated with a divinely inspired fervencie to fulfil the expectation of the ladies and crown the duke's illustrious hopes, changeth his garb, falls to act another part, and from defender turns assailant. Never did art so grace nature nor nature second the precepts of art with so much liveliness and such observancie of time, as when, after he had struck fire out of the steel of his enemie's sword and gained the *feeble* thereof with the *fort* of his own; by angles of the strongest position, he did, by geometrical flourishes of straight and oblique lines, so practically execute the speculative part, that, as if there had been remoras and secret charms in the variety of his motion, the fierceness of his foe was in a trice transqualified into the numness of a pageant. Then was it that, to vindicate the reputation of the duke's family and expiate the blood of the three vanquished gentlemen, he alonged a stoccade *de pied ferme*, then recoyling, he advanced another thrust and lodged it home; after which, retiring again, his right foot did beat the cadence of the blow that pierced the belly of this Italian, whose heart and throat being hit with the two former stroaks, these three franch bouts given in upon the back of the other; besides that, if lines were imagined drawn from the hand that livered them to the places which were marked by them, they would represent a perfect isosceles triangle with a perpendicular from the top angle cutting the basis in the middle. They likewise gave us to understand, that by them he was to be made a sacrifice of atonement for the slaughter of the three aforesaid gentlemen who were wounded in the very same parts of their bodies by other such three venees as these, each whereof being mortal; and his vital spirits exhaling as his blood gushed out, all he spoke was this, that seeing he could not execute, his comfort in dying was that he could not dye by the hand of a braver man; after the uttering of which words, he expiring with the shril clareens of trumpets, bouncing thunder of artillery, bethwacked beating of

Fervencie: *ardour*   Feeble: *middle to point of blade, faible* (fencing term)
Fort: upper to middle point of blade, fort (fencing term)   Remoras: *hindrances*
Alonged: *lunged*   Stoccade: *thrust*   De pied ferme: *firm-footed*   Franch: *open*
Livered: *delivered*   Venees: *thrusts*   Clareens: *shrill sounds*

drums, universal clapping of hands and loud acclamations of joy for so glorious a victory, the aire above them was so rarified by the extremity of the noise and vehement sound, dispelling the thickest and most condensed parts thereof, that, as Plutarch speakes of the Grecians, when they raised their shouts of allegress up to the very heavens at the hearing of the gracious proclamations of Paulus Æmilius in favour of their liberty,[100] the very sparrows and other flying fowls were said to fall to the ground for want of aire enough to uphold them in their flight.

When this sudden rapture was over and all husht into its former tranquility, the noble gallantry and generosity beyond expression of the inimitable Crichtoun did transport them all againe into a new extasie of ravishment, when they saw him like an angel in the shape of a man or as another Mars with the conquered enemie's sword in one hand and the fifteen hundred pistols he had gained in the other, present the sword to the duke as his due and the gold to his high treasurer, to be disponed equally to the three widowes of the three unfortunate gentlemen lately slaine, reserving only to himself the inward satisfaction he conceived for having so opportunely discharged his duty to the House of Mantua.

The reader perhaps will think this wonderful and so would I too, were it not that I know, as Sir Philip Sydney says, that a wonder is no wonder in a wonderful subject[101] and consequently not in him who, for his learning, judgement, valour, eloquence, beauty and good-fellowship, was the perfectest result of the joynt labour of the perfect number of those six deities, Pallas, Apollo, Mars, Mercury, Venus and Bacchus, that hath been seen since the dayes of Alcibiades;[102] for he was reported to have been inriched with a memory so prodigious that any sermon, speech, harangue or other manner of discourse of an hour's continuance, he was able to recite without hesitation after the same manner of gesture and pronuntiation in all points wherewith it was delivered at first; and of so stupendious a judgement and conception, that almost naturally he understood quiddities of philosophy; and as for the abstrusest and most researched mysteries of other disciplines, arts and faculties, the intentional species of them were as readily obvious to the

Allegress: *joy*   Disponed: *distributed*   Quiddities: *subtleties* interiour view and perspicacity of his mind as those of the common visible colours to the external sight of him that will open his eyes to look upon them; of which accomplishment and encyclopedia of knowledge, he gave on a time so marvelous a testimony at Paris, that the words of *Admirabilis Scotus*, the Wonderful Scot, in all the several tongues and idiomes of Europ were, for a great while together, by the most of the echos resounded to the peircing of the very clouds.

To so great a hight and vast extent of praise did the never-too-much-to-be-extolled reputation of the seraphick wit of that eximious man attaine for his commanding to be affixed programs on all the gates of the schooles, halls and colledges of that famous university, as also on all the chief pillars and posts standing before the houses of the most renowned men for literature, resident within the precinct of the walls and suburbs of that most populous and magnificent city, inviting them all, or any whoever else versed in any kinde of scholastick faculty, to repair at nine of the clock in the morning of such a day, moneth and yeer, as by computation came to be just six weeks after the date of the affixes, to the common schoole of the Colledge of Navarre,[103] where at the prefixed time he should, God willing, be ready to answer to what should be propounded to him concerning any science, liberal art, discipline or faculty, practical or theoretick, not excluding the theological nor jurisprudential habits, though grounded but upon the testimonies of God and man, and in any of these twelve languages: Hebrew, Syriack, Arabick, Greek, Latin, Spanish, French, Italian, English, Dutch, Flemish and Sclavonian, in either verse or prose, at the discretion of the disputant; which high enterprise and hardy undertaking by way of challenge to the learnedst men in the world damped the wits of many able scholars to consider whether it was the attempt of a fanatick spirit or lofty designe of a well-poised judgment.

Yet, after a few dayes enquiry concerning him, when information was got of his incomparable endowments, all the choicest and most profound philosophers, mathematicians, naturalists, mediciners, alchymists, apothecaries, surgeons, doctors of both civil and canon law and divines both for

Eximious: *distinguished*   Affixes: *public notices posted up*

107

controversies and positive doctrine, together with the primest grammarians, rhetoricians, logicians and others, professors of other arts and disciplines at Paris, plyed their studys in their private cels for the space of a moneth exceeding hard, and with huge paines and labor set all their braines awork how to contrive the knurriest arguments and most difficult questions could be devised, thereby to puzzle him in the resolving of them, meander him in his answers, put him out of his medium and drive him to a nonplus; nor did they forget to premonish the ablest there of forraign nations not to be unprepared to dispute with him in their own maternal dialects and that sometimes metrically, sometimes otherwayes, *pro libitu.*

All this while the Admirable Scot, for so from thence forth he was called, minding more his hawking, hunting, tilting, vaulting, riding of well-managed horses, tossing of the pike, handling of the musket, flourishing of colours, dancing, fencing, swimming, jumping, throwing of the bar, playing at the tennis, baloon or long catch; and sometimes at the house games of dice, cards, playing at the chess, billiards, trou-madam[104] and other such like chamber-sports, singing, playing on the lute and other musical instruments, masking, balling, reveling; and, which did most of all divert or rather distract him from his speculations and serious employments, being more addicted to and plying closer the courting of handsome ladyes and a jovial cup in the company of bacchanalian blades then the forecasting how to avoid, shun and escape the snares, girns and nets of the hard, obscure and hidden arguments, ridles and demands to be made, framed and woven by the professors, doctors and others of that thrice-renowned university — there arose upon him an aspersion of too great proness to such like debordings and youthful emancipations, which occasioned one less acquainted with himself then his reputation to subjoyn, some two weeks before the great day appointed, to that program of his, which was fixed on the Sorbone-gate, these words: "If you would meet with this monster of perfection, to make search for him either in the taverne or bawdy-house is the readyest way to finde him". By

---

Knurriest: *most knotty*   Meander: *bewilder*   Nonplus: *standstill*
Premonish: *forewarn*   Pro libitu: *at one's pleasure*   Girns: *traps*
Debordings: *excesses*

reason of which expression, though truly as I think, both scandalous and false, the eminent sparks of the university, imagining that those papers of provocation had been set up to nother end but to scoff and delude them in making them waste their spirits upon quirks and quiddities more then was fitting, did resent a little of their former toyle and slack their studyes, becoming almost regardless thereof till the several peals of bells ringing an hour or two before the time assigned, gave warning that the party was not to flee the barriers nor decline the hardship of academical assaults; but, on the contrary, so confident in his former resolution, that he would not shrink to sustaine the shock of all their disceptations.

This sudden alarm so awaked them out of their last fortnight's lethargy, that calling to minde the best way they might, the fruits of the foregoing moneth's labour, they hyed to the forenamed schoole with all diligence; where, after all of them had, according to their several degrees and qualities, seated themselves, and that by reason of the noise occasioned through the great confluence of people which so strange a novelty brought thither out of curiosity, an universal silence was commanded, the Orator of the university in most fluent Latine, addressing his speech to Crichtoun, extolled him for his literature and other good parts and for that confident opinion he had of his own sufficiency in thinking himself able to justle in matters of learning with the whole university of Paris. Crichtoun answering him in no less eloquent terms of Latine, after he had most heartily thanked him for his elogies so undeservedly bestowed, and darted some high encomions upon the university and the professors therein, he very ingenuously protested that he did not emit his programs out of any ambition to be esteemed able to enter in competition with the university but meerly to be honoured with the favour of a publick conference with the learned men thereof. In complements after this manner *ultro citroque habitis*,[105] tossed to and again, retorted, contrerisposted, backreverted and now and then graced with a quip or a clinch for the better relish of the ear, being unwilling in this kind of straining curtesie to yeeld to other, they spent a full half hour

Nother: *no other*   Resent . . . of: *regret*   Disceptations: *disputations*
Literature: *humane learning*   Justle: *contend*   Elogies: *eulogies*

109

and more; for he being the centre to which the innumerable diameters of the discourses of that circulary convention did tend, although none was to answer but he, any of them all, according to the order of their prescribed series, were permitted to reply or comence new motions on any subject in what language soever and howsoever expressed; to all which, he being bound to tender himself a respondent in matter and form suitable to the impugners propounding, he did first so transcendently acquit himself of that circumstantial kinde of oratory that, by well-couched periods and neatly running syllables in all the twelve languages, both in verse and prose, he expressed to the life his courtship and civility; and afterwards, when the Rector of the university, unwilling to have any more time bestowed on superficial rhetorick or to have that wasted on the fondness of quaint phrases which might be better employed in a reciprocacy of discussing scientifically the nature of substantial things, gave direction to the professors to fall on, each according to the dignity or precedency of his Faculty and that, conform to the order given, some metaphysical notions were set abroach, then mathematical; and of those arithmetical, geometrical, astronomical, musical, optical, cosmographical, trigonometrical, statical and so forth through all the other branches of the prime and mother sciences thereof. The next bout was through all natural philosophy according to Aristotle's method from the acroamaticks, going along the speculation of the nature of the heavens and that of the generation and corruption of sublunary things, even to the consideration of the soul and its faculties. In sequel hereof, they had a hint at chymical extractions and spoke of the principles of corporeal and mixed bodies according to the precepts of that art. After this, they disputed of medicine in all its therapeutick, pharmacopeutick and chirurgical parts; and not leaving natural magick untouched, they had exquisite disceptations concerning the secrets thereof. From thence they proceeded to moral philosophy, where, debating of the true enumeration of all vertues and vices, they had most learned ratiocinations about

Statical: *pertaining to weighing*
Acroamaticks: *Aristotle's lectures to close friends and scholars on the esoteric parts of his philosophy*   Sublunary: *terrestrial*
Pharmacopeutick: *pertaining to the mixing or compounding of drugs*

the chief good of the life of man; and seeing the oecumenicks and politicks are parts of that philosophy, they argued learnedly of all the several sorts of governments with their defects and advantages; whereupon perpending that without an established law all the duties of ruling and subjection to the utter ruine of humane society would be as often violated as the irregularity of passion, seconded with power, should give way thereto. The Sorbonist canonical and civilian doctors most judiciously argued with him about the most prudential maximes, sentences, ordinances, acts and statutes for ordering all manner of persons in their consciences, bodyes, fortunes and reputations; nor was there an end put to those literate exercitations till the grammarians, rethoricians, poets and logicians had assailed him with all the subtleties and nicest *quodlibets* their respective habits could afford. Now when, to the admiration of all that were there, the incomparable Crichtoun had, in all these faculties above written, and in any of the twelve languages wherein he was spoke to, whether in verse or prose, held tack to all the disputants who were accounted the ablest scholars upon the earth in each their own profession, and publickly evidenced such an universality of knowledge and accurate promptness in resolving of doubts, distinguishing of obscurities, expressing the members of a distinction in adequate terms of art, explaining those compendious tearms with words of a more easie apprehension to the prostrating of the sublimest mysteries to any vulgar capacity; and with all excogitable variety of learning, to his own everlasting fame, entertained after that kinde the nimble witted Parisians from nine a clock in the morning till six at night; the Rector, now finding it high time to give some relaxation to these worthy spirits which, during such a long space, had been so intensively bent upon the abstrusest speculations, rose up, and saluting the divine Crichtoun, after he had made an elegant panegyrick or encomiastick speech of half an houre's continuance tending to nothing else but the extolling of him for the rare and most singular gifts wherewith God and nature had endowed him, he descended from his chaire and, attended by three or four of the most especial professors,

Oecumenicks: *considerations concerning the universal church*
Perpending: *considering*   Quodlibets: *scholastic debates*

presented him with a diamond ring and a purse full of gold, wishing him to accept thereof, if not as a recompense proportionable to his merit, yet as a badge of love and testimony of the universitie's favour towards him; at the tender of which ceremony there was so great a plaudite in the schoole, such a humming and clapping of hands, that all the concavities of the colledges there about did resound with the eccho of the noise thereof.

Notwithstanding the great honor thus purchased by him for his literary accomplishments and that many excellent spirits to obtaine the like would be content to postpose all other employments to the enjoyment of their studyes, he nevertheless the very next day, to refresh his braines as he said for the toile of the former day's work, went to the Louvre in a buff suit,[106] more like a favorite of Mars then one of the Muses' minions; where, in presence of some princes of the court and great ladies that came to behold his gallantry, he carryed away the ring fifteen times on end and broke as many lances on the Saracen.[107]

When for a quarter of a yeer together he after this manner had disported himself what martially, what scholastically, with the best qualified men in any Faculty so ever that so large a city, which is called the world's abridgement, was able to afford, and now and then solaced these his more serious recreations (for all was but sport to him) with the alluring imbellishments of the tendrer sexe, whose *inamorato* that he might be was their ambition; he on a sudden took resolution to leave the Court of France and return to Italy, where he had been bred for many yeers together; which designe he prosecuting within the space of a moneth without troubling himself with long journeys, he arrived at the Court of Mantua, where immediately after his abord, as hath been told already, he fought the memorable combat whose description is above related. Here was it that the learned and valiant Crichtoun was pleased to cast anchor and fix his abode; nor could he almost otherwayes do without disobliging the duke and the prince his eldest son; by either whereof he was so dearly beloved that none of them would permit him by any means to leave their court, whereof he was

Postpone: *place afterwards*   Buff suit: *military coat made of buff leather*
Inamorato: *beloved*   Abord: *landing*

the only *privado*, the object of all men's love and subject of their discourse; the example of the great ones and wonder of the meaner people; the paramour of the female sexe and paragon of his own: in the glory of which high estimation, having resided at that court above two whole yeers, the reputation of gentlemen there was hardly otherwayes valued but by the measure of his acquaintance; nor were the young unmaryed ladies of all the most eminent places thereabouts any thing respected of one another that had not either a lock of his haire or copy of verses of his composing.

Nevertheless it happening on a Shrove Tuesday at night, at which time it is in Italy very customary for men of great sobriety, modesty and civil behaviour all the rest of the yeer, to give themselves over on that day of carnavale, as they call it,[108] to all manner of riot, drunkenness and incontinency, which that they may do with the least imputation they can to their credit, they go maskt and mum'd with vizards on their faces and in the disguise of a Zanni or Pantaloon[109] to ventilate their fopperies, and sometimes intolerable enormities, without suspicion of being known, that this ever renowned Crichtoun who, in the afternoon of that day, at the desire of my lord duke, the whole court striving which should exceed other in foolery and devising of the best sports to excite laughter (neither my lord, the dutchess nor prince being exempted from acting their parts as well as they could), upon a theater set up for the purpose begun to prank it *a la Venetiana*[110] with such a flourish of mimick and ethopoetick gestures, that all the courtiers of both sexes, even those that a little before that were fondest of their own conceits, at the sight of his so inimitable a garb, from ravishing actors that they were before turned then ravished spectators.

O, with how great liveliness did he represent the conditions of all manner of men! How naturally did he set before the eyes of the beholders the rogueries of all professions from the overweening monarch to the peevish swaine through all the intermediate degrees of the superficial courtior or proud warrior, dissembled churchman, doting old man, cozening lawyer, lying traveler, covetous merchant, rude seaman, pedantick scolar, the amourous shepheard, envious artisan, vain-

Privado: confidant   Ethopoetick: *representing character or manners*

glorious master and tricky servant! He did with such variety display the several humours of all these sorts of people and with a so bewitching energy, that he seemed to be the original, they the counterfeit; and they the resemblance whereof he was the pro-totype. He had all the jeers, squibs, flouts, buls, quips, taunts, whims, jests, clinches, gybes, mokes, jerks, with all the several kinds of equivocations and other sophistical captions, that could properly be adapted to the person by whose representation he intended to inveagle the company into a fit of mirth; and would keep in that miscelany discourse of his which was all for the splene and nothing for the gall, such a climacterical and mercurially digested method that when the fancy of the hearers was tickled with any rare conceit and that the jovial blood was moved, he held it going with another new device upon the back of the first, and another, yet another and another againe, succeeding one another for the promoval of what is a stirring into a higher agitation; till in the closure of the luxuriant period, the decumanal wave of the oddest whimzy of all enforced the charmed spirits of the auditory for affording room to its apprehension suddenly to burst forth into a laughter, which commonly lasted just so long as he had leasure to withdraw behind the skreen, shift off with the help of a page the suite he had on, apparel himself with another and return to the stage to act afresh; for by that time their transported, disparpled and sublimated fancies, by the wonderfully operating engines of his solacious inventions, had from the hight to which the inward scrues, wheeles and pullies of his wit had elevated them, descended by degrees into their wonted stations, he was ready for the personating of another carriage; whereof to the number of fourteen several kinds (during the five hours' space that at the duke's desire, the sollicitation of the court and his own recreation, he was pleased to histrionize it) he shewed himself so natural a representative, that any would have thought he had been so many several actors, differing in all things else save the only stature of the body; with this advantage above the most of other actors, whose tongue with its oral implements is the onely

Buls: *jests*   Mokes: *mockeries*   Climacterical: *cleverly spaced out, climacteric*
Promoval: *furthering*   Decumanal: *immense*   Disparpled: *scattered*
Sublimated: *elevated*

instrument of their mind's disclosing, that, besides his mouth with its appurtenances, he lodged almost a several oratour in every member of his body — his head, his eyes, his shoulders, armes, hands, fingers, thighs, legs, feet and breast, being able to decipher any passion whose character he purposed to give.

First, he did present himself with a crown on his head, a scepter in his hand, being clothed in a purple robe furred with ermyne; after that with a miter on his head, a crosier in his hand and accoutred with a pair of lawn-sleeves; and thereafter with a helmet on his head (the visiere up), a commanding-stick in his hand and arayed in a buff suit with a scarf about his middle. Then in a rich apparel after the newest fashion, did he shew himself like another Sejanus with a periwig daubed with Cypres powder.[111] In sequel of that he came out with a three corner'd cap on his head, some parchments in his hand and writings hanging at his girdle like Chancery bills; and next to that, with a furred gown about him, an ingot of gold in his hand and a bag full of money by his side. After all this he appeares againe clad in a country-jacket with a prong in his hand and a Monmouth-like cap on his head.[112] Then very shortly after with a palmer's coat upon him, a bourdon in his hand and some few cockle-shels stuck to his hat he look't as if he had come in pilgrimage from Saint Michael.[113] Immediately after that he domineers it in a bare, unlined gowne with a pair of whips in the one hand and Corderius in the other; and in suite thereof he honderspondered it[114] with a pair of pannier-like breeches, a mountera cap on his head and a knife in a wooden sheath dagger-ways by his side. About the latter end he comes forth again with a square in one hand, a rule in the other and a leather apron before him; then very quickly after with a scrip by his side, a sheep-hook in his hand and a basket full of flowers to make nosegayes for his mistris. Now drawing to a closure, he rants it first *in cuerpo* and vapouring it with gingling spurs and his armes a *a kenbol*[115] like a Don Diego he strouts it and, by the loftiness of his gate, plaies the Capitan Spavento.[116] Then in the very twinkling of an eye,

Monmouth-like cap: *flat round cap*   Bourdon: *pilgrim's staff*
In suite thereof: *as a sequel*
Honderspondered: *acted like a German mercenary. (See Note 114, p. 227)*
Mountera cap: *Spanish hunter's cap*   In cuerpo: *in his shirt*
Vapouring: *swaggering*   A kenbol: *akimbo*   Strouts: *struts*

you would have seen him againe issue forth with a cloak upon his arm in a livery garment, thereby representing the serving-man; and lastly, at one time amongst those other, he came out with a long gray beard and bucked ruff, crouching on a staff tip't with the head of a barber's cithern and his gloves hanging by a button at his girdle.

Those fifteen several personages he did represent with such excellency of garb and exquisiteness of language, that con-dignely to perpend the subtlety of the invention, the method of the disposition, the neatness of the elocution, the gracefulness of the action and wonderful variety in the so dextrous performance of all, you would have taken it for a comedy of five acts, con-sisting of three scenes each composed by the best poet in the world and acted by fifteen of the best players that ever lived, as was most evidently made apparent to all the spectators in the fifth and last hour of his action which, according to our western account, was about six a clock at night and, by the calculation of that country, half an hour past three and twenty at that time of the yeer; for, purposing to leave of with the setting of the sun, with an endeavour nevertheless to make his conclusion the master-piece of the work, he, to that effect summoning all his spirits together, which never failed to be ready at the cal of so worthy a commander, did by their assistance so conglomerate, shuffle, mix and interlace the gestures, inclinations, actions and very tones of the speech of those fifteen several sorts of men whose carriages he did personate into an inestimable *ollapodrida* of immaterial morsels of divers kinds, sutable to the very ambrosian relish of the Heliconian nymphs,[117] that in the peripetia of this drammatical exercitation, by the inchanted transportation of the eyes and eares of its spectabundal auditorie, one would have sworne that they all had looked with multiplying glasses, and that, like that angel in the Scripture[118] whose voice was said to be like the voice of a multitude, they heard in him alone the promiscuous speech of fifteen several actors; by the various ravishments of the excellencies whereof, in the frolickness of a jocound straine beyond expectation, the

Bucked: *boiled in an alkaline dye and then beaten and rinsed in clear water*
Cithern: *guitar-like instrument (often kept in barbers' shops for use of customers)*
Ollapodrida: *hotchpotch*   Spectabundal: *easy to see*

logofascinated spirits of the beholding hearers and auricularie spectators were so on a sudden seazed upon in their risible faculties of the soul, and all their vital motions so universally affected in this extremitie of agitation that, to avoid the inevitable charmes of his intoxicating ejaculations and the accumulative influences of so powerfull a transportation, one of my lady dutchess' chief maids of honour, by the vehemencie of the shock of those incomprehensible raptures, burst forth into a laughter to the rupture of a veine in her body; and another young lady, by the irresistible violence of the pleasure unawares infused, where the tender receptibilitie of her too too tickled fancie was least able to hold out, so unprovidedly was surprised that, with no less impetuositie of ridibundal passion then as hath been told occasioned a fracture in the other young ladie's modestie, she, not being able longer to support the well-beloved burthen of so excessive delight and intransing joys of such mercurial exhilarations, through the ineffable extasie of an overmastered apprehension fell back in a swown without the appearance of any other life into her then what by the most refined wits of theological speculators is conceived to be exerced by the purest parts of the separated entelechies of blessed saints in their sublimest conversations with the celestial hierarchies. This accident procured the incoming of an apothecarie with restoratives as the other did that of a surgeon with consolidative medicaments.

The Admirable Crichtoun now perceiving that it was drawing somewhat late and that our occidental rays of Phoebus were upon their turning oriental to the other hemisphere of the terrestrial globe, being withall jealous that the uninterrupted operation of the exuberant diversitie of his jovialissime entertainment, by a continuate winding up of the humours there present to a higher, yet higher and still higher pitch above the supremest Lydian note[119] of the harmonie of voluptuousness, should in such a case through the too intensive stretching of the already-super-elated strings of their imagination, with a transendencie overreaching Ela[120] and beyond the well-concerted *gam* of rational equanimitie, involve the remainder of

---

Logofascinated: *fascinated by words*   Ridibundal: *inclined to laughter*
Entelechies: *souls*   Jovialissime: *most good-humoured*   Gam: *gamut*

that illustrious companie into the sweet labyrinth and mellifluent aufractuosities of a lacinious delectation, productive of the same inconveniences which befel the two afore-named ladies; whose delicacie of constitution, though sooner overcome, did not argue but that the same extranean causes from him proceeding of their pathetick alteration might by a longer insisting in an efficacious agencie and unremitted working of all the consecutively imprinted degrees that the capacity of the patient is able to containe, prevaile at last and have the same predominancie over the dispositions of the strongest complexioned males of that splendid society; did, in his own ordinary wearing apparel, with the countenance of a prince and garb befitting the person of a so well bred gentleman and cavalier, κατ ἐξοχήν, full of majesty and repleat with all excogitable civilitie, to the amazement of all that beheld his heroick gesture, present himself to epilogate this his almost extemporanean comedie, though of five hours continuance without intermission; and that with a peroration so neatly uttreed, so distinctly pronounced and in such elegancie of selected termes expressed by a diction so periodically contexed with isocoly of members, that the matter thereof tending in all humility to beseech the highnesses of the duke, prince and dutchess together with the remanent lords, ladies, knights, gentlemen and others of both sexes of that honorable convention, to vouchsafe him the favour to excuse his that afternoon's escaped extravagancies and to lay the blame of the indigested irregularity of his wit's excursions and the abortive issues of his disordered brain upon the customarily-dispensed-with priviledges in those Cisalpinal regions, to authorize such like impertinences at carnavalian festivals; and that although, according to the most commonly received opinion in that country (after the nature of Load-him, a game at cards where he that wins loseth), he who at that season of the year playeth the fool most egregiously is reputed the wisest man, he nevertheless, not being ambitious of the fame of enjoying good qualities by vertue of the antiphrasis of the fruition of bad ones, did meerly

Aufractuosities: *skilfully broken up language of rhetoric*   Lacinious: *prolix*
Κατ ἐξοχήν: *par excellence*   Epilogate: *speak the epilogue*   Isocoly: *equality*
Remanent: *remaining*   Cisalpinal: *on the south side of the Alps*
Antiphrasis: *words used in sense opposite to their usual meaning*

undergo that emancipatorie task of a so profuse liberty and to no other end embraced the practising of such roaming and exorbitant diversions but to give an evident, or rather infallible, demonstration of his eternally bound duty to the House of Mantua and an inviolable testimony of his never-to-be-altered designe, in prosecuting all the occasions possible to be laid hold on that can in any manner of way prove conducible to the advancement of, and contributing to the readiest means for improving those advantages that may best promove the faculties of making all his choice endeavours and utmost abilities at all times, effectual to the long wished for furtherance of his most cordial and endeared service to the serenissime highnesses of my lord duke, prince and dutchess, and of consecrating with all addicted obsequiousness and submissive devotion, his everlasting obedience to the illustrious shrine of their joynt commands. Then, incontinently addressing himself to the lords, ladies and others of that rotonda (which, for his daigning to be its inmate, though but for that day, might be accounted in nothing inferiour to the great Colisee of Rome or Amphitheater at Neems) with a stately carriage and port suitable to so prime a gallant, he did cast a look on all the corners thereof, so bewitchingly amiable and magnetically efficacious as if in his eys had bin a muster of ten thousand cupids, eagerly striving who should most deeply pierce the hearts of the spectators with their golden darts.

And truly so it fell out, that there not being so much as one arrow shot in vain, all of them did love him, though not after the same manner nor for the same end; for, as the manna of the Arabian desarts[121] is said to have had in the mouths of the Egyptian Israelites the very same tast of the meat they loved best, so the princes that were there did mainly cherish him for his magnanimity and knowledge; his courtliness and sweet behaviour being that for which chiefly the noblemen did most respect him; for his pregnancie of wit and chivalrie in vindicating the honour of ladies he was honoured by the knights; and the esquires and other gentlemen courted him for his affability and good fellowship; the rich did favour him for his

Serenissime: *most serene*

119

judgement and ingeniosity and for his liberality and munifi-
cence he was blessed by the poor; the old men affected him for his
constancie and wisdome and the young for his mirth and
gallantry; the scholars were enamoured of him for his learning
and eloquence and the souldiers for his integrity and valour; the
merchants for his upright dealing and honesty praised and
extolled him and the artificers for his goodness and benignity;
the chastest lady of that place would have hugged and imbraced
him for his discretion and ingenuity whilst for his beauty and
comeliness of person he was, at least in the fervency of their
desires, the paramour of the less continent; he was dearly
beloved of the fair women because he was handsom, and of the
fairest more dearly becaus he was handsomer. In a word, the
affections of the beholders, like so many several diameters drawn
from the circumference of their various intents, did all concenter
in the point of his perfection.

After a so considerable insinuation and gaining of so much
ground upon the hearts of the auditory, though in shorter space
then the time of a flash of lightning, he went on as before in the
same thred of the conclusive part of his discourse with a
resolution not to cut it till the over-abounding passions of the
company, their exorbitant motions and discomposed gestures,
through excess of joy and mirth, should be all of them quieted,
calmed and pacified and every man, woman and maid there,
according to their humour, reseated in the same integrity they
were at first; which when, by the articulatest elocution of the
most significant words expressive of the choisest things that
fancie could suggest, and, conforme to the matter's variety,
elevating or depressing, flat or sharply accinating it, with that
proportion of tone that was most consonant with the purpose he
had attained unto, and by his verbal harmony and melodious
utterance setled all their distempered pleasures and brought
their disorderly raised spirits into their former capsuls; he with a
tongue tip't with silver, after the various diapasons of all his
other expressions and, making of a leg for the spruceness of its
courtsie of greater decorement to him then cloth of gold and
purple, farewel'd the companie with a complement of one
period so exquisitely delivered and so well attended by the

Accinating: *accenting*   Diapasons: *melodies*

120

gracefulness of his hand and foot with the quaint miniardise of the rest of his body in the performance of such ceremonies as are usual at a court-like departing; that from the theater he had gone into a lobbie, from thence along three spacious chambers, whence descending a backstaire, he past through a low gallerie which led him to the outer gate, where a coach with six horses did attend him, before that magnificent convention of both sexes (to whom that room, wherein they all were, seemed in his absence to be as a body without a soul) had the full leisure to recollect their spirits which, by the neatness of his so curious a close, were *quoquoversedly* scattered with admiration to advise on the best expediency how to dispose of themselves for the future of that licentious night.

During which time of their being thus in a maze, a proper young lady (if ever there was any in the world) whose dispersed spirits, by her wonderful delight in his accomplishments, were by the power of Cupid with the assistance of his mother, instantly gathered and replaced, did (upon his retiring) without taking notice of the intent of any other, rise up out of her boxe, issue forth at a posterne door into some secret transes, from whence going down a few steps that brought her to a parlour, she went through a large hall, by the wicket of one end whereof, as she entered on the street, she encountered with Crichtoun who was but even then come to the aforesaid coach which was hers; unto which sans ceremony (waving the frivolous windings of dilatory circumstances) they both stepped up together without any other in their company save a waiting gentle-woman that sate in the furthest side of the coach, a page that lifted up the boot thereof and walked by it, and one lacky that ran before with a kindled torch in his hand — all domestick servants of hers, as were the coach-man and postillion who, driving apace and having but a half mile to go, did with all the expedition required set down my lady with her beloved mate at the great gate of her own palace; through the wicket whereof, because she would not stay till the whole were made wide open, they entred both; and injunction being given that forthwith, after the setting up of the coach and horses, the gate should be

Miniardise: *delicacy of behaviour, caressing treatment*   Curious: *ingenious*
Close: *conclusion*   Quoquoversedly: *in every direction*   Posterne door: *private door*

made fast and none (more then was already) permitted to come within her court that night, they joyntly went along a private passage which led them to a lanterne scalier whose each step was twelve foot long; thence mounting up a paire of staires, they past through and traversed above nine several rooms on a floor before they reached her bedchamber; which, in the interim of the progress of their transitory walk, was with such mutual cordialness so unanimously aimed at, that never did the passengers of a ship in a tedious voyage long for a favourable winde with greater uniformity of desire then the blessed hearts of that amorous and amiable couple were, without the meanest variety of a wish, in every jot united.

Nevertheless at last they entred in it, or rather in an Alcoranal paradise[122] where nothing tending to the pleasure of all the senses was wanting. The weather being a little chil and coldish, they on a blew velvet couch sate by one another towards a charcoale fire burning in a silver brasero, whilst in the next room adjacent thereto a pretty little round table of cedar-wood was a covering for the supping of them two together. The cates prepared for them and, a week before that time bespoke, were of the choisest dainties and most delicious junkets that all the territories of Italy were able to afford and that deservedly, for all the Romane Empire could not produce a completer paire to taste them.

In beauty she was supream, in pedigree equal with the best; in spirit not inferiour to any, and in matter of affection a great admirer of Crichtoun, which was none of her least perfections. She many times used to repaire to my lady dutchesse's court, where now and then the prince would cast himself, as à l'improviste, into her way, to catch hold the more conveniently of someone or other opportunity for receiving her employments; with the favour whereof he very often protested, if she would vouchsafe to honour him and be pleased to gratifie his best endeavours with her only gracious acceptance of them, none breathing should be able to discharge that duty with more zeal to her service, nor reap more inward satisfaction in the performance of it; for that his obedience could not be crowned

Lanterne scalier: *winding staircase*   Alcoranal: *belonging to the Koran*
Brasero: *brazier*   A l'improviste: *unexpectedly*

with greater glory then by that of a permanently fixed attendance upon her commandments. His highness' complements, whereof to this noble lady he was at all times very liberal, remained never longer unexchanged then after they were delivered and that in a coine so pretious for language, matter, phrase and elocution, that he was still assured of his being repayed with interest; by means of which odds of her retaliation she, though unknown to her self, conquered his affections and he from thenceforth became her *inamorato*. But with so close and secret a minde did he harbour in his heart that new love and nourish the fire thereof in his veins, that remotely skonsing it from the knowledge of all men, he did not so much as acquaint therewith his most intimate friend Crichtoun; who, by that the sun had deprest our western horizon by one half of the quadrant of his orb, did, after supper with his sweet lady, whom he had by the hand, return againe to the bedchamber wherein formerly they were. And there, without losing of time, which by unnecessary puntilios of strained civility and affected formalities of officious respect, is very frequently but too much lavished away and heedlessly regarded by the young Adonises and fainthearted initiants in the exercises of the Cytheraean Academy,[123] they barred all the ceremonies of Pindarising their discourse[124] and sprucifying it in *à la mode* salutations, their mutual carriage shewing it self as it were in a meane betwixt the conjugal of man and wife, and fraternal conversation of brother and sister; in the reciprocacy of their love transcending both, in the purity of their thoughts equal to this and in fruition of pleasure nothing inferior to the other; for when, after the waiting damsel had, by putting her beautiful mistris into her nocturnal dress, quite impoverished the ornaments of her that daye's wear in robbing them of the inestimably rich treasure which they inclosed, and then performed the same office to the lord of her ladie's affections by laying aside the impestring bulk of his journal abiliaments, and fitting him in the singlest manner possible with the most genuine habit *a la Cypriana*[125] that Cupid could devise; she, as it became an obsequious servant and maid observant of her mistrisse's directions, bidding them good night with the

Skonsing: *hiding*　　Puntilios: *petty formalities*
Pindarising: *mimicking Pindaric style*　　Journal abiliaments: *day clothes*

123

inarticulate voyce of an humble curtesie, locked the doors of the room behind her and shut them both in to the reverence of one another, him to her discretion, her to his mercy and both to the passion of each other; who then, finding themselves not only together but alone with other, were in an instant transported both of them with an equal kinde of rapture; for as he looked on her and saw the splendor of the beams of her bright eyes and with what refulgency her alabaster-like skin did shine through the thin cawle of her Idalian garments,[126] her appearance was like the antartick oriency of a western aurore or acronick rising of the most radiant constellation of the firmament; and whilst she viewed him and perceived the portliness of his garb, comeliness of his face, sweetness of his countenance and majesty in his very chevelure, with the goodliness of his frame, proportion of his limbs and symmetry in all the parts and joints of his body which through the cobweb slenderness of his Cyllenian vestments were represented almost in their *puris naturalibus*;[127] his resemblance was like that of Aeneas to Dido,[128] when she said that he was in face and shoulders like a god; or rather to her he seemed as to the female deities did Ganimed[129] when, after being carried up to heaven, he was brought into the presence of Jupiter.

Thus for a while their eloquence was mute and all they spoke was but with the eye and hand, yet so persuasively, by vertue of the intermutual unlimitedness of their visotactil sensation, that each part and portion of the persons of either was obvious to the sight and touch of the persons of both. The visuriency of either, by ushering the tacturiency of both, made the attrectation of both consequent to the inspection of either. Here was it that passion was active and action passive, they both being overcome by other and each the conquerour. To speak of her hirquitalliency at the elevation of the pole of his microcosme or of his luxuriousness to erect a gnomon on her horizontal dyal, will perhaps be held by some to be expressions full of obscoeness and offensive to the purity of chaste ears; yet seeing she was to be his

Cawle: *network*   Oriency: *lustre*   Acronick: *at sunset*   Portliness: *stateliness*
Chevelure: *head of hair, wig*   Visotactil: *involving both sight and touch*
Visuriency: *desire of seeing*   Attrectation: *touching with hands*
Hirquitalliency: *strongly voiced delight*   Gnomon: *rod, pin*

wife and that she could not be such without consummation of marriage, which signifieth the same thing in effect, it may be thought, as *definitiones logicae verificantur in rebus*,[130] if the exerced act be lawful, that the diction which suppones it can be of no great transgression, unless you would call it a solaecisme or that vice in grammar which imports the copulating of the masculine with the feminine gender.

But as the misery of the life of man is such that bitterness for the most part is subsequent to pleasure and joy the prognostick of grief to come, so the Admirable Crichtoun — or to resume my discourse where I broke off — I say it hapened on a Shrove Tuesday at night, that the ever-renowned Crichtoun was warned by a great noise in the streets to be ready for the acting of another part; for the prince who, till that time from the first houre of the night inclusively for the space of four hours together with all his attendants, had done nothing else but rant it, roar and roam from one taverne to another with hautbois, flutes and trumpets, drinking healths, breaking glasses, tossing pots, whitling themselves with Septembral juyce,[131] tumbling in the kennel and acting all the devisable feats of madness, at least so many as in their irregular judgements did seem might contrevalue all the penance they should be able to do for them the whole Lent thereafter; being ambitious to have a kiss of his mistris' hand, for so, in that too frolick humour of his, he was pleased to call this young lady, before he should go to bed; with nine gentlemen at his back and four pages carrying waxe tapers before him, come to the place where Crichtoun and the foresaid lady were (though the prince knew nothing of Crichtoun's being there) and knocks at the outer gate thereof. No answer is made at first for the whole house was in a profound silence and all of them in the possession of Morphee[132] save that blessed pair of pigeon-like lovers in whom Cupid, for the discharge of Hymenaean rites,[133] had inspired a joynt determination to turne that whole night's rest to motion. But the fates being pleased otherways to dispose of things then as they proposed them, the clapper is up again and they rap with a flap till a threefold clap

Exerced: *exercised ('exerced act' is a technical, logical term, indicating an act performed)*   Hautbois: *wooden double-reeded instruments of high pitch*
Whitling: *intoxicating*

125

made the sound to rebound. With this the porter awakes, looks out at a lattice window of his lodge and, seeing them all with masks and vizards on their faces, asked them what their desire was or what it might be that moved them to come so late in such a disguise. The prince himself answered that they were gentlemen desirous only to salute my lady, which courtesie when obtained, they should forthwith be gone. The porter advertiseth the page and tells him all, who doing the same to the waiting gentlewoman, she, to receive orders from her mistris, opens the chamber doore, enters in, relates the story and demands direction from my lady who immediately bids her call the page to her. She does it; he comes, and enquiring what the will of her *signoria* was with him, she enjoynes him to go down and beseech those gentlemen to be pleased to have her excused for that night because she was abed and not so well as she could wish to bear them company; yet if they conceived any fault in her, she should strive to make them amends for it some other time. The page accordingly acquits himself of what is recommended to him; for after he had caused open the wicket of the gate and faced the street, he first saluted them with that court-like dexterity which did bespeak him a well-educated boy and of good parentage, then told them that he was commanded by his lady mistris to intreat them, seeing she knew not what they were and that their wearing of vizards did in civility debar her from enquiring after their names, to take in good part her remitting of that their visit to another time by reason of her present indisposure and great need of rest; which if they should have any pretext to except against, she would heartily make atonement for it and give them satisfaction at any other time.

The prince's answer was that he thought not but that he should have been admitted with less ceremony and that though the time of the night and his lady mistris her being in a posture of rest might seem to plead somewhat for the non-disturbance of her desired solitariness, that nevertheless the uncontrolled priviledges of the season exempting them from all prescribed, and at all other times observed, boundaries, might in the carnavale-eeve and supremest night of its law-transcendent jollities, by the custome of the whole country, very well apologize for that trespass. Which words being spoken he, without giving the page leisure to reply, pretending it was cold in the streets, rusht in at the open wicket even into the court with all his gentlemen and torch-bearers, each one whereof was no less cup-shotten then himself. The page, astonished at such unexpected rudeness, said with an audible voice, "What do you mean, gentlemen? Do you intend to break in by violence and at such an undue time enforce my lady to grant you admittance? Look, I pray you, to your own reputations; and if regardless of any thing else, consider what imputation and stain of credit wil lye upon you, thus to commit an enormous action because of some colour of justifying it by immunities of set times, grounded upon no reason but meer toleration, without any other warrant then a feeble inveterate prescription. Therefore let me beseech you, gentlemen, if you love your selves and the continuation of your good names or tender any kind of respect to the honor of ladys, that you would be pleased of your own accords to chuse rather to return from whence you came or go whither elswhere you will, then to imagin any rational man wil think that your masks and vizards can be sufficient covers wherewith to hide and palliate the deformedness of this obtrusive incivility."

One of the prince's gentlemen, whose braines the fumes of Greek and Italian wines had a little intoxicated, laying hold only upon the last word, all the rest having escaped both his imagination and memory like an empty sound which makes no impression, and most eagerly grasping at it like a snarling curr that in his gnarring snatcheth at the taile, ecchoes it, "Incivility?" Then, coming up closer to him and saying, "How now Jackanapes! Whom do you twit with incivility?" he gave him such a sound thwhack over the left shoulder with his sword, scabard and all, that the noise thereof reached to all the corners of my Ladye's bedchamber; at which the generous page, who, besides his breeding otherwayes, was the son of a nobleman, being a little commoved and vexed at an affront so undeservedly received and barbarously given, told the esquire who had wronged him, that if he had but had one drop of any good blood within him, he never would have offered to strike a gentleman that wanted a weapon wherewith to defend himself; and that, although he was but of fourteen yeers of age and for strength but as a springal or stripling in regard of him, he should nevertheless

Cup-shotten: *drunk*   Gnarring: *growling*   Springal: *youth* (would any of those other nine gentlemen, as he called them, be pleased to favour him but with the lend of a sword) take upon him even then and on that place to humble his cockescomb, pull his crest a little lower down and make him faine, for the safety of his life, to acknowledge that he is but a base and unworthy man. Whilst the gentleman was about to have shapen him an answer, the prince being very much taken with the discretion, wit, garb and courage of the boy, commanded the other to silence; and forthwith taking the speech in hand himself, commended him very much for his loyalty to his mistris and, for his better ingratiating in the page's favour, presented him with a rich saphir to shew him but the way to my ladye's chamber, where he vowed that, as he was a gentleman, he would make no longer stay then barely might afford him the time to kiss her hands and take his leave. The sweet boy, being more incensed at the manner of that offer of the prince, whom he knew not, then at the discourtesie he had sustained by his aforesaid gentleman, plainly assured him that he might very well put up his saphir into his pocket againe, for that all the gifts in the world should never be able to gaine that of him which had not ground enough in reason for persuading the grant thereof without them.

After that the prince and Pomponacio, for so they called the page, had thus for a long time together debated to and againe the reasons for and against the intended visit with so little success on either side, that the more artifice was used in the rhetorick, the less effect it had in the persuasion; the prince, unwilling to miss of his mark, and not having in all the quivers of his reason one shaft wherewith to hit it, resolved to interpose some authority with his argumentations and, where the foxe's skin could not serve, to make use of the lyon's: to the prosecuting of which intent, he with his vinomadefied retinue resolved to press in upon the page and maugre his will, to get up staires and take their fortune in the quest of the chamber they aimed at; for albeit the stradling as wide as he could of pretty Pomponacio at the door whereat they made account to force their passage, did for a while retard their designe because of their chariness to struggle with so hopeful a youth and tender imp of so great expectation,

To and againe: *back and forth*   Vinomadefied: *maddened with wine*
Maugre: *despite*   Hopeful: *promising*

yet at last being loath to faile of their end, by how indirect meanes soever they might attaine thereto, they were in the very action of crowning their violence with prevalency, when the admirable and ever-renowned Crichtoun, who at the prince's first manning of the court taking the alarm, step'd from the shrine of Venus to the oracle of Pallas Armata;[134] and by the help of the waiting gentlewoman having apparelled himself with a paludamental vesture after the antick fashion of the illustrious Romans, both for that he minded not to make himself then known, that to walk then in such like disguise was the anniversary custome of all that country, and that all, both gentlemen and others standing in that court, were in their mascaradal garments; with his sword in his hand like a messenger from the gods, came down to relieve the page from the poste whereat he stood sentry; and when, as the light of the minor planets appeares not before the glorious rayes of Titan, he had obscured the irradiancy of Pomponacio with his more effulgent presence and that under pretext of turning him to the page to desire him to stand behind him, as he did, he had exposed the full view of his left side so far as the light of torches could make it perceivable to the lookers on, who being all *in cuerpo* carying swords in their hands in stead of cloaks about them, imagined really, by the badge or cognizance they saw neer his heart, that he was one of my ladie's chief domestick servants; he addressed his discourse to the prince and the nine gentlemen that were with him; neither of all whereof, as they were accoutred, was he able (either by the light of the tapers or that of the moon, which was then but in the first week of its waxing, it being the Tuesday next to the first new moon that followed the Purification Day)[135] to discern in any manner of way what they were; and for that he perceived by their unstedfast postures, that the influence of the grape had made them subjects to Bacchus, and that their extranean-like demeanour towards him, not without some amazement, did manifest his certainty of their not knowing him; he therefore with another kind of intonation, that his speech might not bewray him, then that which waited upon his usual note of utterance, made a

Paludamental: *like the military cloak worn by Roman generals*   Antick: *archaic*
Extranean-like: *distanced*   Bewray: *expose*

pithy panegyrick in praise of those that endeavoured by their good fellowship and bacchanalian compagnionry to cheer up their hearts with precious liquour and renew the golden age; whence descending to a more particular application, he very much applauded the ten gentlemen for their being pleased, out of their devotion to the Lyaean god,[136] who had with great respect been bred and elevated amongst the nymphs, not to forget amidst the most sacred plying of their symposiasms that duty to ladyes which was incumbent on them to be performed in the discharge of a visite. Then wheeling neatly about to fetch another careere, he discreetly represented to them all the necessary circumstances at such a visit observable and how the infringing of the meanest title or particle of any one thereof would quite disconcert the mutual harmony it should produce and bring an unspeakable disparagement to the credits and honors of all guilty of the like delinquency. In amplifying hereof and working upon their passions, he let go so many secret springs and inward resorts of eloquence, that being all persuaded of the unseasonableness of the time and unreasonableness of the suit, none of them for a thousand ducats that night would have adventured to make any further progress in that after which, a little before, they had been so eager; so profound was the character of reverence toward that lady, which he so insinuatingly had imprinted into the hearts of them all; wherefore they, purposing to insist no longer upon the visitatory design, did cast their minds on a sudden upon another far more hairbrained consideration; when the prince to one of his chief gentlemen said, "We wil do this good fellow no wrong. Yet, before we go hence, let us try what courage is in him, that after we have made him flee for it, we may tomorrow make one excuse for all to the lady whom he serveth. Do not you see," sayes he, "how he dandleth the sword in his hand as if he were about to braveer us and how he is decked and trimm'd up in his cloaths like another Hector of Troy? But I doubt if he be so martial. He speaks too well to be valiant. He is certainly more Mercurial then military. Therefore let us make him turn his back, that we may spie if, as another Mercury, he hath any wings on his heels."

This foolish chat no sooner was blattered out to the ears of

Blattered: *blethered*   Braveer: *act the bravo towards*

130

three of his gentlemen that were nearest to him but the sudden drawing of their swords, though but in jest, made the other six who heard not the prince, as if they had bin mad to adventure the rashness wherewith the spirit of wine had inspired them against the prudensequal and invincible fortitude of the matchless Crichtoun; who, not being accustomed to turn his back to those that had any project against his brest, most manfully sustained their encounter; which, although furious at first, appearing nevertheless unto him because of the odds of ten to one not to have been in earnest, he for twenty several bouts did but ward their blows and pary with the fort of his sword till, by plying the defensive part too long, he had received one thrust in the thigh and another in the arme; the trickling of his blood from the wounds whereof prompted his heroick spirit as at a desperate stake to have at all or none, to make his tith outvy their stock and set upon them all.[137] In which resolution, when from the door whereat he stood he had lanched forth three paces in the court, having lovely Pomponacio behind him to give him warning in case of surprisal in the reer and all his ten adversaries in a front before him, who, making up above a quadrant of that periphery whereof his body was the center, were about, from the exterior points of all their right shoulder-blades alongst the additional line of their armes and tucks, to lodge home in him so many truculent semi-diameters; he, retrograding their intention and beginning his agency where they would have made him a patient, in as short space as the most diagrammatically-skilled hand could have been able to describe lines representative of the distance 'twixt the earth and the several *kardagas*[138] or horary expeditions of the sun's diurnal motion from his aequinoxial horizontality to the top of his meridian hight, which, with the help of a ruler, by six draughts of a pen is quickly delineated, livered out six several thrusts against them; by vertue whereof he made such speedy work upon the respective segments of that debauch'd circumference through the red ink marks which his streight-drawn stroaks imprinted, that being alonged from the

Prudensequal: *following from prudence*
Tith: *thrusting sword, share. (See Commentary p. 229)*
Stock: *sword, capital. (See Commentary p. 229)*   Tucks: *rapiers*
Retrograding: *reversing*

center-point of his own courage and with a thunderbolt-like swiftness of hand radiated upon their bodies, he discussed a whole quadrant of those ten, whereof four and twenty make the circle and, laying six of the most inraged of them on their backs, left in the other four but a sextant of the aforesaid ring to avenge the death of their dismal associates.

Of which quaternity, the prince being the most concerned in the effects of this disaster as being the only cause thereof, though his intentions levelled at another issue, and like to burst with shame to see himself loadned on all sides with so much dishonour by the incomparable valour of one single man, did set forward at the sword's point to essay if in his person so much lost credit might be recovered; and to that purpose comming within distance, was upon the advancing of a thurst in quart,[139] when the most agil Crichtoun, pareing it in the same ward, smoothly glided along the prince's sword and being master of its feeble, was upon the very instant of making his highness very low and laying his honor in the dust, when one of the three courtiers whom fortune had favoured not to fall by the hand of Crichtoun, cryed aloud, "Hold, hold! Kill not the prince!". At which words the courteous Crichtoun recoyling and putting himself out of distance, the prince pulled off his vizard and, throwing it away, shew his face so fully that the noble-hearted Crichtoun, being sensible of his mistake and sory so many of the prince's servants should have enforced him, in his own defence, to become the actor of their destruction, made unto the prince a very low obeisance and, setting his left knee to the ground as if he had been to receive the honour of knighthood, with his right hand presented him the hilts of his own conquering sword with the point thereof towards his own brest, wishing his highness to excuse his not knowing him in that disguise and to be pleased to pardon what unluckily had ensued upon the necessity of his defending himself, which at such an exigent might have befaln to any other that were not minded to abandon their lives to the indiscretion of others.

The prince, in the throne of whose judgement the rebellious

Quaternity: *group of four*　　Quart: *fourth of the eight parries in fencing*
Pareing: *parrying*　　Ward: *the part of the hilt which protects the hand*

vapours of the tun had installed Nemesis and caused the irascible faculty shake off the soveraignty of reason, being without himself and unable to restraine the impetuosity of the
will's first motion, runs Crichtoun through the heart with his
own sword and kils him; in the interim of which lamentable
accident, the sweet and beautiful lady (who by this time had
slipped her self into a cloth-of-gold petticoat, in the anterior
fente whereof was an asteristick ouch, wherein were inchased
fifteen several diamonds, representative of the constellation of
the primest stars in the signe of Virgo, had enriched a tissue
gown and wastcoat of brocado with the precious treasure of her
ivory body and put the foot-stals of those marble pillars which
did support her microcosme into a paire of incarnation velvet
slippers, embroydered with purle being descended to the lower
door which jetted out to the courtwards where Pomponacio
was standing, with the curled tresses of her discheveled haire
dangling over her shoulders, by the love-knots of whose naturally guilded filaments were made fast the hearts of many
gallant sparks, who from their liberty of ranging after other
beauties were more forcibly curbed by those capillary fetters than
by so many chaines of iron; and in the daedalian windings of the
crisped pleats whereof, did lye in ambush a whole brigade of
Paphian archers[140] to bring the loftiest martialists to stoop to
the shrine of Cupid; and, Arachne-like,[141] now careering, now
caracoling it alongest the polygonal plainness of its twisted
threds, seize on the affections of all whose looks should be
involved in her locks; and, with a presentation exposing to the
beholders all the perfections that ever yet were by the Graces
conferred on the female sexe, all the excellencies of Juno, Venus
and Minerva,[142] the other feminean deities and semi-goddesses
of former ages seeming to be of new revived and within her
compiled as the compactedst abbridgement of all their best
endowments; stepped a pace or two into the court with all the
celerity that the intermixed passions of love and indignation
was able to prompt her to.

During which time, which certainly was very short, because

Fente: *short slit, vent*   Asteristick: *starry*   Ouch: *brooch*
Incarnation: *flesh colour*   Purle: *pearl*   Daedalian: *maze-like*
Careering: *charging, galloping*   Caracoling: *wheeling*

to the motions of her angelically composed body the quantity attending the matter of its constitution was no more obstructive then were the various exquisite qualities flowing from the form thereof, wherein there was no blemish, the eyes of the prince's thoughts and those were with him (for the influences of Cupid are like the actions of generation which are said to be *in instanti*) pryed into, spyed and surveyed from the top of that sublimely framed head, which culminated her accomplishments, down along the wonderful symmetry of her divinely proportioned countenance; from the glorious light of whose two luminaries Apollo might have borrowed rayes to court his Daphne and Diana her Endymion; even to the rubies of those lips, where two Cupids still were kissng one another for joy of being so neer the enjoyment of her two rows of pearles inclosed within them; and from thence through the most graceful objects of all her intermediate parts to the heaven-like polished prominences of her mellifluent and heroinal breast whose porphyr streaks, like arches of the ecliptick and colures, or azimuth and almican-tar circles intersecting other,[143] expansed in pretty veinlets through whose sweet conduits run the delicious streams of nectar wherewith were cherished the pretty sucklings of the Cyprian goddesse, smiled on one another to see their courses regulated by the two niple-poles above them elevated in each their own hemisphere; whose magnetick vertue, by attracting hearts and sympathy in their refocillation, had a more im-powering ascendent over poetick lovers for furnishing their braines with choise of fancy, then ever had the two tops of Parnassus hill, when animated or assisted by all the wits of the Pierian Muses;[144] then from the snow-white galaxy betwixt those gemel-monts whose milken paths, like to the plaines of Thessaly, do by reflexion calefie to that protuberant and convexe ivory whose meditullian node, compared with that other where the ecliptick cuts the aequinoxial, did far surpass it in that property whereby the night is brought in competition with the day; whence, having past the line, and seeming to

In instanti: instantaneous   Ecliptick: *great circle of the celestial sphere*
Colures: *the two great circles which intersect at right angles at the poles*
Refocillation: *revival*   Gemel-monts: *twin-mounts*   Calefie: *heat*
Meditullian: *pertaining to the middle of the earth*

depress the former pole to elevate another, the inward prospect of their minde discovered a new America or land unknown in whose subterranean and intestine cels were secret mines of greater worth then those of either Tibar or Peru;[145] for that, beside the working in them could not but give delight unto the mineralist, their metal was so reciptible for impression and to the mint so plyable, that alchymists profoundly versed in chymical extractions and such as knew how to imbue it with syndon and crown the magisterum with the elixir, instead of treasures merchants bring from the Indias, would have educed little worlds more worth then gold or silver.

All this from their imagination being convoyed into the penitissim corners of their souls in that short space which I have already told, she, rending her garments and tearing her haire like one of the Graces possest with a Fury, spoke thus: "O villains! What have you done? You vipers of men, that have thus basely slaine the valiant Crichtoun, the sword of his own sexe and buckler of ours; the glory of this age and restorer of the lost honor of the Court of Mantua. O Crichtoun, Crichtoun!"

At which last words the prince, hearing them uttered by the lady in the world he loved best and of the man in the world he most affected, was suddenly seazed upon by such extremity of sorrow for the unhappiness of that lamentable mischance, that not being able to sustaine the rayes of that beauty whose percing aspect made him conscious of his guilt, he fell flat upon his face like to a dead man. But knowing *omne simile* not to be *idem*, he quickly arose and to make his body be what it appeared, fixed the hilt of the sword wherewith he had killed Crichtoun fast betwixt two stones at the foot of a marble statue standing in the court, after the fashion of those staves with iron pikes at both ends commonly called Swedish feathers, when stuck into the ground to fence musketeers from the charge of horse; then having recoyled a little from it, was fetching a race to run his brest, which for that purpose he had made open, upon the point thereof, as did Cato Uticensis[146] after his lost hopes of the

Syndon: *thin linen fabric (associated with Christ's shroud)*
Magisterum: *philosopher's stone*
Elixir: *preparation intended to change base metals into gold*   Penitissim: *innermost*
Omne simile: similar in all respects   **Idem:** *the same*

135

recovery of the Commonwealth of Rome; and assuredly, according to that his intent, had made a speedy end of himself but that his three gentlemen, one by stopping him in his course, another by laying hold on him by the middle and the third by taking away the sword, hindred the desperate project of that autochthony. The prince being carryed away in that mad, frantick and distracted humour, befitting a bedlam better then a *serralio*, into his own palace, where all manner of edge-tools were kept from him all that sad night for fear of executing his former designe of self-murther; as soon as to his father, my lord duke, on the next morning by seven a clock, which by the usual computation of that country came at that season of the yeer to be neer upon fourteen hours or fourteen a clock, the story of the former night's tragedy was related and that he had solemnly vowed he should either have his son hanged or his head struck off for the committing of a so ingrate, enormous and detestable crime, one of his courtiers told him that by all appearance his son would save his highness' justice a labour and give it nothing to do, for that he was like to hang himself or after some other manner of way to turn his own Atropos.[147]

The whole court wore mourning for him full three quarters of a yeer together. His funeral was very stately and on his hearse were stuck more epitaphs, elegies, threnodies and epicediums then, if digested into one book, would have outbulkt all Homer's works; some of them being couched in such exquisite and fine Latin, that you would have thought great Virgil and Baptista Mantuanus[148] for the love of their mother-city had quit the Elysian fields[149] to grace his obsequies; and other of them, besides what was done in other languages, composed in so neat Italian and so purely fancied, as if Ariosto, Dante, Petrark and Bembo[150] had been purposely resuscitated to stretch even to the utmost their poetick vein to the honour of this brave man, whose picture till this hour is to be seen in the bedchambers or galleries of the most of the great men of that nation, representing him on horseback with a lance in one hand and a book in the other; and most of the young ladies likewise that were any thing handsome, in a memorial of his worth had his effigies in a little oval tablet of

Autochthony: *son of the soil*　　　Threnodies: *dirges*　　　Epicediums: *funeral odes*

136

gold hanging 'twixt their breasts and held for many yeers together that metamazion or intermammilary ornament an as
necessary outward pendicle for the better setting forth of their
accoutrements as either fan, watch or stomacher. My lord duke,
upon the young lady that was Crichtoun's mistris and future
wife, although she had good rents and revenues of her own by
inheritance, was pleased to conferr a pension of five hundred
ducats a yeer. The prince also bestowed as much on her during
all the days of his life, which was but short, for he did not long
enjoy himself after the cross fate of so miserable an accident. The
sweet lady, like a turtle bewailing the loss of her mate, spent all
the rest of her time in a continual solitariness and resolved, as
none before Crichtoun had the possession of her body, that no
man breathing should enjoy it after his decease.

The verity of this story I have here related concerning this
incomparable Crichtoun may be certified by above two
thousand men yet living, who have known him; and truly of his
acquaintance there had been a far greater number but that
before he was full thirty two yeers of age, he was killed as you
have heard. And here I put an end to the Admirable Scot.

The scene of the choicest acts of this late heros of our time
having been the country of Italy, the chief State whereof is
Venice, it cannot be amiss as I have done for Spaine, France,
Holland, Denmark, Swedland and Germany, that I make
mention of these four Scotish Colonels: Colonel Douglas,
Colonel Balantine, Colonel Lyon and Colonel Anderson who,
within these very few yeers, have done most excellent service to
the Venetian Commonwealth. Nor can I well forget that sea-
captain, Captain William Scot, whose martial atchievements
in the defence of that state against the Turks may very well
admit him to be ranked amongst the colonels. He was vice-
admiral to the Venetian fleet and the onely renowned bane and
terror of Mahometan navigators. Whether they had galleys,
galeoons, galiegrosses or huge warships, it was all one to him. He
set upon all alike, saying still, the more they were, the manyer he
would kill and the stronger that the encounter should happen to
be, the greater would be his honour and his prise the richer. He

Pendicle: *pendant*   Galiegrosses: *great galleys*

oftentimes so cleared the archipelago of the Mussulmans[151] that the Ottoman family at the very gates of Constantinople would quake at the report of his victories; and did so ferret them out of all the creeks of the Adriatick Gulph and so shrewdly put them to it that sometimes they did not know in what part of the Mediterranean they might best shelter themselves from the fury of his blows. Many of their mariners turned land-souldiers for fear of him, and of their maritime officers, several took charge of caravans to escape his hand, which for many yeers together lay so heavy upon them that he was cryed up for another Don Jean d'Austria or Duke d'Orea[152] by the enemies of that Scythian generation — in spight of which and the rancour of all their unchristian hearts, he dyed but some eighteen moneths ago in his bed of a feaver in the Isle of Candia.

Now as besides those colonels above recited, many other Scotish colonels since the jubilee of 1600 till the yeer 1640 have faithfully served the Venetian State against both the Christian and Turkish emperours; so in the intervals of that time have these following Scotish colonels been in the service of the King of Pole against both the Moscoviter, Turk and Swed: to wit, Colonel Lermond, Colonel Wilson, Colonel Hunter, Colonel Robert Scot, Colonel Gordon, Colonel Wood, Colonel Spang, Colonel Gun, Colonel Robertson, Colonel Rower and several others.

And seeing we are come so far on in the deduction of the Scotish colonels who for the space of thirty or fourty yeers, without reckoning the last ten, have been so famous for their valour in the continent of Europe, from whence the Isle of Britain excludes it self, that neither thick nor thin, hunger nor plenty, nor heat nor cold was said to have been able to restraine them from giving proof thereof; and that from the hot climates of Spaine, Italy and France we have, in prosecuting the threed of this discourse, travelled through those of a mediocer temper — of the Low Countries, Denmark and Hungary — even to the cold regions of Germanie, Swedland and Pole; I hold it expedient before I shut up this enumeration of Scotish colonels into a period, that the very Scyths and Sarmats,[153] even to the almost subarctick incolaries, be introduced to bear record of the

Incolaries: *inhabitants*

138

magnanimity of the Scotish nation; which nevertheless, because I would not trespass upon the reader's patience in making the nomenclature too prolixe, I make account to do by setting down only the names of those Scotish colonels that served under the great Duke of Moscovy[154] against the Tartar and Polonian: viz. Colonel Alexander Crawford, Colonel Alexander Gordon, Colonel William Keith, Colonel George Mathuson, Colonel Patrick Kinindmond and Colonel Thomas Garne who, for the height and grosseness of his person, being in his stature taller, and greater in his compass of body then any within six kingdomes about him, was elected King of Bucharia,[155] the inhabitants of that country being more inclined to tender their obedience to a man of a burly pitch like him (whose magnitude being every way proportionable in all its dimensions and consisting rather in bones then flesh, was no load to the minde nor hindrance to the activity of his body) then to a lower-sized man, because they would shun equality as near as they could with him of whom they should make choice to be their sovereign; they esteeming nothing more disgraceful nor of greater disparagement to the reputation of that state then that their king should, through disadvantage of stature, be looked down upon by any whose affaires, of concernment perhaps for the weal of the crown, might occasion a mutual conference face to face. He had ambassadors sent to him to receive the crown, scepter, sword and all the other royal cognizances belonging to the Supreme Majesty of that nation; but I heard him say, that the only reason why he refused their splendid offers and would not undergo the charge of that regal dignity was because he had no stomack to be circumcised. However, this uncircumcised Garne, agnamed the Sclavonian and upright Gentile, for that he loves good fellowship and is of a very gentile conversation, served as a colonel together with the forenamed five and other un-mentioned colonels of the Scotish nation in that service against the Crim Tartar[156] under the command of both his and their compatriot, Sir Alexander Leslie, generalissimo of all the forces of the whole empire of Russia; which charge, the wars against the Tartarian beginning afresh, he hath re-obtained and is in the plenary enjoyment thereof, as I believe, at this same instant

Pitch: *stature*   Gentile: *courteous*   Crim: *Crimean*

time, and that with such approbation for fidelity and valour that never any hath been more faithful in the discharge of his duty nor of a better conduct in the infinite dangers through which he hath past.

I shall only here by the way, before I proceed any further, make bold to desire the reader to consider, seeing so short a space as thirty, or four and thirty yeers time hath produced so great a number of colonels and others above that degree of the Scotish nation, universally renowned for their valour and military atchievements in all the forraign and transmarine countries, states and kingdoms of Christendome, what vast number of lieutenant-colonels, majors, captaines, lieutenants, ensignes etc. besides the collateral officers of an army, such as adjutants, quartermasters, commissaries, scoutmasters, marshals and so forth through all the other offices belonging to the milice of a nation (either by sea or land) should be found of Scotishmen to have been since the yeere one thousand and six hundred in the many several outlandish wars of Europe; which, I cannot think, if prejudicacy be laid aside, but that it will so dispose the reader that he will acknowledge the Scotish nation to have been an honorable nation, and that of late too, in their numerousness of able and gallant men totally devoted to the shrine of Mars; of which sort, as I have omitted many worthy and renowned colonels abroad, so will I not insist upon the praise of two of our countrymen, Sir John Hume of Eatoun by name and Francis Sinclair, natural son to the late Earl of Catnes; the first whereof in his travels through Italy, by his over-mastering, both at the blunt and sharp, the best swordsmen and fence-masters of that country, acquired the reputation of the skilfullest man in the world at the rapeer-point; yet being killed at a battel in Denmark some few yeers agoe, to shew that there wanted not another of the same Scottish nation to supply his place and to inherit every whit as deservedly that hight of fame conferred on him for his valour, the most couragious and magnanimous acts of the aforesaid Francis Sinclair will manifest it to the full with almost the universal testimony of all Spaine, Italy and Germany which for many yeers together were the theaters of his never-daunted prowess. To relate all the duels

Outlandish: *foreign*

wherein he hath been victorious and but to sum them together, it would amount to a greater number then all the lessons that the most consciencious master of escrime that is, doth usually give in a whole three yeers space to him whom he intends to make a proficient in that faculty. Therefore in stead of all, as by the dimension of Hercules' foot one may judge of the stature of his body, and by the taste of a spoonful, as the saying is, to know what kinde of liquor is in a tun, I will only make mention of two actions of his, one done at the emperour's court in Vienne[157] and the other at Madrid in Spaine.

The first was thus. A certain gallant nobleman of High-Germany, who by the stile of Conquerour, without any other addition, in duels, wherein he had overthrown all those of any nation that ever coped with him, having repaired to the great city of Vienne to accresce his reputation in some more degrees by the subjection of any proud spirit there; eager in that sort of contestation whereof he heard there were many, and notice being given to him of this Sinclair, who had a perfect sympathy with him in that kind of adventuring humour, they very quickly met with one another and had no sooner exchanged three words, when time and place being assigned for debating the combate, they determined to take nothing in hand till first it were made known who should, to the very hazard of their lives, bear clear away the palme and reap the credit of the bravest champion. But the news thereof being carryed to the emperor, who being unwilling that the victor should terminate the concertation in the blood of the vanquished, and yet desirous for his own sport that by them somewhat might be done before him in matter of tryal which of them should prove most skilful in the handling of his armes, he enjoyned them at a perfixed time in his own presence to decide the controversie with foyles; and for the better animating them thereto, assured them that which of them soever should give the other the first three free bouts should, for his salary or *epinicion*, have a paire of spurs of beaten gold set with diamonds. The combatants very heartily embraced the condition and were glad to turn the sharp to blunt to gaine the gold spurs; by which means, their hope of overcoming on both sides having cheerfully brought them to the appointed place and

Perfixed: *determined*   Epinicion: *prize for victory*

time designed for the purpose, they had no sooner adjusted themselves in equal termes for foyles and every thing else befitting that jeopardless monomachy, but Sinclair at first, before he came within full distance, to try the manner of his adversarie's play made a flourish or two of very nimble and most exquisite falsifyings; whereat the other, conceiving them for really intended thrusts, was so disordred in his motion that, offering to ward where he needed not and taking the alarm too hot, Sinclair was so confident of his own sufficiency against that High-Dutchman,[158] that when he had askt the Emperor for how many franch bouts his majesty would adjudge the spurs to be gained and that the emperor's answer was, "For the first three"; Sinclair replied, if he did not give him five on end he should be content to forfeit the spurs and two hundred crowns besides; whereupon, immediately facing his adversary, to let him know that many ward without a cause that cannot pary when they should, with the coinstantanean swiftness of hand and foot gave him *de pied ferme* a terrible slap on the breast, wherewith the German lord did so stagger, that before he could fully recover himself the blow was doubled and redoubled with a sound thwack on the back of those, seconded with another bounce, not leaving him till with a push and a thump again he had hit him seven several times and that with the same confidence and facility that the usher of a fencing-hall useth to alonge against his master's plastron. The emperour, by the thud of each stroak, which furthered his counting, having reckoned beyond the number of the five promised bouts and unwilling Sinclair should lack of his due or the other have his ribs broken, cryed aloud, "Hola! Forbear! Enough!". Whereupon the duellists desisting, the emperor required them both to stand before him; who, seeing the seven marks which the button of Sinclair's foyle, whitened with chalk, had imprinted in the other's black sattin doublet and how they lay in order after the manner of the situation of the seven stars of the Little Bear, laughed heartily for he was a peece of an astronomer and a great favourer of mathematicians. Then, addressing his speech to Sinclair, who had so much natural arithmetick as to know that seven included

Monomachy: *duel*   Alonge: *lunge*
Plastron: *leather-covered wadded shield worn over the breast*   A peece of: *somewhat of*

five, asked him why, in livering in of his thrusts, he exceeded the promised number, seeing five was sufficient for gaining of the prize; and why, being pleased to make them seven, he had fixed them in their stations after the fashion of a Charlewaine?[159] Sinclair, to whom though astronomy might have signified somewhat to eat for any thing he knew of the science, had nevertheless the perspicacity to make the word Charlewaine serviceable to his present purpose, very promptly answered, "Sir, I did so place them in honour of my master, CHARLES, King of Great Britain; and gave in two venees more then I was obliged to, to give your Caesarean Majesty to understand that in the two kingdoms of England and Scotland, whereof that isle consists, there are many thousands more expert then I in matter of martial feats". At which answer the emperor was so well pleased, that he gave him the spurs as his due for the first five and a gold chaine for the other two.

In the mean while for the emperor's better diversion, a certain Spanish hidalgo of the Archduke Leopoldo's court[160] made bold to relate to his Imperial Majesty how the said Francis Sinclair had in the city of Madrid performed a more notable exploit and of far greater adventure, which was this.

Eight Spanish gentlemen being suspicious of Sinclair's too intimate familiarity with a kinswoman of theirs, whom they called *Prima* (that is to say, a she-cozen) did all together set upon him at one time with their swords drawn; which unexpected assault moved him to say, "Gentlemen, I doubt not but you are valiant men. Therefore, if you would have your desire of me, my intreaty is only that you would take it as it becomes men of valour and that by trying your fortune against mine at the sword's point one after another". The Spaniards pretending to be men of honour, not only promised to do what he required but, the better to assure him that they would prove faithful to him in their promise, swore all of them upon a cross which they made with their swords, that they would not faile therein should it cost them all their lives. In the extremity that Sinclar was, this kind of unhoped for honest dealing did very much incourage him, especially he knowing that he and they all had but Toledo-blades,[161] whose fashion was then to be all of one length and size.

Livering in: *delivering*   Charlewaine: *The Plough (astron.)*

In a word, conforme to paction, they fell to it and that most cleverly, though with such fatality on the Spanish side, that in less then the space of half an hour he killed seven of them epassyterotically (that is, one after another), gratifying the eighth, to testifie he had done no wrong to the rest, with the enjoyment of his life, who, rather then to undergoe the hazard of the destiny of his forerunners, chused to abandon his vindicative humour and leave unrevenged the blood and honour of his male and female cosens.

Much more may be said of him but that I will not now supererogate in magnifying the fulfilment of the reader's expectation by the performance of more then I promised; being resolved for brevitie's sake to pass over with silence many hundreds of our country (such as Robert Scot who was the deviser of leathern guns)[162] that were in other parts much esteemed for their inventions of warlike engines.

And that since the yeer a thousand and six hundred, before which time no action hath been performed anywhere, nor from that time till this within the Isle of Britain by any of those colonels and others whom I have here before recited, for which I have praised them or otherwaies mentioned any of them but by way of designation of their names in relation to their service abroad; nor amongst them all have I nominated above five or six that either served in or did so much as look upon the wars of England, Scotland and Ireland; and yet I expect not to merit blame, albeit of those general persons and colonels of the Scotish nation (whereof there is a great multitude) that have served since the yeer 1641 in these our late wars of England, Scotland and Ireland, I make no mention because *multitudo* is no more *virtus* then *magnitudo*; for though there be some, and those but very some, amongst them that have been pretty well principled in reason and had true honor before their eyes; yet seeing the great mobil of the rest, by circumvolving them into a contrary motion hath retarded their action and made their vertue abortive, in not expressing their names I do them favour, by such concealment obviating the imputation which they deserve

Conforme to paction: *in accordance with the bargain*   Gratifying: *requiring*
Multitudo is no more *virtus* then *magnitudo*: *a large number is no more a virtue than size*   Mobil: *'play' on prime mover and rabble*

for having been in so bad company and undersphering themselves to the bodies of those vaster orbs, whether of the state, milice or Church of Scotland, whose rapidity of violence might hurry them into a course quite opposite to the goodness of their own inclination.

For whoever they be (whether civil or ecclesiastical) of the Scotish nation, whom the English can with any kind of reason upbraid with covetousness, the commons of Scotland with oppression, or other states and countryes with treachery and dissimulation, it is my opinion that their names should not otherwayes be recorded but as beacons are set up where there are dangerous passages by sea, that such thrifty navigators, whether coetaneans or successors, as intend to saile with safety into the harbour of a good conscience, may thereby avoid the rocks and shelves of their greedy, tyrannous and hypocritical dealings: nor can it be a sufficient excuse for any of those officers to say they thought they could not offend God therein for that the Kirk did warrant them in what they did, seeing they might very well know that it becometh such as would take upon them a charge over and against the lives of others in the respective preservation and destruction of their souldier friends and foes, to have principles within themselves for the regulating of their outward actions and not to be driven like fools for advice sake to yeeld an implicite obedience to the oracles of the Delphian presbytery[163] whose greatest enthusiasts, for all its cryed up infallibility, have not possibly the skill to distinguish betwixt rape-seed and musket-powder. If any say that by taking such a course, their motion seems to be the more celestial because, in imitation of the upper orbs, it is furthered by the assistance of an external intelligence, I answer that according to the opinion of him in whose philosophy they read those separated animations, to each of the heavens is allowed an informant as well as assisting soul; and though that were not, the intelligences are so far different that there is hardly any similitude whereupon to fixe the comparison, for those superior ones are pure *simplicissim* acts, insusceptible of passion and without all matter or potentiality of being affected with any alteration; but these are gross, mixed patients, subject to all the disorders of the inferiour appetites,

Rape-seed: *seed of the turnip*   Simplicissim: *most simple*

plunged in terrestrial dross and for their profit or lucre in this world lyable to any new impressions.

That the gentry, then, and nobility of Scotland, whereof for the most part did consist those fresh water officers,[164] should by their co-drawing in the Presbyterian yoak, have plowed such deep and bloody furrows upon the backs of the commons of their own native soyle, is not only abominable but a thing ridiculous and an extream scandal to the nation; for when some laird or lord there, whose tender conscience could embrace no religion that was not gainefull, had, for having given his voice perhaps to the augmentation of a minister's stipend or done such like thing tending to the glory of the new Diana of Ephesus,[165] obtained a commission for the levying of a regiment of horse, foot or dragoons under pretext of fighting for God against the malignants and sectaries, then was it that, by uncessant quarterings, exacting of trencher money and other most exorbitant pressures upon the poor tenandry of that country, such cruelty and detestable villany was used and that oftentimes by one neighbour to another under the notion of maintaining the Covenant and the cause of God, that hardly have we heard in any age of such abominations done by either Turk or infidel, and all out of a devotion to the blessed sum of money which the master of these oppressed tenants, for saving of his land from being laid wast, must needs disburse; for most of those kirkofficers of regiments and their *subordinados* were but very seldom well pleased with the production of either man or horse, how apt soever they might seem to prove for military service; alledging some fault or other to the horse, and that the man, for lack of zeal (for any thing they knew) to the Covenant, might procure a judgement from heaven upon the whole army; that therefore they would take but money, thereby the better to enable them to provide for such men and horses as they might put confidence into. And if it chanced, as oftentimes it did, that a country gentleman, out-putter of foot or horse, being scarce of money, should prove so untractable as to condescend to nothing but what literally he was bound to, then by vertue of the power wherewith they were intrusted to see their souldiers well clothed,

Trencher money: *feudal due for supplying Lord's table*

armed and accommodated with transport-money and other such appurtenances, they had such a faculty of undervaluing whatever was not good silver and gold that, to make up the deficiencies according to their rates would extend to so great a sum that hardly could any lyable to a levy that was refractary to their desire of having money, save so much as one single sixpence by his emission of either horse or foot; so fine a trick they had with their counterfeit religion to make an honest poor gentleman glad to chuse the worst of two evils for shunning a third of their own contrivance, worse then they both.

And when at any time the innocent gentlemen, in hope of commiseration, would present their grievances to the respective committees of the shires, seldom or never was there any prevention of or reparation for the aforesaid abuse, especially in the north of Scotland; of all parts whereof the committees of the shires of Innernass and Ross,[166] whether joyntly or separately sitting, proved the most barbarous and inhumane; it being a commonly received practise amongst their logerheadistick wisdoms, not only to pass these and such like enormities with the foresaid officers but to gratifie them besides for the laying of a burthen upon their neighbours, which they should have undergone themselves. Yea, to such a height did their covetousness and hypocrisie reach that the better to ingratiate themselves in the favors of the souldiery for the saving of their pence, when the officers, out of their laziness, would be unwilling to travel fourty or fifty miles from their quarters for the taking up of mantenance or any arreer due of horse- and foot-levies, they took this savage and unchristian course: they would point at any whom they had a peck at, pretending he was no good Covenanter and that he favoured toleration; and for that cause, being both judges and parties themselves, would ordaine him, under pain of quartering and plundring, to advance to the insatiable officers so much money as the debt pretended to be due by those remote inhabitants, though meer strangers to him, did extend to; by which means it ordinarily fell out that the civillest men in all the country and most plyable to good order were the greatest sufferers; and the basest, the greedyest and the

Refractary: *opposed*
Logerheadistick: *thickheaded (i.e. pertaining to the logic of a dumbwit)*

147

most unworthy of the benefit of honest conversation, the onely men that were exempted and had immunities.

Now when many of these laird and lord kirk-officers had, by such unconscionable means and so diametrically opposite to all honour and common honesty, acquired great sums of money, then was it that, like good Simeons of iniquity,[167] they had recourse to their brother Levi for framing of protestations; their conscience not serving them to fight for a king that was like to espouse a malignant interest; under which cover, free from the tempest of war, like fruitful brood geese they did stay at home to hatch young chickens of pecunial interest out of those prodigious egs which the very substance of the commons had laid down to them, with a curse, to sit upon.

Yet, if for fashion sake, at the instigation of inferior officers, who were nothing so greedy as they, some shew of muster was to be made of souldiers to be sent to Sterlin leaguer or anywhere else, then were these same very men, whom, out of their pretended zeal to the good cause they had formerly cast either for malignancy or infencibility, and in lieu of each of them accepted of fifty or three-score dolars, more or less, inrolled in their troops or companies; when for the matter of three or four dolars with the consent of a cup of good ale and some promise of future plunder, they had purchased their good wils to take on with them; they approving themselves by such insinuating means good servants in being able by the talent of their three dolars, to do the state that service for the which the poor country gentleman must pay threescore and be forced to quit his man to boot.

Truly those are not the Scotish colonels whom I intend to commend for valour, it being fitter to recommend them to posterity as vipers who, to work out a livelihood to themselves, have not stuck to tear the very bowels of their mother-country and bury its honour in the dust.

Such were not those Scotish colonels I formerly mentioned whose great vassalages abroad and enterprises of most magnanimous adventures, undertaken and performed by them in other countries, might very well make a poorer climate then Scotland enter in competition with a richer soyle.

Sterlin leaguer: *the Stirling siege*   Infencibility: *unfit for military service*

148

Yet seeing the intellectual faculties have their vertues as well as the moral, and that learning in some measure is no less commendable then fortitude; as those afore-named Scotish men have been famous beyond sea for the military part, so might I mention thrice as many moe of that nation as I have set down of warlike officers, who since the yeer one thousand and six hundred have deserved in all those aforesaid countryes of France, Italy, Spaine, Flanders, Holland, Denmark, Germany, Pole, Hungary and Swedland, where they lived, great renown for their exquisite abilities in all kind of literature; the greatest part of whose names I deem expedient for the present to conceal, thereby to do the more honor to some whose magnanimity and other good parts now to commemorate would make one appear, in the opinions of many, guilty of the like trespass with them that in the dayes of Nero called Rome by its proper name after he had decreed to give it the title of Neroniana.[168]

Nevertheless being to speak a little of some of them before I lanch forth to cross the seas, I must salute that most learned and worthy gentleman and most indeared minion of the Muses, Master Alexander Ross,[169] who hath written manyer excellent books in Latine and English (what in prose, what in verse) then he hath lived yeers; and although I cannot remember all, yet to set down so many of them as on a sudden I can call to minde, will I not forget — to the end, the reader, by the perusal of the works of so universal a scholar, may reap some knowledge when he comes to read.

His *Virgilius Evangelizans* in thirteen several books, a peece truly, which when set forth with that decorement of plates it is to have in its next edition will evidently shew that he hath apparelled the evangelists in more splendid garments and royal robes then, without prejudice be it spoken, his compatriots Buchanan and Jhonstoun have in their paraphrastick translation of the Psalmes done the king and prophet David. His four books of the Judaick wars, intituled *De Rebus Judaicis Libri Quatuor*, couched in most excellent hexameters; his book penned against a Jesuite in neat Latine prose, called *Rasura Tonsoris*; his *Chymera Pythagorica contra Lansbergium*; his *Additions to Wollebius and Ursinus*; his book called *The new Planet, no Planet*; his

Decorement: *decoration*

Meditations upon Predestination; his book intituled *The Pictures of the Conscience*; his *Questions upon Genesis*; his *Religion's Apotheosis*; his *Melissomachia*; his *Virgilius Triumphans*; his *Four Curious Books of Epigrams* in Latin elegiacks; his *Mel Heliconium*; his *Colloquia Plautina*; his *Mystagogus-poeticus*; his *Medicus Medicatus*; his *Philosophical Touchstone*; his *Arcana Microcosmi*; his *Observations upon Sir Walter Rawley*; his *Marrow of History* or *Epitome of Sir Walter Rawleigh's Works*; his great *Chronology* in the English tongue, set forth in folio, deducing all the most memorable things that have occurred since the Macedonian war till within some ten or twelve yeers to this time; and his many other learned treatises, whose titles I either know not or have forgot.

Besides all these volumes, books and tractates here recited, he composed above three hundred exquisite sermons which, after he had redacted them into an order and diction fit for the press, were by the merciless fury of Vulcan destroyed all in one night to the great grief of many preachers to whom they would have been every whit as useful as Sir Edwards Cook's reports are to the lawyers.[170] But that which I as much deplore and am as unfainedly sory for, is that the fire which on that fatal night had seazed on the house and closet where those his sermons were consumed, had totally reduced to ashes the very desks wherein were locked up several metaphysical, physical, moral and dialectical manuscripts whose conflagration, by philosophers is as much to be bewailed, as by theologically-affected spirits was that of his most divine elucubrations.

This loss truly was irrecoverable; therefore by him at last digested because he could not help it; but that some losses of another nature, before and after that time by him sustained, have as yet not been repaired lyeth as a load upon this land, whereof I wish it were disburthened, seeing it is in behalf of him who for his piety, theological endowments, philosophy, eloquence and poesie, is so eminently qualified, that, according to the metempsychosis of Pythagoras,[171] one would think that the souls of Socrates, Chrysostome, Aristotle, Ciceron and Virgil[172] have been transformed into the substantial faculties of that entelechy, wherewith by such a conflated transanimation he is informed and sublimely inspired. He spends the substance

Redacted: *put together*   Metempsychosis: *transmigration of the soul* of his own lamp for the weal of others. Should it not then be recruited with new oyle by those that have been enlightened by it? Many enjoy great benefices and that deservedly enough for the good they do to their coaevals onely. How much more meritoriously should he then be dealt with whose literate erogations reach to this and after-ages? A lease for life of any parcel of land is of less value then the hereditary purchase thereof; so he of whom posterior generations reap a benefit ought more to be regarded then they whose actions perish with themselves. Humane reason and common sense it self instructeth us that dotations, mortifications and other honorary recompences should be most subservient to the use of those that afford literatory adminicularies of the longest continuance for the improvement of our sense and reason.

Therefore could I wish, nor can I wish a thing more just, that this reverend, worthy and learned gentleman, Master Rosse, to whom this age is so much beholden, and for whom posterity will be little beholden to this age if it prove unthankful to him, were, as he is a favorite of Minerva, courted by the opulent men of our time as Danae was by Jupiter,[173] or that they had as much of Maecenas' soul[174] as he hath of Virgil's; for if so it were or that this isle of all Christendom would but begin to taste of the happiness of so wise a course, vertue would so prosper and learning flourish by his encouragements and the endeavours of others in imitation of him, that the Christians needed lie no longer under the reproach of ignorance which the Oriental nations fixe upon them[175] in the termes of seeing but with one eye. But in the instance of Great Britain alone, to vindicate in matter of knowledge the reputation of this our Western world, make the Chineses by very force of reason of whose authority above them they are not ashamed, be glad to confess that the Europæans as well as themselves look out with both their eyes and have no blinkard minds. Of which kind of brave men, renowned for perspicacy of sight in the ready perceiving of intellectual objects and that *in gradu excellenti*, is this Master Rosse; the more ample

---

Erogations: *bestowal of gifts*   Posterior: *later*   Dotations: *endowments*
Mortifications: *disposals of property*   Adminicularies: *aids*
In gradu excellenti: at the highest level

expressing of whose deserved elogies that I remit unto another time, will I hope be taken in better part that I intend to praise him againe, because *laus* ought to be *virtutis assecla*[176] and he is alwayes doing good.

Therefore lest I should interrupt him, I will into France, Spain and other countries to take a view of some great scholars of the Scotish nation who of late have been highly esteemed for their learning in forraign parts: of which number he that first presents himself is one Sinclair,[177] an excellent mathematician, Professor Regius and possessor of the Chaire of Ramus (though long after his time) in the University of Paris. He wrote, besides other books, one in folio, *De Quadratura Circuli*. Of the same profession and of his acquaintance there was one Anderson,[178] who likewise lived long in Paris and was for his abilities in the mathematical sciences accounted the profoundlyest principled of any man of his time. In his studyes he plyed hardest the equations of algebra, the speculations of the irrational lines, the proportions of regular bodies and sections of the cone; for though he was excellently well skilled in the theory of the planets and astronomy, the opticks, catoptricks, dioptricks, the orthographical, stereographical and schenographical projections, in cosmography, geography, trigonometry and geodesie, in the staticks, musick and all other parts or pendicles, sciences, faculties or arts of or belonging to the disciplines mathematical in general or any portion thereof in its essence or dependances; yet taking delight to pry into the greatest difficulties, to soar where others could not reach and, like another Archimedes, to work wonders by geometry and the secrets of numbers; and having a body too weak to sustaine the vehement intensiveness of so high a spirit, he dyed young, with that respect nevertheless to succeeding ages that he left behind him a posthumary book intituled *Andersoni Opera*, wherein men versed in the subject of the things therein contained will reap great delight and satisfaction.

There was another called Doctor Seaton,[179] not a Doctor of

Catoptricks: *the reflection of light (Part of science of optics dealing with)*
Dioptricks: *the refraction of light (Part of science of optics dealing with)*
Schenographical: *drawing in perspective*
Staticks: *science dealing with the causes of weight*

Divinity but one that had his degrees at Padua and was *doctor utriusque juris*; for whose pregnancy of wit and vast skill in all the mystries of the civil and canon laws, being accounted one of the ablest men that ever breathed, he was most heartily desired by Pope Urbane the Eighth to stay at Rome and, the better to encourage him thereto, made him chief professor of the Sapience,[180] a Colledge in Rome so called; where, although he lived a pretty while with great honor and reputation, yet at last, as he was a proud man, falling at some ods with Il Collegio Romano,[181] the supreamest seat of the Jesuites and that wherein the general of that numerous society hath his constant residence, he had the courage to adventure coping with them where they were strongest and in matter of any kind of learning to give defiance to their greatest scholars; which he did do with such a hight of spirit and in such a lofty and bravashing humour that although there was never yet that ecclesiastical incorporation wherein there was so great universality of literature or multiplicity of learned men, he nevertheless, misregarding what estimation they were in with others and totally reposing on the stock or basis of his own knowledge, openly gave it out that if those *Teatinos*[182] (his choler not suffering him to give them their own name of Jesuites) would offer any longer to continue in vexing him with their frivolous chat and captious argumentations to the impugning of his opinions (and yet in matters of religion they were both of one and the same faith), he would, like a Hercules amongst so many Myrmidons,[183] fal in within the very midst of them, so besquatter them on all sides and, with the granads of his invincible arguments, put the braines of all and each of them in such a fire that they should never be able, pump as they would, to finde in all the celluls thereof one drop of either reason or learning wherewith to quench it.

This unequal undertaking of one against so many, whereof some were greater courtiers with his Papal Holiness then he, shortened his abode at Rome and thereafter did him so much prejudice in his travels through Italy and France that when at any time he became scarce of money, to which exigent his

Doctor utriusque juris: Doctor of both Canon and Civil law
Bravashing: *swaggering*   Teatinos: *Theatines. (See Commentary p. 234)*
Besquatter: *bespatter with filth*   Granads: *grenades*

prodigality often brought him, he could not as before expect an *ayuda de costa* as they call it or *viaticum* from any prince of the territories through which he was to pass because the chanels of their liberality were stopped by the rancour and hatred of his conventual adversaries.

When nevertheless he was at the lowest ebb of his fortune, his learning and incomparable facility in expressing any thing with all the choicest ornaments of, and incident varieties to the perfection of the Latine elocution, raised him to the dignity of being possessed with the Chair of Lipsius[184] and professing humanity (in Italy called *buone letere*) in the famous University of Lovan; yet, like Mercury unapt to fix long in any one place, deserting Lovan he repaired to Paris, where he was held in exceeding great reputation for his good parts and so universally beloved that both laicks and churchmen, courtiers and scholars, gentlemen and merchants, and almost all manner of people willing to learn some new thing or other (for, as sayes Aristotle,[185] every one is desirous of knowledge) were ambitious of the enjoyment of his company and ravished with his conversation. For besides that the matter of his discourse was strong, sententious and witty, he spoke Latine as if he had been another Livy or Salustius;[186] nor, had he been a native of all the three countryes of France, Italy and Germany, could he have exprest himself, as still he did when he had occasion, with more selected variety of words, nimbler volubility of utterance or greater dexterity for tone, phrase and accent in all the three languages thereto belonging.

I have seen him circled about at the Louvre with a ring of French lords and gentlemen, who hearkned to his discourse with so great attention that none of them, so long as he was pleased to speak, would offer to interrupt him, to the end that the pearles falling from his mouth might be the more orderly congested in the several treasures of their judgements; the ablest advocates, barristers or counselors at law of all the Parlement of Paris, even amongst those that did usually plead *en la chambre dorée*, did many times visit him at his house to get his advice in hard debatable points. He came also to that sublime pitch of good diction even in the French tongue that there having past by

Ayuda de costa: financial help   *Viaticum: provision for a journey*

vertue of a frequent intercourse several missives in that idiom betwixt him and le Sieur de Balzak,[187] who, by the quaintest Romancealists[188] of France and daintiest complementers of all its lushious youth, was almost uncontrollably esteemed in eloquence to have surpassed Ciceron; the straine of Seaton's letters was so high, the fancy so pure, the words so well connexed and the cadence so just, that Balzak, infinitely taken with its fluent yet concise oratory, to do him the honor that was truly due unto him, most lovingly presented him with a golden pen in acknowledgement of Seaton's excelling him both in retorick and the art of persuasion; which gift proceeding from so great an oratour and for a supereminency in that faculty wherein himself, without contradiction, was held the chiefest of this and all former ages that ever were born in the French nation, could not chuse but be acounted honorable. Many learned books were written by this Seaton in the Latine tongue whose titles, to speak ingenuously, I cannot hit upon.

There was another Scotish man named Cameron[189] who within these few yeers was so renowned for learning over all the provinces of France that, besides his being esteemed for the faculties of the minde the ablest man of all that country, he was commonly designed, because of his universal reading, by the title of 'The Walking Library'; by which, he being no less known then by his own name, he therefore took occasion to set forth an excellent book in Latine, and that in folio, intituled *Bibliotheca Movens*, which afterwards was translated into the English language.

To mention those former Scotish men and forget their compatriot Barclay,[190] the author of *Argenis, Icon Animorum* and other exquisite treatises, translated out of Latine into the languages almost of every country where use is made of printing, would argue in me a great neglect. It shall suffice nevertheless for this time that I have named him, for I hope the reader will save me a labour and extoll his praises to as great hight when he shall be pleased to take the paines to peruse his works.

Yet that the learning of the travelers of the Scotish nation may not seem to be tyed to the climate of France (although all Scots by the privilege of the laws of that kingdome be naturalized French, and that all the French kings since the days of Charlemaine, which is about a thousand yeers since, by reason of their fidelity to that crown, have put such real confidence in the Scots, that whithersoever the King of France goeth, the Scots are nearest to him of any and the chief guard on which he reposeth for the preservation of his royal person): there was a Scotish man named [Colvil][191] who in the yeer 1627 had a pension of King Philip the Fourth of six hundred ducats a yeer for his skilfulness in the Hebrew, Caldean, Syriack, Aethiopian, Samaritan and Arabick tongues beyond all the Christians that ever were born in Europe. The service he did do the Spanish king in those languages (especially the Arabick and Caldean) which, after great search made over all his ample territories and several other kingdoms besides for some able man to undergo the task, could not be got performed by any but him, was to translate into Latine or Spanish some few books of those six hundred great volumes, taken by Don Juan de Austria at the Battel of Lepanto[192] from the great Turk, whch now lye in the great library of the magnifick Palace of the Escurial, some seven leagues westward from Madrid and otherwayes called San Lorenço el Real. Of those and many other mental abilities of that nature, he gave after that most excellent proofs both at Rome, Naples and Venice.

That most learned Latine book in folio, treating of all the mathematical arts and sciences, which was written by that Scotish gentleman Sempil, resident in Madrid, sheweth that Scotish spirits can produce good fruits even in hot climates.

Another named Gordon, of the Scotish nation likewise, wrote a great Latin book in folio of chronology, which is exceeding useful for such as in a short time would attaine to the knowledge of many histories.

Another Gordon, also beyond sea, penned several books of divinity in an excellent stile of Latin. Of which kinde of books, but more profoundly couched, another Scot named Turneboll wrote a great many. These four eminent Scots[193] I have put together because they were societaries by the name of Jesus vulgarly called Jesuits; some whereof are living as yet, and none of those that are not dyed above fourteen yeers ago.

Methinks I were to blame, should I in this nomenclature leave out Dempster, who for his learning was famous over all Italy, had made a learned addition to Rossinus[194] and written several other excellent books in Latin, amongst which that which doth most highly recommend him to posterity is the work which he penned of five thousand illustrious Scots, the last liver whereof, as is related in the 56. page of this book, dyed above fifty yeers since; for which, together with the other good parts wherewith he was endowed, himself was truly illustrious.

Balfour, a professor of philosophy in Bourdeaux,[195] wrote an excellent book in Latine upon the morals. So did another of the Scotish nation, named Donaldson, upon the same very subject and that very accurately. Primrose, a Scotish man who was a preacher in French at Bourdeaux[196] and afterwards became one of the three that preached in the French church at London, wrote several good books both in Latin and French. Doctor Liddel penned an exquisite book of physick and so did Doctor William Gordon and both in the Latine tongue, which two doctors were for their learning renowned over all Germany. Pontaeus,[197] a Scotish man, though bred most of his time in France, by several writings of his obvious to the curious reader gave no small testimony of his learning.

There was a professor of the Scottish nation within these sixteen yeers in Somure,[198] who spoke Greek with as great ease as ever Cicero did Latine and could have expressed himself in it as well and as promptly as in any other language; yet the most of the Scotish nation never having astricted themselves so much to the propriety of words as to the knowledge of things, where there was one preceptor of languages amongst them, there were above forty professors of philosophy. Nay, to so high a pitch did the glory of the Scotish nation attaine over all the parts of France and for so long time together continued in that obtained hight, by vertue of an ascendant the French conceived the Scots to have above all nations in matter of their subtlety in philosophical disceptations, that there hath not been till of late, for these several ages together, any lord, gentleman or other in all that country who being desirous to have his son instructed in the principles of philosophy, would intrust him to the discipline of any other then a Scotish master; of whom they were no less proud then Philip was of Aristotle, or Tullius of Cratippus.[199] And if it occurred, as very often it did, that a pretender to a place in any French university, having in his tenderer yeers been

Astricted: *limited*

157

subserulary to some other kind of schooling, should enter in competition with another aiming at the same charge and dignity whose learning flowed from a Caledonian source, commonly the first was rejected and the other preferred; education of youth in all grounds of literature under teachers of the Scotish nation being then held by all the inhabitants of France to have been attended, *caeteris paribus*, with greater proficiency then any other manner of breeding subordinate to the documents of those of another country. Nor are the French the only men have harboured this good opinion of the Scots in behalf of their inward abilities: but many times the Spaniards, Italians, Flemins, Dutch, Hungarians, Sweds and Polonians have testified their being of the same mind by the promotions whereunto, for their learning, they in all those nations at several times have attained.

Here nevertheless it is to be understood that neither these dispersedly-preferred Scots were all of one and the same religion nor yet any one of them a Presbyterian. Some of them were and are as yet popish prelates such as the Bishop of Vezon;[200] and Chalmers, Bishop of Neems;[201] and Signor Georgio Con,[202] who wrote likewise some books in Latine, was by his intimacy with Pope Urban's nephews, Don Francesco, Don Antonio and Don Taedaeo Barbarini and for his endeavoring to advance the Catholico-pontificial interest in Great Britain, to have been dignified with a cardinal's hat which, by all appearance, immediately after his departure from London he would have obtained as soon as he had come to Rome, had death not prevented him by the way in the city of Genua. But had he returned to this island with it, I doubt it would have proved ere now as fatal to him as another such like cap in Queen Marie's time had done to his compatriot Cardinal Betoun.[203]

By this, as it is perceivable that all Scots are not Presbyterians nor yet all Scots Papists, so would not I have the reputation of any learned man of the Scotish nation to be buryed in oblivion because of his being of this or this, or that, or yon, or of that other religion; no more then if we should cease to give learning and moral vertues their due in the behalfe of pregnant and good spirits born and bred in several climates; which to withhold

Subserulary: *subjugated*

from them, whether Periscians, Heteroscians or Amphiscians,[204] would prove very absurd to the humane ingenuity or ingenuous humanity of a true cosmopolite.

For we see how the various aspects of the heavens in their asteristick and planetary influences, according to the diversity of our sublunary situations, disposeth the inclinations of the earth's respective inhabitants differently; whence, as is said in the 87. page of this book, the Spaniards are proud, the French inconstant, the Italians lascivious etc. and every nation almost in their humour, not only discrepant from one another but each having some disorderly motion which another hath not, makes the other to be possessed with some irregularity which the former wants.

We know the Hollanders are more penurious then the High-Germans and they more intemperate then the Spaniards, who againe are more lecherous then the Hollanders. Now seeing *ex malis moribus bonae oriuntur leges*[205] and that vices, like diseases of the body, must be cured by contraries, it will cleerly follow, there being vices contrary to other as well as vice to vertue, that the laws curbing those vices in the opposite extreams must needs be very disssonant from one another.

Do not we see that in Holland to play the merchant is accounted honorable, athough it be thought disgraceful in High-Germany for a gentleman to use any kind of traffick? The Spaniard holds him worse then a beast that is at any time drunk, yet the Dutchman esteems him no good fellow that sometimes is not. The Hollander deems him unworthy of the name of man that fornicates before he marry, but the Spaniard hardly doth repute him a man who hath not exercised those male abilities whereby he is distinguished from the woman.

Thus according to the genius of each climate; statutes, acts and ordinances being instituted for the regulating of men's actions and our obedience to superior powers by custome becomming, as it were, natural, we by experience finde that the religion wherewith men are most accustomed lyes best to their consciences.

For that it is so, we know by the vehemency of fidimplicitaries, of whom some will chuse to lose their lives before they quit their

Asteristick: *relating to the stars*   Fidimplicitaries: *strong or fanatical believers*

religion, although they be altogether ignorant of what they should believe till they ask the minister; whose custome, to make their consciences subservient to their choler, is to principle them with the negative faith without any great positive doctrine, for so begins the Covenant;[206] of which kind of zealous disciples was that covenanting gentleman who burnt a great many historical and philosophical books, thinking they had been books of Popery, he taking them to be such because of the red letters he saw in their titles and inscriptions.

Nor shall we need to think it strange that in the world there are so many several religions, if we consider that the divers temperaments of our bodies alter our inclinations, from whose disparity arise repugnant laws which long obedience makes it seem a sacriledge to violate. In my opinion, truly, there is nothing more natural then variety; yea, and that sometimes with opposition. Are not we composed of the four elements, which have their contrary as wel as symbolizing qualities? And doth not the manner of their mixture and the degrees, by more or less, of the qualities from thence flowing in the constitution of men's bodies disagree in all the persons of the world? Hence some are melancholious, some phlegmatick, some cholerick and some sanguinean, and every one of those more or less according to the humour that affects him in its quantity and quality.

Thus if men were left to themselves, every one would have a several religion. But seeing to reap good from one another we must to one another apply our selves, and that this application without conformity would prove destructive, therefore is it that the individuals of mankinde have been still pleased to forego some natural interest they had in peculiar differences, the better to erect an uniformity in their society for that self-preservation, which is the chief end of their designes.

This making either a king or state, we come then to have laws imposed on us according to the climate or disposition of the people. And although I know there be a difference betwixt divine and humane institutions and that it is fitting wicked thoughts be punished as well as words or actions, yet do I appeal to the judgement of any that will, in casting his eye upon the world as it is and still hath been, consider but the various governments in the regulating of the deeds of the consciences of men; if he finde it not to be true that over the whole universe amongst the Christians, Jews, Paynims and Mahumetans, both in this and former ages, religions almost have been still distinguished by secular soveraignties, each state having its own profession and the faith of one climate being incompatible with that of another; and yet in the duties commonly observed 'twixt neighbor and neighbor in matter of buying and selling, trucking, changing and such like sociable commutations, there is as great unanimity by the most part of the world maintained even in the bonds of honesty, as if, as they know what pleaseth God should please them, they were of the opinion of Tamarlain,[207] who believed that God was best pleased with diversity of religions, variety of worship, dissentaneousness of faith and multiformity of devotion.

For this cause prescinding from the religion of any of my compatriots, which if displeasing to God will no doubt at last displease themselves and hurry upon them that punishment which we ought not to aggravate before its time by detaining from them what praise to them is due for the natural and moral accomplishments wherewith God hath endowed them for our benefit; for in praising them, we praise God who hath made them the instruments of doing us good.

These three profound and universal scholars of the Scotish nation: Tyry of the House of Drumkilbo, Mackbrek and Brown[208] deserve a rank in this list of men of literature as well as Chisum, the Bishop of Vezon and others of the Romish faith above mentioned and for whose praises I have already apologized. Tyry wrote books of divinity in a most acurate straine and, being assistant to the general of the Jesuites, was the second person of all that vast ecclesiastical republick which reacheth as far as to the outmost territories of all the Christian kings and states of the whole continent of the world; a higher place then which amongst them no stranger ever attained to in Italy, which is the place of their supremest jurisdiction. Mackbrek is eminent for his literature in Pole and Brown in Germany and both of them authors of good books.

To hit upon the names of others such as these of the Scotish nation, renowned for learning even in remoter parts of the

Trucking: *bartering*   Dissentaneousness: *diversity of opinion.*
Apologized: *written in justification of*

world, it would be a task not so proper for any as for the great traveler Lithco,[209] a compatriot likewayes of theirs, who in nineteen yeers space traveled three times by land over all the known parts almost of Europe, Asia and Africk, as by a book of a pretty bulk in quarto set forth by himself is more evidently made manifest. The said Lithco also is an author of several other books. And so was Simon Graham,[210] a great traveler and very good scholar, as doth appear by many books of his emission. But being otherwayes too licentious and given over to all manner of debordings, the most of the praise I will give him wil be to excuse him in these terms of Aristotle — *Nullum magnum ingenium sine mixtura dementiae.*[211]

Some other eminent men for literature of the Scotish nation, besides those formerly rehearsed, have been much esteemed of abroad, although they were no Roman Catholicks; such as Doctor John Forbas[212] who was a professor of divinity in Leyden and wrote an excellent book of divinity in folio, called *Irenicon.* Doctor Read likewise was an able scholar, as may appear by his book of Anatomy and other learned writtings.

Now seeing I am from beyond sea bringing the enumeration of my scholars homewards, I cannot forget the names of Doctor Balcanquel, Doctor Sibbalds, Doctor Stuart and Doctor Michel, all able divines and sometimes beneficed men in England.

How much the Protestant faith oweth to Doctor Robert Baron[213] for his learned treatises against Turnebol the Jesuite, *De Objecto Formali Fidei,* I leave to be judged by those that have perused them. To the conversation of Doctor William Lesly,[214] who is one of the most profound and universal scholars now living, his friends and acquaintance of any literature are very much beholding but to any books of his emission nothing at all; whereat every one that knoweth him wondreth exceedingly and truly so they may; for though scripturiency be a fault in feeble pens and that Socrates the most learned man of his time set forth no works, yet can none of these two reasons excuse his not evulging somewhat to the publike view, because he is known to have an able pen whose draughts would grace the paper with

Scripturiency: *mania for writing*   Evulging: *displaying* impressions of inestimable worth; nor is the example of Socrates able to apologize for him unless he had such disciples as Plato and Aristotle who, having seposited in their braines the scientifick treasures of their master's knowledge, did afterwards in their own works communicate them to the utility of future generations. Yet that this Caledonian Socrates, though willing, could not of late have been able to dispose of his talent, did proceed from the merciless dealings of some wicked Anites, Lycons and Melits[215] of the Covenant, the cruelty of whose perverse zeal will keep the effects of his vertue still at under, till by the persuasion of some honest Lysias[216] the authority of the land be pleased to reseat him into his former condition with all the encouragements that ought to attend so prime a man.

Doctor John Gordon, sometime minister of Elgin, Doctor William Hogstoun and Doctor James Sibbett are men who have given great proof of their learning as well by treatises which they have divulged, as in all manner of academical exercitations. Doctor William Guild[217] deserveth by himself to be remembred both for that he hath committed to the press many good books tending to the edification of the soul and bettering of the minde, and that of all the divines that have lived in Scotland these hundred yeers he hath been the most charitable and who bestowed most of his own to publike uses. The lovingness of his heart dilates it self to many and the center of his desires is the common weal. In matter of great edifices — where he builds not, he repaires; and many churches, hospitals, colledges and bridges have been the objects of his beneficence. But to shew the vertue of this man beyond thousands of others richer then he, even of those that had a nearer and more immediate call to the performance of such charitable offices, when he was Principal of the old Colledge of Aberdeen and that at a time when, by reason of the sword everywhere raging through the land, all schooles almost were laid waste, so great was his industry, so prudent his government and so liberal his erogations that the number of the scholars there, all the time that he ruled, did by threescore and ten a yeer exceed the greatest confluence that ever was therein since the foundation of that University; to which I wish all

Seposited: *reserved*   At under: *undervalued*

happiness because of him for whom this book is intended, who learned there the elements of his philosophy under the conduct of one Master William Seaton,[218] who was his tutor; a very able preacher truly and good scholar and whom I would extoll yet higher but that being under the consistorian lash, some critick presbyters may do him injury by pretending his dislike of them for being praised by him who idolizeth not their authority.

The same reason invites me not to insist upon the praises of Master William Lauder, preacher at Ava,[219] a good divine and excellent poet both in Latine and English. And for the same cause must I forbear to spend encomions upon that worthy gentleman, Master David Leech[220] who is a most fluent poet in the Latine tongue, an exquisite philosopher and profound theolog.

Seeing I am come to speak againe of Scotish poets which have flourished of late, the foresaid Master Leech hath an elder brother named John[221] who hath set forth four or five most excellent books of epigrams and eclogues in the Latine tongue. One Master Andrew Ramsey[222] likewise hath been the author of books of very good epigrams in Latine. Several others in that nation are and have been of late very good Latine poets, amongst which I must needs commemorate Doctor Arthur Jhonstoun,[223] a physician by profession, yet such a one as had been so sweetly imbued by the springs of Helicon that before he was fully three and twenty yeers of age he was laureated poet at Paris and that most deservedly, as may appear by his *Parergon*, his *Paraphrastick Translation of the Psalmes* (wherein if he excell not, I am sure he equaleth Buchanan) and some other treatises by name to me unknown.

His brother also, Doctor William Jhonstoun, was a good poet in Latine and a good mathematician, acknowledged to be such (which was none of his meanest praises) by Master Robert Gordon of Straloch,[224] one of the ablest men of Scotland in the mathematical faculties and who, of all mathematicians, hath done it most honor by having taken the paines to set down all the shires and countries thereof in most exact geographical maps; which designe, though intended, essayed and blocked by many others, yet was never brought to its full and compleat perfection

Consistorian: *Presbyterian*

164

but by this gentleman of the name of Gordon, intituled the Laird of Straloch; who, being loath his vertue and learning should expire with himself, hath the most hopeful and best educated children of any whosoever within two hundred miles of his house.

These mathematical blades put me in mind of that Doctor Liddel, of whom, for his abilities in physick, I made mention in p. 157. which I had reason to do because of his learned books written in Latin, *De Diaeta, De Febribus* and *De Methodo Medicinae*; who for his profoundness in these siences of sensible immaterial objects was everywhere much renowned, especially at Francfort de Maine, Francfort on the Oder and Heidelberg, where he was almost as well known as the monstrous bacchanalian tun that stood there in his time. He was an eminent professor of the mathematicks, a disciple of the most excellent astronomer Tycho Brahe and condisciple of that worthy Longomontanus.[225] Yet in imitation of Aristotle whose doctrine with great proficiency he had imbued, esteeming more of truth then of either Socrates or Plato, when the new star began to appear in the constellation of Cassiopeia, there was concerning it such an intershocking of opinions betwixt Tycho Brahe and Doctor Liddel evulged in print to the open view of the world, that the understanding reader could not but have commended both for all; and yet, in giving each his due, praised Tycho Brahe most for astronomy and Liddel for his knowledge above him in all the other parts of philosophy.

As this Doctor Liddel was a gallant mathematician and exquisite physician, so being desirous to propagate learning to future ages and to make his own kindred the more enamoured of the sweetness thereof, especially in mathematical sciences, he bequeathed fourty pounds English money a yeer[226] to the new Colledge of the University of Aberdeen for the maintenance of a mathematical professor, with this *proviso*, that the neerest of his own kinsemen, *caeteris paribus*, should be preferred before any other. This any rational man would think reasonable; nor was it truly much controverted for the space of fourteen or fifteen yeers together after the making of the legacy; at which time his nephew on the brother's side being a childe and but then initiated to the rude elements of Latine, one Doctor William Jhonstoun was preferred to the place because there was none at that time of Doctor Liddel's consanguinity able to discharge it; a reason verily relevant enough.

But by your leave, good reader, when Doctor William Jhonstoun dyed[227] and that Doctor Liddel's nephew, Master Duncan Liddel by name, was then of that maturity of age and provection of skil in most of the disciplines mathematical, as was sufficient for the exercise of that duty and the meriting of his uncle's benefice, did the good men, rulers at the helme there, make any conscience of the honest Doctor's latter will? No, forsooth! The oracle must be first consulted with. The ministerian philoplutaries — my tongue forks it, I have mistaken it seems one word for another, I should have said philosophers — thought fit otherwayes to dispose thereof; for, say they, Master Duncal Liddel hath committed the hainous sin of fornication and begot a young lass with childe. Therefore his uncle's testament must be made void in what relates to his enjoyment of that dotation. O brave logick and curious commentary upon a later will for the better explication of the mind of the defunct! Which Presbyterian doctrine, had it bin in request in the daies of Socrates, what fine pass would the world have been brought to ever since that time by that ignorance which should have over-clouded us through our being destitute of the works of Plato, Aristotle and Euclid with all the scholiasts that have glossed on them these two thousand yeers past; for by all appearance those three prime Grecians would have been forced in their younger yeers to betake themselves to some other profession then philosophy for want of a master to instruct them in the principles thereof; for the Presbytery of Athens, no doubt, would have pearched up poor Socrates upon a penitentiary pew and outed him of his place for having two wives at once, neither whereof, whether Xantippe or Myrto,[228] was either so handsome or good as Master Liddel's concubine; and in lieu of that trespasser supplyed the academical chaire with the breech of a more sanctified brother whose zealous jobernolisme would never have affected the anti-Presbyterian spirits of Plato, Euclid or Aristotle nor gained to his schoole any disciples who should have been able from such a muddy fountain to derive any clear

Provection: *advancement*   Philoplutaries: *lovers of wealth*
Jobernolisme: *stupidity*

springs of learning to after ages, nor benefit posterity with any other kind of literate works then such as the pretended holy men and accusers of Socrates — Anitus, Lycon and Melitus by name — did set forth; which to the eyes of both body and minde have ever since their time been of the colour of the Duke of Vandome's cloak,[229] invisible.

But if one durst make bold to speak to those great professors of piety, I would advise them out of the evangile to take the beam out of their own eye before they meddle with the moat that is in their neighbor's, and to consider that the sin of theft which they committed in robbing Master Liddel of his due is a far more hainous transgression then that single fornication for which, besides the forfeiture of what was mortified to him, he was by them for a long time together most rigorously persecuted.

Nor do I think their fault can be better expiated then by fulfilling the contents of the legacy and investing Liddal in his own right; which that I may seem to avouch with the better ground of reason, I dare almost persuade my self that there is not any within the isle of Britain with whom, taking in all the mathematical arts and sciences together, practical and theoretick, he will not be well pleased upon occasion to adventure a dispute for superiority in the most, and that with a willingness to forego and renounce any claim, title or priviledge he can or may pretend to for the Chaire of mathematical professor in new Aberdeen, in case of non-prevalency.

This is more, some will say, then his outside doth promise, and that to looke to him one would not think he had such abilities. What then? Do not we see in apothecaries' shops, pots of the same worth and fashion containe drugs of a different value, and sometimes the most precious oyntment put in the coursest box? So may a little and plaine man in outward shape inclose a minde high and sublime enough; a giant-like spirit in a low stature being able to overtop a colossus with pygmaean endowments.

But were there no other *remora* or obstruction to retard his intended progress in mathematical designes, the inward qualifications of his minde to the advancement of those sciences would quickly raise his person to a greater estimation. Yet truly, as he is in London for the present, I can no better compare him

Mortified: *bequeathed through death*

167

then to an automatary engine wherein there are many several springs, resorts and wheels which, though when once put into a motion would produce most admirable effects, are nevertheless forced for want of a convenient agent to give them the due brangle, to lye immobile and without efficacy.

Such an agent is a Mecaenas, a patron, a promover of learning, a favorer of the Muses and protector of scholars; in the production of which kind of worthy men, were this land alone but a little more fertil, not only Great Britain but the whole world besides would be the better for it.

As for such of the Scotish nation as of late have been famous for English poesie, the first that occurs is Sir William Alexander, afterwards created Earle of Sterlin.[230] He made an insertion to Sir Philip Sidney's *Arcadia* and composed several tragedies, comedies and other kind of poems, which are extant in a book of his in folio, intituled *Sterlin's Works*. The purity of this gentleman's vein was quite spoiled by the corruptness of his courtiership — and so much the greater pity — for by all appearance, had he been contented with that mediocrity of fortune he was born unto and not aspired to those grandeurs of the court, which could not without pride be prosecuted nor maintained without covetousness, he might have made a far better account of himself. It did not satisfie his ambition to have a laurel from the Muses and be esteemed a king amongst poets, but he must be king of some new-found-land, and (like another Alexander indeed, searching after new worlds) have the soveraignty of Nova Scotia. He was born a poet and aimed to be a king. Therefore would he have his royal title from King James, who was born a king and aimed to be a poet.

Had he stopped there, it had been well. But the flame of his honour must have some oyle wherewith to nourish it. Like another King Arthur he must have his knights, though nothing limited to so small a number; for how many soever that could have looked out but for one day like gentlemen and given him but one hundred and fifty pounds sterlin without any need of a key for opening the gate to enter through the Temple of Vertue, which in former times was the only way to honour, they had a scale from him whereby to ascend unto the platformes of Vertue,

Resorts: *mechanical springs*   Brangle: *shaking*

168

which they, treading underfoot, did slight the ordinary passages and, to take the more sudden possession of the Temple of Honour, went upon obscure by-paths of their own towards some secret angiports and dark postern-doors, which were so narrow that few of them could get in till they had left all their gallantry behind them. Yet such being their resolution, that in they would and be worshipful upon any tearms, they misregarded all formerly-used steps of promotion, accounting them but unnecessary, and most rudely rushing in unto the very sanctuary, they immediately hung out the orange colours to testifie their conquest of the honour of knight-baronet.

Their king nevertheless, not to staine his royal dignity or to seem to merit the imputation of selling honor to his subjects, did for their money give them land, and that in so ample a measure that every one of his knight-baronets had for his hundred and fifty pounds Sterlin, heritably disponed unto him six thousand good and sufficient acres of Nova Scotia ground, which being but at the rate of six pence an acre, could not be thought very dear, considering how prettily in the respective parchments of disposition they were bounded and designed fruitful corne land, watered with pleasant rivers running alongst most excellent and spacious meadows; nor did there want abundance of oaken groves in the midst of very fertil plaines, for if they wanted any thing, it was the scrivener or writer's fault, for he gave order, as soon as he received the three thousand Scots marks, that there should be no defect of quantity or quality, in measure or goodness of land, and here and there most delicious gardens and orchards with whatever else could in matter of delightful ground best content their fancies, as if they had made purchase amongst them of the Elysian fields or Mahumet's paradise.

After this manner my Lord Sterlin for a while was very noble and, according to the rate of Sterlin money, was as twelve other Lords in the matter of that frankness of disposition, which not permitting him to dodge it upon inches and ells, better and worse, made him not stand to give to each of his champions territories of the best and the most. And although there should have happened a thousand acres more to be put in the charter or writing of disposition then was agreed upon at first, he cared not.

Angiports: *narrow openings in a wall*

Half a piece to the clerk was able to make him dispense with that. But at last, when he had inrolled some two or three hundred knights who, for their hundred and fifty peeces each, had purchased amongst them several millions of Neocaledonian acres, confirmed to them and theirs for ever under the great seal, the affixing whereof was to cost each of them but thirty peeces more; finding that the society was not like to become any more numerous and that the ancient gentry of Scotland esteemed of such a whimsical dignity as of a disparagement rather then addition to their former honor, he bethought himself of a course more profitable for himself and the future establishment of his own state; in prosecuting whereof without the advice of his knights who represented both his houses of parliament, clergy and all, like an absolute king indeed, disponed heritably to the French for a matter of five or six thousand pounds English money, both the dominion and propriety of the whole continent of that kingdom of Nova Scotia, leaving the new baronets to search for land amongst the Selenits in the moon or turn Knights of the sun; so dearly have they bought their orange riban[231] which, all circumstances considered, is and will be no more honorable to them or their posterity then it is or hath been profitable to either.

What I have said here is not by way of digression but to very good purpose and pertinent to the subject in hand; for as armes and arts commonly are paralleled, and that Pallas goes armed with a helmet, I held it expedient, lest the list of the scholars set down in this place should in matter of pre-eminence be too far overpeered by the roll of the souldiers above recited, that my Lord Sterlin should here represent the place of a king for the literatory part, as well as there did the great uncircumcised Garne for the military, and bring Nova Scotia in competition with Bucharia.

Besides this Lord Alexander, Drummond and Wishart[232] have published very good poems in English; nor is Master Ogilvy to be forgot,[233] whose translation of Virgil and of the fables of Aesop in very excellent English verses most evidently manifesteth that the perfection of the English tongue is not so

Disponed: *made over*

narrowly confined but that it may extend it self beyond the natives on this side of Barwick.

I might have named some more Scotish poets both in English and Latine but that besides, as I often told, I intend not to make a compleat enumeration of all, there is a Latin book extant which passeth by the name of *Deliciae Poetarum Scotorum* wherein the reader may finde many, even of those that have lived of late yeers, whom I have here omitted, as I have done several other able men of the Scotish nation in other faculties, such as Master David Chalmers[234] who in Italy penned a very good book and that in neat Latine, treating of the antiquities of Scotland and had it printed at Paris; as also one Simson[235] who wrote in Latine four exquisite books of hieroglyphicks, and one Hart in the city of London[236] at this present, who wrote the *Fort Royal of Scripture*, etc.

The excellency of Doctor William Davison in alchymy above all the men now living in the world, whereof by his wonderful experiments he giveth daily proof, although his learned books published in the Latine tongue did not evidence it, meriteth well to have his name recorded in this place. And after him Doctor Leeth, though in time before him, designed in Paris, where he lived by the name of Letu, who, as in the practise and theory of medicine he excelled all the doctors of France, so in testimony of the approbation he had for his exquisiteness in that faculty, he left behinde him the greatest estate of any of that profession then, as the vast means possest by his sons and daughters there as yet can testifie.

Amongst those eminent doctors of physick, I ought not to forget Doctor Fraser who was made doctor at Toulouse with the universal approbation and applause of that famous university and afterwards succeeded to Doctor Arthur Jhonstoun's place of Physician in Ordinary to the late king. There is another Scotish gentleman likewise, of the name of Wallace, in France called Devalois, who enjoyeth and hath so done these many yeers the dignity of a prime counseller of the Parlament of Grenoble, the capital city of the province of Dauphiné, and is withal the chief favourite and the only trustee of the Grand Mareshal de Criky.[237]

Now as in this heterogenean miscellany we have proceeded from the body to the purse, that is, metonymically from the physician to the lawyer, so after the same desultory method, which may be well excused in this unpremeditated and almost extemporanean treatise, we may for the soul's sake, which in this later age (so far as metaphors may with proper significations enter in competition) hath been no less subject to poverty and diseases than any of the former two, have another hint at some of our late Scotish divines; the first whereof, and that *prioritate dignitatis*, that to my memory presenteth himself, is Doctor William Forbas,[238] Principal once of the Colledge of New Aberdeen and afterwards made Bishop of Edenburgh; who was so able a scholar that since the daies of *Scotus Subtilis*, there was never any that professed either divinity or philosophy in Scotland that in either of those faculties did parallel him. He left manuscripts of great learning behind him, which, as I am informed, were bought at a good rate by Doctor Laud,[239] late Archbishop of Canterbury and Primate of England; whose spiritual brother, Spotteswood,[240] late Archbishop of Saint Andrews and Chancellor of Scotland was likewise endowed with a great deal of learning, by means whereof, although he wrote many good books, yet that wherein he bestowed most pains was a large book in folio, intituled *The History of the Church of Scotland*, which I believe was never printed. Yet the manuscript thereof, written with Spotteswod's own hand, I saw presented at Whitehall in the lobby betwixt the little gallery and privy chamber, now called the Admiralty Court, by Maxwel late Bishop of Rosse, to the late king who even then delivered it to his Secretary of State for Scotland, William Earl of Lanerick by name,[241] who was the same Duke Hamiltoun of Hamiltoun that was killed at Worcester and only brother to James, Duke by the same aforesaid title, who two yeers before that lost his head at Westminster in the palace-yard. But what became of that manuscript[242] afterwards I cannot tell. But this I know, that the tenderer thereof, upon his knees to his late majesty, as the gift of a deceased man (for the author dyed but the very day before)[243] Master John Maxwel by name, was a very learned man and author of some good books. Yet lest the reader's humour should be inflamed with the mentioning of these three malignant prelates, I must afford him for antidote another trinity of a

Prioritate dignitatis: by priority of standing

contrary operation, all in one dose, the ingredients wherof are Henderson, Gillespick and Rutherford, named Alexander, George and Samuel, all Masters truly and have been so to my knowledge these twelve yeers past; which three have been or are (for the first two of them are dead) very able and learned men; whose books nevertheless (for they were all authors) I will in some things no otherwayes commend then Andraeas Rivetus,[244] Professor of Leyden, did the doctrine of Buchanan and Knox; whose rashness, in apologizing for them, he ascribed *praefervido Scotorum ingenio, et ad audendum prompto*.[245]

Truly and without flattery be it spoken, for I believe none that knows me will twit me with that vice, the nation of Scotland hath besides those I have here nominated produced several excellent spirits and that of late too, whose abilities, by the Presbyterian persecution and the indigence it hath brought upon them, have been quite smothered and hid as a candle under a bushel.

Many learned books written in Scotland, for want of able and skillful printers[246] and other necessaries requisite for works of such liberal undertaking have perished; and sometimes after they are ready for the press, if the author in the interim happen to dy, the wife and children, for the most part, like rats and mice that preferr the chest where the bread and cheese is kept to the coffer wherein is the silver and gold, to save a little money make use of the aforesaid papers without any regard to the precious things contained in them — to fold perhaps their butter and cheese into, or to other less honorable employments. So unfortunate a thing it is that either good spirits should be struck with penury or that their writings should fall into the hands of ignorants.

That poverty is an enemy to the exercise of vertue and that *non facile emergunt quorum virtutibus obstat res angusta domi*,[247] is not unknown to any acquainted with plutocracy or the soveraign power of mony. But if the great men of the land would be pleased to salve that sore, which possibly would not be so expensive to them as either their hawks or hounds, then peradventure would these ingenious blades sing out aloud and cheerfully with Martial, "*Sint Maecenates non deerunt, Flacce, Marones*";[248] and it might very probably be, and that in a short space, that by such gallant incitements, through a vertuous emulation who should

173

most excell other, Scotland would produce for philosophy, astronomy, natural magick, poesie and other such like faculties, as able men as ever were Duns Scotus, Sacroboscus, Reginaldus Scotus[249] and other compatriots of these three Scots whose names I would not insert in the roll of the rest because they flourished before the yeer 1600.

Now as I have not mentioned any Scotish man to praise him for eminent actions done by him, either in the field or schoole, preceding the yeer 1600; which if I had had a minde to do, I would not have omitted the naming of the several Constables of France, admirals and generals of armies that have been of the Scotish nation in the French service; neither would I have forgot the high and honorable employments the Scots had of Charlemaine, the first occidental Emperor; nor the great exploits performed by the Scots under the conduct of Godfrey de Bullion[250] in the conquest of Jerusalem and afterwards under his successors in the kingdoms of Syria, Antiochia and Egypt against the Saracens; nor what was done by the Scots in defence of the territories of Spaine against the Moores and Aethiopians; as also I would have spoken a little of the Dukes of Chasteau le Roy and Dukes of Aubigny that were Scots;[251] and of Count Betun and Count de Mongomery[252] who killed the King of France in tilting.

So is it that of all those I have named, whether for milice or literature, so far short I have faln in the number of the whole, that not only hath the greatest part of them all been natives of the north of Scotland, but hardly have both the south and west of that country produced the fifth part of them; such a fruitful seminary hath that otherwayes obscure climate of the world proved in the affording of excellent spirits both for armes and arts. Whether what I have related here of the warriors and scholars of the Scotish nation that have been famous abroad be not for uncontrollable truths received in other countries by those that have been eye-witnesses to their actions, I appeal to Sir Oliver Fleemin, Master of the Ceremonies, and to Master Dury;[253] who, as they are both men of good judgement and have been travelers in other states and kingdoms, so am I certainly persuaded that they cannot be altogether estranged from the report of the good reputation of those their compatriots in the places through which they passed; which I believe the rather, for that most of them do know Sir Oliver Fleemin to be a man of excellent good parts, wise in counsel, experienced in affaires of state, true to his trust and in six or seven of the chief languages of Christendome the ablest, liveliest and most pertinent spokesman of this age; and that also they are not ignorant of the most eminent endowments wherewith Master John Dury (in Germany and France, where his learning is highly extolled, intituled Duraeus) hath his minde qualified and imbellished. In reason he is strongly principled and alloweth prudence to be a directress of his actions. He doth not subordinate his faith to the affaires of the world, although it agree not with his faith to gainestand an established authority. He holds it more lawful to yeeld obedience to a power set up above us, then to the hazard of the ruine of a country to erect another. He loveth an honest peace and the wayes that tend to it, and with thankfulness payeth the favours of protection. He reverenceth the all-seeing providence in the change of government and, where it commandeth, there he yeelds allegiance. But if the reader would have a more genuine character of his worth and that which shall represent him with a greater liveliness, his best course will be to have recourse to the perusal of the several treatises composed by him, whereof he hath emitted good store.

Notwithstanding all I have written in praise of Sir Oliver Fleemin and Master John Dury, I would expatiate my pen a little more at large upon this encomiastick straine in behalf of them both, but that I hope ere long to extoll them againe by way of duty, when they shall be pleased out of their love and respect to Sir Thomas Urquhart, who is the only man of whom this book is intended, for whether he be the author or some other that is but a friend or servant of his, it is not material, seeing the furtherance of his weal and credit of his country is the meer scope thereof and end whereat it buts, to interpone their favour with the members of the Parliament and Councel of State, seeing they are the only two of the Scotish nation that as yet have any kind of intimacy with either of these High Courts, and second him in his just demands to the obtaining of what in this tractate is desired in his name. And although nothing of those kinde of good offices hath by them hitherto been performed to

Buts: *aims*   Interpone: *place between*

him, lest perhaps their offering to open their mouth for any in whom there was suspicion of malignancy might breed dislike and diminution of trust, yet must I needs desire them now to lay aside those needless fears and groundless apprehensions and, like real friends indeed, bestir themselves to do that gentleman a courtesie which cannot chuse, though *per impossible* he were unthankful, but carry along with it like all other actions of vertue its own remuneration and reward; and if by mischance, which I hope shall not occur, their forwardness in sollicitation procure a reprehensory check, then let them lay the blame upon this page which I shall take upon my shoulder and bear the burthen of all; there is no inchantment there.

But that '*Amicus certus in re incerta cernitur*'[254] was a saying of King James, of whom to make no mention amongst the literate men of the Scotish nation that have flourished since 1600, would argue in me no less debility of memory then Massala Corvinus was subject to, who forgot his own name;[255] for besides that he was a king, history can hardly afford us amongst all the kings that ever were (Solomon and Alfonso of Aragon being laid aside)[256] any one that was neer so learned as he; as is apparent by that book in folio, intituled *King James his Works*[257] and several other learned treatises of his which in that book are not contained.

In this list of armes and arts-men, King James obtaines a rank amongst the scholars because the souldiery did repute him no favourer of their faculty. His Majesty is placed last, as in a Parliamentary procession, and bringeth up the reer as General Ruven leads on the van; for as Ruven was such a meer souldier that he could neither read nor write, so King James was such a meer scholar that he could neither fight by sea nor land. He thought James the Peaceable a more royal stile then William the Conqueror and would not have changed his motto of '*Beati pacifici*'[258] for the title of '*Sylla Felix*',[259] although it had been accompanyed with the victory over a thousand Mariuses. Yet in his dayes were the Scots in good repute and their gallantry over almost all countries did deserve it.

Then was it that the name of a Scot was honorable over all the world and that the glory of their ancestors was a passport and

Per impossibile: by an impossibility

safe-conduct sufficient for any traveler of that country. In confirmation whereof, I have heard it related of him who is the τὸ οὗ ἕνεκα²⁶⁰ of this discourse and to whose weal it is subordinated, that after his peragration of France, Spaine and Italy, and that for speaking some of those languages with the liveliness of the country accent, they would have had him pass for a native, he plainly told them, without making bones thereof, that truly he thought he had as much honour by his own country which did contrevalue the riches and fertility of those nations by the valour, learning and honesty, wherein it did parallel if not surpass them. Which assertion of his was with pregnant reasons so well backed by him that he was not much gainesaid therein by any in all those kingdoms.

But should he offer now to stand upon such high terms and enter the lists with a spirit of competition, it fears me that in stead of laudatives and panegyricks, which formerly he used, he would be constrained to have recourse to vindications and apologies, the toyle whereof, in saying one and the same thing over and over again with the misfortune of being the less believed the more they spoke, hath proved of late almost insupportable to the favourers of that nation, whose inhabitants in forraign peregrinations must now altogether in their greatest difficulties depend upon the meer stock of their own merit with an abatement of more then the half of its value by reason of the national imputation; whilst in former times men of meaner endowments would in sharper extremities, at the hands of stranger-people, have carryed thorow with more specious advantages by the only vertue of the credit and good name of the country in general; which, by twice as many abilities as ever were in that land, both for martial prowess and favour of the muses, in the persons of private men can never in the opinion of neighbour states and kingdoms be raised to so great a hight as publick obloquy hath deprest it. For as that city whose common treasure is well stored with money, though all its burgers severally be but poor, is better able to maintaine its reputation then that other, all whose citizens are rich without a considerable bank; (the experience whereof history gives us in the

Tò οὗ ἕνεκα: effective cause   Peragration of: *travelling across*

deduction of the wars betwixt the Venetians and Genois);[261] even so will a man of indifferent qualifications, the fame of whose country remaineth unreproached, obtaine a more amicable admittance to the societies of most men then another of thrice more accomplished parts, that is the native of a soyle of an opprobrious name; which, although after mature examination it should seem not to deserve, yet upon the slipperiest ground that is of honor questioned, a very scandal once emitted will both touch and stick.

This maintaining of the reputation of the Scots in these latter dayes hath at several times in forraign countries occasioned adventuring of the single combate against such inconsiderate blabs, as readily upon any small though groundless misreport are prodigal of reproaches and cast aspersions on men of the most immaculate carriage. Many instances hereof I could produce, but to avoid prolixity I will refer the manifestation of the truth thereof to the testimony of Captain John Mercer[262] whom I might have nominated for his excellency in the sword with Sir John Hume of Eatoun and Francis Sinclair but that in a treatise of this nature, where the subjected matter doth not all at once present it self to the memory, to place each one in order as he comes is *methodo doctrinae* nothing repugnant to the true series of the purpose in hand.

What ascendant he hath over others at the single rapeer hath been many times very amply expressed by my Lord of New-castle and the late Earl of Essex, and, as I am informed, by this same Earl of Salisbury, besides divers others who have been eye-witnesses to the various proofs he hath given of his exquisiteness in the art of defence; amongst whom Sir John Carnegy and Sir David Cuningham are best able to relate what with their own eyes they saw him do at Angiers, a city in France, where, after many exasperating provocations, he at last, to vindicate both his own fame and that of his native country, overthrew in the presence of sundry gentlemen and ladies one of the most re-nowned for the faculty of escrime that was in all that kingdom. Some such trials are reported to have been undergone by him here in England, with so much applause and deserved approbation as from the mouths of men very skilful in that

Deduction: *detailed account*   Blabs: *tale-tellers*   Carriage: *conduct*
Methodo doctrinae: according to a systematic method   Escrime: *fencing*

gladiatory profession hath extracted, out of their sincerity of heart, an unfained commendation of being the best sword-man of the Isle of Great Britain. Which I say, not to disparage any of the English nation, for that I know there are in it as truly valourous men as any one breathing in the world and of as good conduct for the improving of their courage and making it effectual against their declared enemies; but that he hath some secret puntilios in the exercise of the single sword-fight, by pursuing all manner of wards with falsifying, binding and battering of the sword after a fashion of his own, with all due observance of time and distance; by providing, in case the adversary after a *finda*, going to the *parade*, discover his brest to *caveat* and give him in a thrust in *quart* with *ecarting* and *volting* the body, to alonge a stoccade *coupée au ventre les deux pieds en sautant* and other such excellents feats, which the judgement conceiving and the eye perceiving, the hand and foot by vertue of a constant practise execute with an incredible nimbleness and agility; to the perfection whereof although a martially-disposed gentleman do never attaine, it can no more derogate from his eminency in military employments then it doth eclipse the credit of a commander-in-chief of cavalry not to make a well-managed horse to go so neatly *terre à terre*, the *incavalar*, the *ripolone*, the *passades*, the *corvetti*, the *serpegiar*, the two steps and a leap, the *mezere*, the *gallop galliard, le saut de mouton* and other such like pleasant aires, as would a *cavallerizo* or master of the noble art of riding. Notwithstanding the frequent hazards which many besids this Capt. Mercer, whom now I will not nominate, have run themselves upon in defence of the good name of the Scots, the nature nevertheless of common spirits is, without any fore-cast of danger, to proclaim the disease of some to be a leprosie cleaving to the body of the whole nation.

Finda: feint   *Parade: parry*
Caveat: disengage (fence) by shifting one's sword from one side to the other of the adversary's sword   *Ecarting: stepping aside*   *Volting: turning around*
Stoccade: *thrust*   *Terre à terre: from place to place*   *Incavalar: mounting*
Ripolone: (meaning uncertain)
Passades: moving horse backwards and forwards over same ground
Corvetti: curvets   *Serpegiar: weaving, zigzagging*
Mezere: high school movement, high steps of front and back feet
Gallop galliard: brisk dance for two horses   *Saut de mouton: leapfrog*
Aires: *artificial motions of a managed horse*

Which custom truly as it is disapprovable for that the innocent do thereby suffer for the fault of the guilty, so do I the more dislike it that the gentleman who in this treatise is the most concerned, when, after that to my knowledge he had received some favour with expectation of greater ones, it no sooner happened (by his servants or some else) to be known of what country he was, but immediately the effectual courtesies formerly intended towards him were exchanged into meer superficial complements and general civilities, with this assurance nevertheless that out of their respects to him they should abstaine in all times comming from doing any injury to his compatriots; which hope of preservation of his countrymen upon the basis of his single reputation from the danger of future prejudice, did afford him no small contentment, although the name of his country in matter of himself did prove a very dismal obstruction to the prosecuting of his own good fortune; and, to speak ingenuously, seeing it is the case of many good spirits and worthy gentlemen besides him, I could heartily wish, as no man is anywhere praised for his mother's being in such or such a place at the instant of his birth, that also nowhere any should receive the least detriment either in his means or estimation for his parents' residence when he was born.

Those productions of meer chance and concomitances of what is totally out of the reach of our power to command were understood by the wise and generous men of old to deserve so little influence for procuring good or bad to the enjoyers of them, that Anacharsis, although a native of Scythia,[263] which was then a more savage country then at this time it is, albeit now it be the seminary of a wilder people then ever Scotland did bring forth, was by Greece, the most judicious nation in the world, with great applause inrolled in the sacred septenary of the most highly-renowned men for prudence and true wisdom that ever lived there; and Oxales,[264] notwithstanding his being a highlander of Genua and born amidst the barren mountains of Liguria, was nevertheless by the mighty Emperour Tamarlain, although a stranger and of a different religion to the boot, dignified with the charge and title of one of the prime generals of that vast Asiatick army which overthrew the Turkish Bajazet.

Septenary: *group of seven*

In imitation of which specious and remarkable examples, that the state of this isle, without regard to ephestian or exotick country, exterior concernements, adjuncts of fortune or any thing beyond the sphere of our will's activity, should consider of men according to the fruits, whether good or bad, true or false, of the several acts and habits respectively which, before the interior faculties by frequent iteration were therewith affected, did at first depend upon our own election, it is both my desire and expectation, for that the gentleman whose interest I hereby intend to promove doth openly defie very calumny it self to be able to lay any thing to his charge either for tergiversation, covetousness or hypocrisie, the three foule blots wherewith his country is stained by those that, for the blemish of a few, would asperse the whole and upon all lay the imputation of faults done but by some.

I dare swear with a safe conscience that he never coveted the goods of any, nor is desirous of any more in matter of worldly means then the peaceable possession of what is properly his own. He never put his hand to any kinde of oath nor thinks fit to tye his conscience to the implicite injunctions of any ecclesiastical tyranny. He never violated trust; always kept his parole and accounted no crime more detestable then the breach of faith. He never received money from king nor parliament, state nor court, but in all employments, whether preparatory to or executional in war, was still his own paymaster and had orders from himself. He was neither in Duke Hamilton's engagement nor at the field of Dunbar;[265] nor was he ever forced in all the several fights he hath been in to give ground to the enemy before the day of Worcester battel. To be masked with the vaile of hypocrisie he reputes abominable and gross dissimulation to contrast the ingenuity of a free-born spirit. All flattering, smoothing and flinching for by-ends he utterly disliketh and thinks no better of adulatory assentations then of a gnatonick sycophantizing or parasitical cogging. He loves to be open-hearted and of an explicite discourse, chusing rather by such means to speak what is true to the advantage of the good then to conceal wickedness under a counterfeit garb of devotion.

Ephestian: *domestic*   Tergiversation: *prevarication*
Assentations: *servile signs of agreement*   Gnatonick: *parasitical*
Cogging: *wheedling*

181

By virtue of which liberty, though reasonably assumed by him and never exceeding the limits of prudential prescription, he in a little book lately published of the genealogy of his House, had (after the manner of his predecessors, who for distinction sake were usually entituled by appellative designations) his proper name affected with the agnominal addition of the word '*parresiastes*', which signifieth one that speaks honestly with freedom; not but that above all things he approveth of secrecy in the managing of affaires of moment and holdeth the life of all great businesses to consist in the closeness of counsel whilst they are in agitation; but as a woman should not sit with her face masked in the company of her friends at dinner, nor a man keep himself alwaies skulking behinde a buckler where there is no appearance of a foe — so should the affectedness of a servil silence utterly be exploded when veracity of elocution is the more commendable quality.

This bound he never yet transgressed and still purposeth to be faithful to his trust. I am not now to dispute the mutual relation of protection and obedience; and how far, to the power God hath placed above us in imitation of Christ, we are bound to succumb. Those that are throughly acquainted with him know his inclinations, both that he will undertake nothing contrary to his conscience; that he will regulate his conscience by the canons of a well-grounded faith and true dictamen of reason and that to the utmost of his power he will perform whatever he promiseth. As for those that know him not and yet would in the censure of him as liberally criticize it as if they were his cardiognosts and fully versed in his intentions: if they be not men in whom he is concerned, as having authority above him, he will never vex his brain nor toyle his pen to couch a fancy or bestow one drop of inke upon them for their satisfaction. It doth suffice him that the main ground of all his proceedings is honesty; that he endeavoreth the prosecuting of just ends by upright means and, seeing the events of things are not in the power of man, he voluntarily recommendeth unto providence the overruling of the rest. He hath no prejudicate principles nor will he be wedded to self-opinions.

Buckler: *small round shield*   Dictamen: *dictate*
His cardiognosts: *those who knew his heart*

And yet, as I conceive it, he believeth that there is no government, whether ecclesiastical or civil, upon earth that is *jure divino*, if that divine right be taken in a sense secluding all other forms of government, save it alone, from the priviledge of that title; those *piae fraudes* and political whimsies being obtruded upon tender consciences to no other end but that, without expense of war, they might be plyable in their obedience to the injunctions of the vice-gerents of the law, meerly by deterring them from acting any thing contrary to the will of the primitive legislator for fear of celestial punishment.

As for pacts and covenants, it is my opinion that he thinks they are no further obligatory and consequently, being annihilated, no more to be mentioned much less urged, when the ground whereupon they were built or cause for which they were taken, are not in vigour to have any more influence upon the contracters: for *idem est non esse et non operari*; *non entium nullae sunt affectiones* and *sublato fundamento tolluntur et omnia quae illi superstruuntur.*[266]

I am confident the consistorian party will be so ill pleased with the freedom of this expression, that they will account him a malignant or a sectary[267] that hath penned it. Therefore, in my conceit, to use their cavilling idiom, a malignant and independent wil better sympathize with one another then either of them with the presbyter, whose principles how consistent they are with monarchy or any other kind of temporal soveraignty, let any man judge that is versed in the story of Geneva, the civil wars of France and Bohemia and history of Queen Mary of Scotland;[268] although what hath been done by the kirkists these last dozen of yeers had been altogether buryed in oblivion, that nothing had been known of their unanimous opposition by the Presbyterian armies at Dunslaw, Newburne, Marston Moor and Hereford to the late king's designes, crowned by his own imprisonment at Newcastle and Holmby; and that after proclaiming Charles the Second at the Market Cross of Edenburgh, king of the three realms of England, Scotland and Ireland, that they had wounded him and shed his blood in the persons of the peerage of Huntely and Montrose had been utterly forgotten.

Piae fraudes: pious frauds   Vice-gerents: *deputy rulers*

What gallant subjects these Presbyterians have been, are for the present and will prove in times coming to any kinde of secular power you may perceive by King James his *ΒΑΣΙΛΙΚΟΝ ΔΩΡΟΝ*, the late king's *ΕΙΚΩΝ ΒΑΣΙΛΙΚΗ* and this young king's *ΒΑΣΙΛΙΚΟΣ ΑΔΥΝΑΣΤΗΣ*;[269] they to basilical rule or any other temporal soveraignty, being in all its genders and that at all occasions as infectious as ever was the basilisk's sight to the eye of man.

For of a king they onely make use for their own ends and so they will of any other supreme magistracie that is not of their own erection. Their kings are but as the Kings of Lacedemon whom the Ephors presumed to fine[270] for any small offence; or as the puppy kings which, after children have trimmed with bits of taffata and ends of silver-lace and set them upon wainscoat cupboards besides marmalade and sugar-cakes, are oftentimes disposed of, even by those that did pretend so much respect unto them, for a two-peny custard, a pound of figs or mess of cream.

Verily I think they make use of kings in their consistorian state as we do of card-kings in playing at the hundred;[271] any one whereof, if there be appearance of a better game without him, and that the exchange of him for another incoming card is like to conduce more for drawing of the stake, is by good gamesters without any ceremony discarded: or as the French on the Epiphany day use their *Roy de la Febve* or King of the Bean;[272] whom, after they have honoured with drinking of his health and shouting aloud, *"Le Roy boit, le Roy boit"*, they make pay for all the reckoning, not leaving him sometimes one peny rather then that the exorbitancie of their debosh should not be satisfied to the full. They may be likewise said to use their king as the players at nine-pins do the middle kyle, which they call the king, at whose fall alone they aim, the sooner to obtain the gaining of their prize; or as about Christmas we do the King of Misrule whom we invest with that title to no other end but to countenance the bacchanalian riots and preposterous disorders of the family where he is installed.

The truth of all this appears by their demeanour to Charles the Second whom they crowned their king at Sterlin[273] and who, though he be for comeliness of person, valour, affability, mercy,

Basilical: *royal*   Hundred: *card game*   Debosh: *debauch*   Kyle: *skittle*

184

piety, closeness of counsel, veracity, foresight, knowledge and other vertues, both moral and intellectual, in nothing inferiour to any of his hundred and ten predecessors, had nevertheless no more rule in effect over the Presbyterian Senate of Scotland then any of the six foresaid mock-kings had above those by whom they were dignified with the splendour of royal pomp.

That it is so, I appeal to the course taken by them for assisting him whom they called their king against them whom I must confess they hate more then him. For admitting of none to have any charge in state, church or army but such as had sworn to the eternity of the Covenant and inerrability of the Presbyterian See, lest otherwise, like Achan's wedge,[274] they should bring a judgement upon the land; some lords and many others so principled, after that by their king they had been intrusted with commissions to levie regiments of both horse and foot together with other officers subordinate to them, did, under pretext of making the king a glorious king and the Covenant to triumph at the gates of Rome, with a pseudo-sanctimonial trick of zeal-legerdemain-subtilty and performing the admirable feats of making a little weak man, unfit for military service, a tall, strong and warlike champion and that onely by the sweet charm of laying twenty rexdolars upon his head and shoulders; as also by the archangelical inchantment of fifteen double angels, had the skill to make an Irish hobbie or Galloway nag as sufficient for their field-fight as any Spanish genet or Naples courser.

In prosecution of which wonderful exploits, some of them approved themselves such exquisite alchymists that many of both the cavalry and infantry with their arms, ammunition and apparel, were by them converted into pure gold and silver; by means whereof, although the army shrunk into half the proposed number in both horse, foot and dragoons, and all the most necessary accommodations for either camp, leaguer or march was chymically transformed into the aforesaid welbeloved metal, they nevertheless put such undoubted confidence into the goodness of their cause, that, by vertue thereof, no less miraculous acts were expected and promised by the prophecies of their Neo-Levites out of scripture, to be atchieved

Rexdolars: *silver coins*   Double angels: *golden coins*
Hobbie: *ambling or pacing horse*   Genet: *small (Spanish) horse*
Courser: *swift horse*

by them against the malignants and sectaries then those of Gideon with his water-lappers and Jonathan[275] with his armour-bearer against the Midianites and Philistims. To so great a height did their presumption reach; and yet when it came to the push, those that had received greatest profit by the country assessments and ruined with cruellest exactions the poor yeomanry were the first that returned homewards, being loth to hazard their precious persons lest they should seem to trust to the arm of flesh.

Notwithstanding this backsliding from martiall prowess of the godly officers, with the epenthesis of an l, in which number I inrol not al but the greater part of those that were commissionated with the Scot-Ecclesiastical approbation, their rancour and spleen being still more and more sharpned against the English nation, they in their tedious pharisaical prayers before supper and sesquihoral graces upon a dish of skink and leg of mutton would so imbue the mindes of the poor swains on whose charge they were, with vaticinations of help from heaven against the Sennacheribs[276] that were about to infest Hezekiah's host and the peace of their Israel, that the innocent sufferers having sustained more prejudice by quartering, plundering and continual impositions of those their hypocritical countrymen then ever their predecessors had done by all the devastations of the ancient English, Saxons, Danes and Romanes; the holier they were in outward shew, their actions proving still the more diabolical; they, in recompence of those aerial or rather fiery ejaculations, recommended the avenging of their wrongs to God, and heartily loaded them, and that deservedly, with as many curses and execrations as they had lost of pence. The pretty effect of a good cause and result sutable to the project of making the jure-divine presbytery a government which, besides its universality and eternity, should in matter of dominion be, for its sublimity, placed above all the potentates on the earth; preferring by that account a Scotish Moderator to a Romane Dictator, although they minded not that such as claimed most right to this *generalissima*-jurisdiction were, unknown to themselves, chained in fetters of iron as slaves to the tyrannie of two insolent masters, the concupiscible and irascible appetites.

Epenthesis: *Interposition of a letter or a syllable in the midst of a word*
Sesquihoral: *lasting an hour and a half*   Skink: *ham*

Who doubteth, that is not blinded with the ablepsie of an implicite zeal, but that by such contrivements the three foresaid dominions together with Wales were as fully projected to be subject to the uncontrolable commands of the Kirk as the territories of Romania, Urbino, Ferrara and Avignon to the See of Rome; though with this advantage on the Pope's side, that joynt to the power wherewith he is invested by his Papality, he ruleth over those parts by the right of a secular prince, which title they cannot pretend to.

Were those kirkmen free from covetousness and ambition, whereinto that most of them are no less deeply plunged then any laick in the world, sufficient proof within these two yeers hath been given in Scotland by their laying claim to the fifth part of all the rents of the land under the notion of tythes, devesting noblemen of their rights of patronages and bringing their persons to stand before them on penitentiary pews, like so many varlets, in mendiciary and gausapinal garments; not so much for any trespass they had committed, as thereby to confirm the soveraignty of their hierarchical jurisdiction, which is neither monarchical, aristocratical nor democratical but a meer plutarchy, plutocracy or rather plutomanie, so madly they hale after money and the trash of this world. If so, I say, they were not guilty of suchlike enormities and that according to their talk of things above, their lives were answerable or yet the result of their acts when all together in assemblies, synods or presbyteries, they are congregated into one body, then to require such matters might in some measure seem excusable, because an unfeigned zeal to the furtherance of learning, piety and good works should be seconded with power and wealth; but that for a meer aerial discourse of those whose hearts are ingulphed in the dross of worldly affections, others should part from their own means and dignities to enrich the wives and children of hypocrites is a crying sin before God, contrary to Saint Paul's admonition,[277] who accounteth men infidels that do so, and the abusing of those benefits he hath vouchsafed to allow us for the maintenance of our families and provision for posterity.

Is there any more common saying over all Scotland in the

Ablepsie: *blindness*   Mendiciary: *fitting for beggars*
Gausapinal: *made of frieze*   Plutomanie: *insane pursuit of wealth*

mouthes of the laicks then that the minister is the greediest man in the parish, most unwilling to bestow any thing in deeds of charity, and that the richer they become (without prejudice be it spoken of some honest men amongst them) the more wretched they are; grounding that assertion on this, that by their daily practice both severally and conjunctly, it is found that for their splendour and inrichment most of them do immire their spirits into earthly projects, not caring by what sordid means they may attain their aims; and if they make any kinde of sermocination tending in outward appearance to godliness, which seldom they do, being enjoyned by their ecclesiastical authority to preach to the times, that is, to rail against malignants and sectaries or those whom they suppose to be their enemies, they do it but as those augurs of old of whom Aulus Gellius speaking, saith, "*Aures verbis ditant alienas, suas ut auro locupletent crumenas*".[278]

I know I touch here a string of a harsh sound to the Kirk, of a note dissonant from their proposed harmony and quite out of the systeme of the intended oecumenick government by them concerted. But seeing there are few will be taken with the melody of such a democratical hierarchie, that have not preallably been stung with the tarantula of a preposterous ambition, I will insist no longer on this purpose; and that so much the rather, that he, whose writings I in this tractate intermix with my own, tempers his Heliconian water with more hony then vinegar and prefers the epigrammatical to the satyrick straine; for although I think there be hardly any in Scotland that proportionably hath suffered more prejudice by the Kirk then himself; his own ministers, to wit, those that preach in the churches whereof himself is patron: Master Gilbert Anderson, Master Robert Williamson and Master Charles Pape by name, serving the cures of Cromarty, Kirkmichel and Cullicudden, having done what lay in them for the furtherance of their owne covetous ends, to his utter undoing; for the first of those three, for no other cause but that the said Sir Thomas would not authorize the standing of a certain pew (in that country called a desk) in the church of Cromarty, put in without his consent by a professed enemy to his House, who had plotted the ruine thereof

---

Sermocination: *sermon*   Oecumenick: *universal*   Preallably: *previously*
Standing: *continuance in existence*

and one that had no land in the parish, did so rail against him and his family in the pulpit at several times, both before his face and in his absence, and with such opprobrious termes, more like a scolding tripe-seller's wife then good minister, squirting the poyson of detraction and abominable falshood, unfit for the chaire of verity, in the eares of his tenandry, who were the onely auditors, did most ingrately and despightfully so calumniate and revile their master, his own patron and benefactor, that the scandalous and reproachful words striving which of them should first discharge against him its steel-pointed dart, did oftentimes like clusters of hemlock or wormewood dipt in vinegar stick in his throat; he being almost ready to choak with the aconital bitterness and venom thereof, till the razor of extream passion by cutting them into articulate sounds and very rage it self in the highest degree by procuring a vomit, had made him spue them out of his mouth into rude, indigested lumps like so many toads and vipers that had burst their gall.

As for the other two, notwithstanding that they had been borne, and their fathers before them, vassals to his House, and the predecessor of one of them had shelter in that land by reason of slaughter committed by him, when there was no refuge for him anywhere else in Scotland; and that the other had never been admitted to any church had it not been for the favour of his foresaid patron who, contrary to the will of his owne friends and great reluctancy of the ministry it self, was both the nominater and chuser of him to that function, and that before his admission, he did faithfully protest he should all the days of his life remain contented with that competency of portion the late incumbent in that charge did enjoy before him; they nevertheless behaved themselves so peevishly and unthankfully towards their forenamed patron and master that, by vertue of an unjust decree both procured and purchased from a promiscous knot of men like themselves, they used all their utmost endeavours, in absence of their above-recited patron, to whom and unto whose House they had been so much beholding, to outlaw him and declare him rebel by open proclamation at the market-cross of the head town of his owne shire in case he did not condescend

Aconital: *poisonous*

189

to the grant of that augmentation of stipend which they demanded, conforme to the tenour of the above-mentioned decree; the injustice whereof will appear when examined by any rational judge.

Now the best is, when by some moderate gentlemen it was expostulated why against their master, patron and benefactor they should have dealt with such severity and rigour, contrary to all reason and equity, their answer was they were inforced and necessitated so to do by the synodal and presbyterial conventions of the Kirk under paine of deprivation and expulsion from their benefices. I will not say, "κακοῦ κόρακος κακὸν ᾠον",[279] but may safely think that a well sanctified mother will not have a so ill-instructed brat and that *injuria humana* cannot be the lawfull daughter of a *jure divino* parent.

Yet have I heard him, notwithstanding all these wrongs, several times avouch that from his heart he honoureth the ministerial function and could wish that each of them had a competency of livelihood, to the end that for not lacking what is necessary for him, he might not be distracted from the seriousness of his speculative imploiments, with which above all things he would have one busied that were admitted to that charge, and to be a man of a choice integrity of life and approved literature; he alwayes esteeming philosophy in all its mathematical, natural and prudential demonstrations, rules and precepts, so convenient for inbellishing the minde of him whose vocation it is to be sequestred from the toil of worldly affairs, that the reason and will of man being thereby illuminated and directed towards the objects of truth and goodness, a churchman or pretender to divinity, regardless of those sciences, might be justly suspected to be ignorant of God, by caring so little for the knowledge of his creatures and upon a sacred text oftentimes to make an unhallowed comment.

I have heard him likewise say he would be glad that in every parish of Scotland there were a free schoole and a standing library in the custody of the minister (with this proviso, that none of the books should be embezeled by him or any of his successors and he impowered to persuade his parishioners in all he could to be liberal in their dotations towards the school and

Injuria humana: human injury   *Jure divino: by divine law*

magnifying of the library); to the end that besides the good would thereby redound to all good spirits, it might prove a great encouragement to the stationer and printer; that being the noblest profession amongst merchants and this amongst artificers: as also to intreat the civil magistrate, by the severity of the law to curb the insolency of such notorious and scandalous sinners as should prove unpliable to the stamp of his wholesome admonitions.

As for his wife and children, if he follow the footsteps of Solomon and ask sincerely for wisdom of God before he wed, he will undoubtedly endow him with wealth sufficient for both; for whoever marieth, if he be wise, will either have a vertuous or a monyed woman to his marriage bed, by means of either whereof, the discretion and foresight of a judicious husband will provide a dowry for her and education for her issue, which, in a well policied country, is better then a patrimony.

The taking of this course will advance learning, further piety, improve all moral vertues, establish true honour in the land, make trades flourish, merchandise prosper, the yeomanry industrious, gentlemen happy and the ministers themselves richer then when their mindes were totally bent on the purchase of money; for, as patterns of godliness without morosity, and literature without affectation, being men qualified as aforesaid by their sweetness of conversation and influence of doctrine, they would gaine so much ground upon the hearts of their acquaintance that countrymen would not onely gratifie them dayly and load them with variety of presents but would also after their decease rather chuse to starve themselves then suffer the wives and children of persons so obliging to be in any want or indigence, specially if the traffick and civility of Scotland were promoved by a close union with England, not heterogeneal (as timber and stone upon ice stick sometimes together, bound by the frost of a conquering sword) but homogeneated by naturalization and the mutual enjoyment of the same priviledges and immunities; which design being once by King James set abroach, although some of his compatriot subjects, out of ambition to be called rather profound scholars and nimble wits

Homogeneated: *made the same*   Set abroach: *published*

then good countrymen and loyal counsellors, did pertinaciously withstand the motion.

Yet seeing a wedge of wainscot is fittest and most proper for cleaving of an oaken tree and that Sir Francis Bacon,[280] otherwise designed by the titles of Lord Verulam and Viscount Saint Alban's, was pleased to make a speech thereupon in the honorable House of Commons in the fifth year of King James his raign in this dominion, it is the humble desire of the author that the States of this isle vouchsafe to take notice of his reasons, he being both a wise man and a good English man, after the manner as followeth.

He begins his discourse thus:

"It may please you, Master Speaker, preface will I use none but put my self upon your good opinions to which I have been accustomed beyond my deservings; neither will I hold you in suspense what way I will chuse but now at the first declare my self, that I mean to counsel the House to naturalize the nation of Scotland; wherein nevertheless I have a request unto you which is of more efficacy to the purpose I have in hand then all that I shall say afterwards, and it is the same request which Demosthenes did more then once in great causes of estate make to the people of Athens,[281] that when they took into their hands the balls, whereby to give their voices, according as the manner of them was, they would raise their thoughts and lay aside those considerations which their private vocations and degrees might minister and represent unto them, and would take upon them cogitations and mindes agreable to the dignity and honour of the estate.

"For, Master Speaker, as it was aptly and sharply said by Alexander to Parmenio,[282] when upon their recital of the great offers which Darius made, Parmenio said unto him, 'I would accept these offers were I as Alexander,' he turned it upon him again, 'So would I,' saith he, 'were I as Parmenio'; so in this cause, if an honest English merchant — I do not single out that state in disgrace, for this island ever held it honorable, but onely for an instance of private profession — if an English merchant should say, 'Surely I would proceed no further in the union were I as the king', it might be reasonably answered, 'No more would the king, were he as an English merchant': and the like may be said of a gentleman in the country, be he never so worthy or sufficient; or of a lawyer, be he never so wise or learned; or of any other particular condition in this kingdome: for certainly, Master Speaker, if a man shall be onely or chiefly sensible of those respects which his particular affection and degree shall suggest and infuse into him and not enter into true and worthy considerations of estate, we shall never be able aright to give counsel or take counsel in this matter; for if this request be granted, I account the cause obtained."

Having begun his speech after this manner, he proceeds yet further, and first he fully answers all the arguments concerning inconveniencies that have been alledged to ensue in case of giving way to this naturalization. Next he discloseth what greater inconveniencies would assuredly befal this land if they did not condescend to the union; and lastly, what gaine and benefit would redound to England by meanes thereof; all which he displayeth in that learned speech with such exquisite reasons and impartial judgement, that, without prejudicacie of opinion and sense-perverting passion, there is nothing to be said against it.

He resteth not here, but in another passage thereof, after his having acknowledged the difference or disparity betwixt the two nations in matter of external means, giving therein the advantage to England as the richer country, he expresseth himself in these words: "Indeed it must be confessed that for the goods of the mind and body they are *alteri nos*; for, to do them but right, we know in their capacity and understandings they are a people ingenious, in labour industrious, in courage valiant, in body hard, active and comely. More might be said, but in commending them we do but in effect commend ourselves, for they are of one part and continent with us and the truth is we are participant both of their vertues and vices", etc.

He says furthermore, in illustration of the inconveniences which England will incur in case of non-naturalizing the Scots, that "whatsoever several kingdoms or estates have been united in soveraignty, if that union hath not been fortified and bound in with a further union and namely that which is now in question (of naturalization) this hath followed, that at one time or other they have broken, being upon all occasions apt to relapse and revolt to the former separation. Of this assertion, the first

Alteri nos: above us   Continent with: *joined to*

example that I will set before you is of the memorable union which was between the Romans and the Latines,[283] which continued from the battel at the Lake of Regilla for many yeers until the Consulship of Caius Plautius and Lucius Aemilius Mammercus; at which time there began, about this very point of naturalization, that war which was called *Bellum Sociale*,[284] being the most bloody and pernicious war that ever the Romane state endured; wherein, after numbers of battels and infinite sieges and surprisals of towns, the Romanes in the end prevailed and mastered the Latines; and as they had the honour of the war, so, looking back into what perdition and confusion they were neer to have been brought, they presently naturalized them all."

Immediately thereafter, setting before our eyes the example of Sparta and the rest of Peloponnesus[285] their associates, he saith thus: "The state of Sparta was a nice and jealous state of this point of imparting naturalization to their confederates. But what was the issue of it? After they held them in a kind of society and amity for divers yeeres, upon the first occasion given, which was no more then the surprisal of the castle of Thebes by certain desperate conspirators in the habit of masters, there insued forthwith a general revolt and defection of their associates, which was the ruine of their state, never after to be recovered."

In the same discourse he introduceth another example, though of latter times, which is this, that notwithstanding the kingdome of Aragon had, in the persons of Ferdinand and Isabella, been united with the rest of Spain[286] and that it had so continued for many years, yet because it was severed and divided from the other kingdoms of Spaine in this point of naturalization, it fell out so that, long after that, upon the voice of a condemned man out of the grate of a prison towards the street, that cryed, "*Libertad! Libertad!*" there was raised a dangerous rebellion which with great difficulty was supprest with an army royal; after which victory nevertheless to shun further inconvenience, they were incorporated with Castile and the remanent regions of Spaine. Pisa likewise being united unto Florence[287] without the benefit of naturalization, upon the first sight of Charls the Eighth of France his expedition into Italy, did

Jealous: *vigilant*

revolt. Yet afterwards it was reunited and did obtain the foresaid benefit."

A little after, the better to persuade the Parliament to the said naturalization of the Scots, he subjoineth these words, "On the other part, Master Speaker, because it is true which the logicians say, *opposita juxta se posita clarius elucescunt*,[288] let us take a view and we shall find that wheresoever kingdoms and states have been united and that union incorporated by the bond of naturalization mutually, you shall never observe them afterwards, upon any occasion of trouble or otherwise, to break and sever again; as we see most evidently before our eyes in our provinces of France — that is to say, Guyen, Provence, Normandy, Britain which, notwithstanding the infinite infesting troubles of that kingdome, never offered to break again. We see the like effect in all the kingdomes of Spain which are mutually naturalized — as Castile, Leon, Valencia, Andaluzia, Granada, Murcia, Toledo,[289] Catalonia and the rest, except Aragon which held the contrary course and therefore had the contrary success. And lastly we see the like effect in our nation, which never rent asunder after it was united, so as we now scarce know whether the Heptarchy was a true story or a fable.[290] And therefore, Master Speaker, when I revolve with my self these examples and others so lively expressing the necessity of a naturalization, to avoid a relapse into a separation, I must say I do believe (and I would be sory to be found a prophet in it) that except we proceed with this naturalization, though not perhaps in his majestie's time, who hath such interest in both nations, yet in the mean time of his descendents, these realmes will be in continual danger to divide and break again. Now if any man be of that careless mind, *maneat nostros ea cura nepotes*;[291] or of that hard mind to leave things to be tried by the sharpest sword, sure I am he is not of Saint Paul's opinion, who affirmeth that whosoever useth not foresight and provision for his family is worse then an infidel; much more if we shall not use foresight for these two kingdomes that comprehend in them so many families but leave things open to the peril of future division."

And so forth going on very efficaciously in confirmation of the premises, he proceeds to the benefits which arise to England by knitting the knot surer and straiter between these two realms by communicating naturalization to Scotland. His words are these: "The benefits may appeare to be two: the one surety, the other greatness. Touching surety, Master Speaker, it was well said by Titus Quintus the Romane,[292] touching the state of Peloponnesus, that the tortoise is safe within her shell (*testudo intertegumen tuta est*); but if there be any parts that lie open, they endanger all the rest. We know well that although the state at this time be in a happy peace, yet for the time past the more ancient enemy is the French and the more late the Spaniard; and both these had as it were their several postern-gates whereby they might have approach and entrance to annoy us. France had Scotland and Spaine had Ireland, for these were but the two accesses which did comfort and encourage both these enemies to assaile and trouble us. We see that of Scotland is cut off by the union of these two kingdomes, if that it shall be made constant and permanent. That of Ireland is cut off likewise by the convenient situation of the west of Scotland[293] towards the north of Ireland, where the sore was, which we see being suddenly closed by meanes of this salve; so that as now there are no parts of the state exposed to danger to be a temptation to the ambition of forrainers but their approaches and avenues are taken away; for I do little doubt but these forrainers, who had so little success when they had those advantages, will have much less comfort now that they be taken from them. And so much for surety."

He goes on, "For greatness, Master Speaker, I think a man may speak it soberly and without bravery, that this kingdom of England, having Scotland united, Ireland reduced and shipping maintained is one of the greatest monarchies, in forces truely esteemed, that hath been in the world; for certainly the kingdoms here on earth have a resemblance with the kingdom of heaven which our Saviour compareth not to any great kernel or nut but to a very small graine, yet such a one as is apt to grow and spread; and such do I take to be the constitution of this kingdom, if indeed our country be referred to greatness and power and not quenched too much with the consideration of utility and wealth. For, Master Speaker, was it not, think you, a true answer that Solon of Greece made to rich King Croesus of Lydia,[294] when he shewed unto him a great quantity of gold that he had gathered together in ostentation of his greatness and might? But Solon said to him, contrary to his expectation, 'Why,

Sir, if another come that hath better iron then you, he will be lord of all your gold'. Neither is the authority of Machiavel[295] to be despised, who scorneth that proverb of state, taken first from a speech of Mucianus, that moneys are the sinews of war, and saith, 'There are no true sinews of war but the very armes of valiant men'.

"Nay more, Master Speaker, whosever shall look into the seminary and beginning of the monarchies of the world, he shall finde them founded in poverty. Persia, a country barren and poor in respect of Media, which they reduced; Macedon, a kingdome ignoble and mercenary untill the time of Philip the son of Amintas; Rome had a poor and pastoral beginning; the Turks, a band of Sarmachian Scyths that in a vagabond manner made incursion upon that part of Asia which is called Turcomania, out of which, after much variety of fortune, sprung the Ottoman family, now the terrour of the world.

"So we know the Goths, Vandals, Alans, Huns, Lombards, Normans and the rest of the northern people in one age of the world made their descent and expedition upon the Roman Empire and came, not as rovers to carry away prey and be gone againe, but planted themselves in a number of rich and fruitful provinces, where not only their generations but their names remaine to this day. Witness Lombardy; Catalonia, a word composed of Goth and Alan;[296] Andaluzia, a name corrupted from Vandalitia;[297] Hungaria; Normandy and others. Nay the fortune of the Swisses of late yeers, which are bred in a barren and mountanous country, is not to be forgotten; who first ruined the Duke of Burgundy, the same who had almost ruined the kingdom of France, what time after the battel near Granson[298] the rich jewel of Burgundy, prised at many thousands, was sold for a few pence by a common Swisse that knew no more what a jewel meant then did Aesop's cock;[299] and again the same nation in revenge of a scorn was the ruine of the French king's affaires in Italy, Lowis the Twelfth;[300] for that king, when he was pressed somewhat rudely by an agent of the Swissers to raise their pensions, broke into words of choler. 'What,' saith he, 'will those villains of the mountaines put a task upon me?' Which words lost him his dutchy of Milan and chased him out of Italy.

Seminary: *origin*

197

"All which examples, Master Speaker, do well prove Solon's opinion of the authority and majesty that iron hath over gold." For confirmation hereof, a little after he says, "Seeing the nation of Spaine, which of ancient time served many ages first under Carthage, then under Rome, after under Saracens, Goths and others, should of late yeers take unto them that spirit as to dream of a monarchy in the West, only because they have raised from some wild and unarmed people mines and stores of gold; and, on the other side, that this Island of Britain, seated and named as it is, and that hath, I make no question, the best iron in the world — that is, the best souldiers of the world — shall think of nothing, but accompts and audits, *meum* and *tuum* and I cannot tell what, is truly very strange." Finally, he closeth that his speech with this period. "I have spoken, Master Speaker, out of the fountaine of my heart. *Credidi, propter quod loquutus sum*;[301] I believed, therefore I spake. So my duty is performed. The judgement is yours. God direct it for the the best."

In another speech, again used by the said Sir Francis Bacon in the lower House of Parliament by occasion of a motion concerning the union of laws, he spoke thus: "And it please you, Master Speaker, were it now a time to wish as it is to advise, no man should be more forward or more earnest then my self in this wish, that his majestie's subjects of England and Scotland were governed by one law and that for many reasons.

"First, because it will be an infallible assurance that there will never be any relapse in succeeding ages to a separation.

"Secondly, *dulcis tractus pari jugo*;[302] if the draught lie most upon us and the yoak lie least on them, or inverse-wise, it is not equal.

"Thirdly, the qualities and, as I may terme it, the elements of their laws and ours are such as do promise an excellent temperature in the compounded body; for if the prerogative here be too indefinite, it may be the liberty there is too unbounded. If our laws and proceedings be too prolix and formal, it may be theirs are too informal and summary.

"Fourthly, I do discern, to my understanding, there will be no great difficulty in this work; for their laws, by that I can learn, compared with ours, are like their language; for as their

Meum: mine   *Tuum: yours*

language hath the same roots that ours hath but hath a little more mixture of Latine and French, so their laws and customs have the like grounds that ours have with a little more mixture of the civil law and French customs.

"Lastly, the mean to this work seemeth to me no less excellent then the work it self; for if both laws shall be united, it is of necessity for preparation and inducement thereunto, that our own laws be renewed and recompiled, then the which, I think, there cannot be a work more politick, more honorable nor more beneficial to the subjects of the land for all ages; for this continual heaping up of laws without digesting them maketh but a chaos and confusion and turneth the laws many times to become but snares to the people, and therefore this work I esteem to be indeed a work, rightly to terme it, heroical, and that which (if I might live to see) I would not desire to live after; so that for this good wish of union of laws I do consent to the full."

A little after he sayes that "This union of laws should not precede the naturalization nor go along with it *pari passu* but altogether succeed it, and that not in the precedence of an instant but in distance of time, because the union of laws will ask a great time to be perfected both for the compiling and for the passing of them; during all which time, if this mark of strangeness should be denied to be taken away, I fear it may induce such a habit of strangeness as will rather be an impediment then a preparation to further proceeding."

And albeit in the conclusion of his speech he saith that he holdeth this motion of union of laws very worthy and arising from very good minds but not proper for that time, yet do I think that for this time and as the juncture of affaires is for the present, it is very proper and expedient.

Therefore although in some parcels of the foresaid discourse not here recited many pregnant reasons to those that opposed the naturalization of the Scots, because that nation was annexed to England by inheritance and not conquest, be exhibited; to shew that the grant of the benefit thereof should not be obstructed, for that Scotland was not a conquered country, as also why the Scots' unwillingness to receive the English laws

Pari passu: step for step

199

should be no impediment to their naturalization, and that in Robert Calvin's case,[303] which is extant to be seen in the seventh book of Sir Edward Cook's *Reports*, many excellent things are deduced in favour of the *postnati* of that realm, notwithstanding the diversity of laws and Scotland's then unacknowledged subordination to the meer authority of this land; yet seeing the face of affairs is quite altered from what it was then and that the English civility and good carriage may gain so much upon the affections of the people there as to make them in a very short space to be of the same customs, manners and language with them, I do really believe if Sir Francis Bacon and Sir Edward Cook were now living, that both of them would unanimously advise the state and soverainty of this island to allow unto Scotland, which neither is nor never was a kingdom more then Wales was of old, the same priviledges and immunities in every thing that Wales now hath and which the Scots have in France, a transmarine country, to enjoy everywhere in all things the emoluments and benefits competent to the free-born subjects of England; and to this effect to impower that nation with liberty to chuse their representatives to be sent hither to this their soveraigne parliament, that the publick trustees of England, Scotland and Wales may at Westminster jointly concur for the weal of the whole Isle, as members of one and the same incorporation. These two knights, one whereof was Lord High Chancellor of England and the other Atturny General and Lord Chief Justice of the Common Pleas, were good and wise men, full of honour, free from prevarication and by-respects, learned lawyers, excellent scholars, fluent orators and, above all, worthy, loving and sincere patriots of England; for which cause I hope so many exquisite qualities, meeting as it were in one constellation by vertue of a powerfull influence upon the mindes of the supreame senate of the land, will incline the hearts of every one not to dissent from the judgement and approbation of these two so eminent judges and zealous English men; and that so much the rather, that to the accomplishment of so commendable a work we are conducted by nature it self, which, having made us *divisos orbe Britannos*,[304] sheweth by the

Postnati: 'those born after' (the union of 1603)

antiperistatick faculty of a fountain or spring-well in the summer season (whose nature is to be the colder within it self the greater circumobresistance of heat be in the aire which surrounds it), that we should cordially close to one another, unite our forces and the more vigourously improve the internal strength we have of our selves, the greater that the outward opposition and hostility appear against us of the circumjacent outlandish nations which inviron us on all sides.

This was not heeded in ancient times by reason of the surquedry of the old English, who looked on the Scots with a malignant aspect; and the profound policie of the French in casting, for their own ends, the spirit of division betwixt the two nations to widen the breach. But now that the English have attained to a greater dexterity in encompassing their *faciendas* of state and deeper reach in considering what for the future may prove most honourable and lucrative, will, like an expert physician to a patient sick of a consumption in his noble parts, who applieth cordials and not corosives, and lenitives rather then cauters, strive more, as I imagine, to gain the love and affection of the Scots, thereby to save the expence of any more blood or mony then for overthrowing them quite in both their bodies and fortunes, to maintain the charge of an everlasting war against the storms of the climate, the fierceness of discontented people, inaccessibility of the hills and sometimes universal penury, the mother of plague and famine; all which inconveniences may be easily prevented without any charge at all by the sole gaining of the hearts of the country.

By which means — patching up old rents, cementing what formerly was broken and by making of ancient foes new friends — we will strengthen our selves and weaken our enemies and raise the Isle of Britain to that height of glory that it will become formidable to all the world besides.

In the mean while the better to incorporate the three dominions of England, Scotland and Wales and more firmly to consolidate their union, it were not amiss in my opinion that (as

---

Antiperistatick: *in opposition to its surroundings*
Circumobresistance: *surrounding opposition*   Circumjacent: *surrounding*
Surquedry: *arrogance*   Faciendas: *achievements*
Lenitives: *gentle laxative medicines*   Cauters: *red hot irons*

little rivers which use to lose their names when they run along into the current of a great flood) they have their own peculiar titles laid aside and totally discharged into the vast gulph of that of Great Britain.

But if upon any emergent occasion it be thought fit to make mention of Ireland and the several dominions of Britain in an orderly enumeration; to place Ireland, as I conceive it, before Scotland is very preposterous; not but that Ireland is a far more fertil country and that the Irish may be as good as any men; that the Scots in these latter yeers may be much degenerated from the magnanimity of their forefathers and that the succeeding progeny may perhaps prove little better, or as you will; for be the soile or climate never so good or bad, with a permanence or rather immutability in either of those qualities, the respective natives and inhabitants thereof will nevertheless, according to the change of times, be subject to a vicissitude of vice and vertue, as may appear by the inclinations of the Greeks and Romans now, compared with those of their ancestors in the days of Xerxes and Hannibal; but onely that I conceive priority to be more due to Scotland, although I should speak nothing of its more immaculate reputation both abroad and at home, and of a longer series of soveraigns that swayed scepter there in a continuate, uninterrupted succession, and that because of its greater conformity with and proximity to the nation of England; the people whereof, if they would imitate the fashion of the warlike Romans, should say 'Scots and Irish' as the Romans did 'Latines and Gaules' or 'Latins and Sicilians' by reason of the Latins' vicinity and nearer adjacence to Rome; although Sicilie was more fruitfull and opulent then Latium and the Gaules more populous and every whit as fierce in the field as the Latins.

I am afraid that I have trespassed a little upon the patience of the reader by insisting so long in my discourse upon Scotland. Yet in regard of my obligation and bound duty to the author of the above-recited lost papers, whose native soyle it is, I could hardly do less, seeing it is for the good of him that this whole tractate is compiled, and to his behalf who expects not (as has been said already in the 181. page and abundantly proved by the fifteenth axiom) either recompense or punishment for his country's sake. He likewise hopeth by vertue of the said axiom that his being a meer prisoner of war without any further delinquencie will not militate much against him if the subjects of the land, by inventions of his, attain to what is conducible to them in saving of expence, as by the discovery proferred to the publick he is able to make good when required thereto; that either money or lands, if not both, should be due to him for the disclosure of so prime a secret is clearly demonstrated by the sixteenth; and that the State will be no less courteous and favourable to him then to any other prisoner of war proportionably, is plainly evidenced by the seventeenth. That the supreme authority of the isle in matter of the liberty of his person and that of his brothers and menial servants, together with the enjoyment of his own houses, lands and rents, free from sequestration, confiscation, composition and garisoning, should allow him the same conditions granted to any other no more deserving then himself is manifestly proved by the eighteenth; therefore he should obtaine the greater favours, as aforesaid, is proved by the nineteenth, and that if no other prisoner of all his country be truly competent but to himself alone, the ample character, in all its branches (as it is specified in the 181, 182 and 183 pages) which I have given of him and could not conceal, being much less then his due; then, in stead of a recompence for the surplusage of wherein others are defective, which he covets not, none certainly of all the Scotish nation, whether prisoner or other, should receive from the state so great favours and courtesies as himself, because (without prejudice be it spoke to any man) he did from the beginning of these intestine broyles walk in an even if not a more constant track of blameless carriage, free from hypocrisie, covetousness and tergiversation, then any of his compatriots; that notwithstanding the strictness of his allegiance to supreme authority and the many ties of obedience that lie upon any subject whatsoever, he may by vertue of his owne merit deserve a reward from the state, is clear by the twentieth; and that for the imparting of this invention and others to publick acceptance, which are so properly his own that no other braine that ever was or is did contribute any thing to their eduction, he may lawfully claim right to a competency of retribution, is made patent by the one and twentieth.

And lastly, the author desiring no more but the grant of the

Sequestration: *banishment*   Eduction: *development*

foresaid demands, although by the strict rule of commutative justice it should seem to be a reward by too may stages inferior to the discovery of so prime an invention; yet that the state doth him neither wrong nor injustice therein, provided he be not denyed of what he requireth, is fully cleared by the two and twentieth or last axiome.

This apodictick course, by a compositive method theorematically to infer consequences from infallible maximes with all possible succinctness, I thought fit to imbrace, because to have analytically couched those verities by mounting the scale of their probation upon the prosyllogistick steps of variously amplified confirmations would have been a procedure for its prolixity unsuitable to the pregnancy of the state whose intuitive spirits can at the first hearing discerne the strength of manifold conclusions, without the labour of subsuming, in the very bowels and chaos of their principles.

I could truly, having before my eyes some known treatises of the author whose muse I honour and the straine of whose pen to imitate is my greatest ambition, have enlarged this discourse with a choicer variety of phrase and made it overflow the field of the reader's understanding with an inundation of greater eloquence;[305] and that one way, tropologetically, by metonymical, ironical, metaphorical and synecdochical instruments of elocution in all their several kinds artificially affected according to the nature of the subject; with emphatical expressions in things of great concernment, with catachrestical in matters of meaner moment, attended on each side respectively with an epiplectick and exegetick modification; with hyperbolical, either epitatically or hypocoristically as the purpose required to be elated or extenuated, they qualifying metaphors and accompanied with apostrophes; and lastly, with allegories of all sorts, whether apologal, affabulatory, parabolary, aenigmatick

Commutative justice: *the justice which is corrective in transactions between man and man*   Apodictick: *clearly demonstrated*
Prosyllogistick: *pertaining to a syllogism of which the conclusion forms the major or minor premiss of another syllogism*   Tropologetically: *apologetically by way of a trope*
Catachrestical: *improper use (of words)*   Epiplectick: *given to rebuking (rhet.)*
Exegetick: *explanatory*   Epitatically: *in an intensive manner*
Hypocoristically: *with [endearing or] euphemistic terms*
Apologal: *of the nature of a fable*   Affabulatory: *having a moral*
Parabolary: *parabolical*

or paraemial; and on the other part, schematologetically adorning the proposed theam with the most especial and chief flowers of the garden of rhetorick and omiting no figure either of diction or sentence that might contribute to the ear's enchantment or persuasion of the hearer.

I could have introduced in case of obscurity synonymal, exargastick and palilogetick elucidations; for sweetness of phrase, antimetathetick commutations of epithets; for the vehement excitation of matter, exclamations in the front and epiphonemas in the reer. I could have used for the promptlyer stirring up of passion apostrophal and prosopopoeial diversions; and for the appeasing and setling of them, some epanorthotick revocations and aposiopetick restraints. I could have inserted dialogismes, displaying their interrogatory part with communicatively pysmatick and sustentative flourishes; or proleptically with the refutative schemes of anticipation and subjection, and that part which concerns the responsory with the figures of permission and concession.

Speeches extending a matter beyond what it is auxetically, digressively, transitiously, by ratiocination, aetiology, circumlocution and other wayes I could have made use of; as likewise with words diminishing the worth of a thing, tapinotically, periphrastically, by rejection, translation and other meanes, I could have served my self.

There is neither definition, distribution, epitrochism, increment, caracterism, hypotyposis or any schem figurating a speech by reason of what is in the thing to our purpose thereby signified, that I needed to have omitted; nor, had I been so

Paraemial: *proverbial*   Schematologetically: *by means of figured language*
Exargastick: *(meaning uncertain)*   Palilogetick: *repetitive (usually for emphasis)*
Antimetathetick: *having the members of an antithesis inverted*
Epiphonemas: *exclamatory final sentences*
Prosopopoeial: *using the rhetorical device of personification*
Epanorthotick: *recalling a word in order to substitute a stronger or more correct one*
Aposiopetick: *halting for rhetorical effect*
Dialogismes: *discussions in form of dialogue*   Pysmatick: *interrogatory*
Sustentative: *sustaining*   Proleptically: *anticipatively*
Auxetically: *by amplification*   Transitiously: *by transitions*
Aetiology: *giving a reason*   Tapinotically: *by way of diminution (rhet.)*
Epitrochism: *hurried accumulation of several points*
Caracterism: *representation by means of signs or characters*
Hypotyposis: *vivid description of scene or event*

pleased, would I have past by the figurative expressions of what is without any thing of the matter in hand, whether paradigmatical, iconical, symbolical, by comparison or any other kinde of simile; or yet paradoxical, paramologetick, paradiastolary, antipophoretick, cromatick or any other way of figurating a speech by opposition, being formules of oratory whereby we subjoyn what is not expected; confess something that can do us no harme; yeeld to one of the members, that the other may be removed; allow an argument to oppose a stronger; mixe praise with dispraise and so forth through all manner of illustration and decorement of purposes by contrarieties and repugnance.

All those figures and tropes besides what are not here mentioned (these synecdochically standing for all, to shun the tediousness of a too prolixe enumeration) I could have adhibited to the embellishment of this tractate, had not the matter it self been more prevalent with me then the superficial formality of a quaint discourse.

I could have firreted out of topick celluls such variety of arguments tending to my purpose and seconded them with so many divers refutations, confirmations and prosyllogistick deductions, as, after the large manner of their several amplifications according to the rules of art, would, contexed together, have framed a book of a great quarto size in an arithmetical proportion of length to its other two dimensions of bredth and thickness. That is to say, its bredth should exceed the thickness thereof by the same number of inches and no more that it is surpassed by the length; in which, considering the body thereof, could be contained no less then seven quires of paper at least; and yet, notwithstanding this so great a bulk, I could have disposed the contents of its whole subjected matter so appositely into partitions for facilitating an impression in the reader's memory and pesented it to the understanding in so spruce a garb, that spirits blest with leisure and free from the urgency of serious employments, would happily have bestowed as liberally

Paradigmatical: *exemplary*   Paramologetick: *of the nature of an admission*
Paradiastolary: *giving something unfavourable a favourable impression by an expression conveying only part truth*
Antipophoretick: *having an objection refuted by a contrary allegation*
Cromatick: *elaborate*   Adhibited: *admitted*   Topick: *topic*
Celluls: *pigeon-holes*

some few houres thereon as on the perusal of a new-coined Romancy or strange history of love adventures.

For although the figures and tropes above rehearsed seem in their *actu signato*, as they signifie meer notional circumstances, affections, adjuncts and dependences on words, to be a little pedantical and to the smooth touch of a delicate ear somewhat harsh and scabrous, yet in their exerced act, as they suppone for things reduplicatively as things in the first apprehension of the minde by them signified, I could, even in far abstruser purposes, have so fitly adjusted them with apt and proper termes and with such perspicuity couched them as would have been suitable to the capacities of courtiers and young ladies, whose tender hearing, for the most part being more taken with the insinuating harmony of a well-concerted period in its isocoletick and parisonal members then with the never-so-pithy a fancy of a learned subject destitute of the illustriousness of so pathetick ornaments, will sooner convey persuasion to the interior faculties from the ravishing assault of a well-disciplined diction in a parade of curiosly-mustered words in their several ranks and files, then by the vigour and fierceness of never so many powerful squadrons of a promiscuously digested elocution into bare logical arguments; for the sweetness of their disposition is more easily gained by undermining passion then storming reason, and by the musick and symmetry of a discourse in its external appurtenances then by all the puissance imaginary of the ditty or purpose disclosed by it.

But seeing the prime scope of this treatise is to testifie my utmost endeavours to do all the service I can to Sir Thomas Urquhart, both for the procuring of his liberty and intreating the state, whose prisoner he is, to allow him the enjoyment of his own, lest by his thraldome and distress (useful to no man) the publick should be deprived of those excellent inventions whose emission totally dependeth upon the grant of his enlargement and freedom in both estate and person; and that to a state which respecteth substance more then ceremony, the body more then the shadow, and solidity more then ostentation, it would argue great indiscretion in me to become no other waies a suiter for that worthy gentleman then by emancipating my vein upon the

---

Actu signato: function of meaning   Scabrous: *rough*   Isocoletick: *of equal length*
Parisonal: *characterized by exact balance (of clauses)*   Pathetick: *moving, affecting*

full carreer of rhetorical excursions, approving my self thereby like to those navigators, gunners and horsemen who use more saile then ballast, more powder then ball and employ the spur more then the bridle.

Therefore is it, that laying aside all the considerations of those advantages and prerogatives a neat expression in fluent termes hath over the milder sexe and miniard youth, and setting before my eyes the reverence and gravity of those supereminent men to whom my expectation of their non-refusal of my request hath emboldened me to make my addresses, I hold it now expedient without further adoe to stop the current of my pen and, in token of the duty I owe to him whose cause I here assert, to give way to his more literate and compleat elucubrations; which, that they may the sooner appear to the eyes of the world for the advancement of both vertue and learning, I yet once more, and that most heartily, beseech the present state, parliament and Supream Councel of Great Britain to vouchsafe unto the aforesaid Sir Thomas Urquhart of Cromarty knight, heritable sheriff and proprietary thereof, a grant of the releasement of his person from any imprisonment whereunto, at the discretion of those that took his parole, he is ingaged; the possession like-wise of his House of Cromarty, free from garisoning, and the enjoyment of his whole estate in lands without affecting it with any other either publick or private burthen then hath been of his own contracting; and that with the dignities thereto belonging of hereditary sheriffship, patronage of the three churches there and admiralty of the seas betwixt Catnes and Innernass inclusively, with subordination nevertheless to the high admiral of the land; together with all the other priviledges and immunities which, both in his person and that of his predecessors, hath been from time to time accounted due by inheritance to the House of Cromarty, and that for the love of the whole island on which he offereth in compensation to bestow a benefit, under pain of forfeiture of all he hath, of ten times more worth. As this is my humble petition, so is it conform to the desires of all the best spirits of England, Scotland, Wales and Ireland.

> Pity it were to refuse such
> As ask but little and give much.

Miniard: *dainty*   Elucubrations: *studious elucidations*

The list of those Scots mentioned in this book who have been generals abroad within these fifty years.

Sir Patrick Ruven	S. Alexander Lesly,	James King
Gen. Ruderford	Dux foederis	Marquis Lesly
Lord Spence	S. Alexander Lesly, in Moscovy	Marquis Hamilton

The list of other Scotish officers mentioned in this treatise who were all colonels abroad and some of them general persons.

LIEUTENANT-GENERALS	Alexander Ramsay	Col. Edmond
David Lesly	Quartermaster-	Col. Erskin
S. James	General	Alex. Forbas
Livingstoun	Col. Anderson	Alex. Forbas
William Bailif	Earl of Argyle	Arthur Forbas
	Col. Armestrong	Fines Forbas
	Earl of Bacluch	John Forbas
MAJOR-GENERALS	S. James Balantine	Lord Forbas
Lodovick Lindsay	S. William	S. John Fulerton
Robert Monro	Balantine	Thomas Garne
Thomas Ker	S. David Balfour	Alex. Gordon
S. David	S. Henry Balfour	Alex. Gordon
Drummond	Col. Boyd	John Gordon
S. James Lumsden	Col. Brog	Col. Gordon
Robert Lumsden	Col. Bruce	S. Andrew Gray
S. John Hepburn	James Cockburne	William Gun
Lord James	Col. Colon	Col. Gun
Douglas	Lord Colvil	S. Frederick
Watchtoun	Alex. Crawford	Hamilton
Hepburn	Col. Crichtoun	James Hamilton
John Lesly	Alex Cuningam	John Hamilton
	George Cuningam	Hugh Hamilton
	Robert Cuningam	S. Francis
COLONELS	William Cuningam	Henderson
Alexander	George Douglas	S. John Henderson
Hamilton,	Col. Douglas	Thomas Hume
General of the	Col. Douglas	Col. Hunter
Artillery	Col. Edinton	Edward Johnston

209

James Johnston
William Johnston
S. John Innes
Earl of Irvin
William Keith
Jhon Kinindmond
Patrick
    Kinindmond
Thomas
    Kinindmond
William
    Kinindmond
Walter Lecky
Col. Lermond
Alex. Lesly
George Lesly
John Lesly
Robert Lesly
Col. Liddel

Andrew Lindsay
George Lindsay
Col. Lithco
Col. Livingstoun
Robert Lumsden
Col. Lyon
Col. Mathuson
S. John Meldrum
Assen Monro
Fowles Monro
Hector Monro
Obstel Monro
Col. Morison
S. Pat. Morray
Col. Mowat
Col. Ramsey
James Ramsey
Lord Reay
Col. Robertson

Col. Rower
Frances Ruven
John Ruven
L. Sancomb
Col. Sandilands
Robert Scot
James Seaton
James Seaton
S. John Seaton
William Sempil
Francis Sinclair
Col. Spang
James Spence
L. Spynay
Robert Stuart
Thomas Thomson
John Urquhart
Col. Wederburne
Col. Wilson

I have not mentioned here Lieutenant-General John Midletoun, Lieutenant-General Sir William Balfour nor General Major Sir George Monro, etc. because they returned from the forraign countryes, where they did officiate, though in places over both horse and foot of great concernment, before they had obtained the charge of colonels.

As for pricking down into colums those other Scots in my book renowned for literature and personal valour, I held it not expedient; for that the sum of them doth fall so far short of the number I have omitted, that proportioned to the aggregate of all who, in that nation since the yeer 1650, without reckoning any intrusted in military employments either at home or abroad, have deserved praise in armes and arts, joyntly or disjunctively, it would bear the analogy, to use a lesser definite for a greater indefinite, of a *subnovitripartient* eights; that is to say in plain English, the whole being the dividend and my nomenclature the divisor, the quotient would be nine with a fraction of three-eights; or yet more clearly, as the proportion of 72 to 675.

FINIS

ERRATA

Page 106, line 7. for *Paulus Æmilius* read *Titus Flaminius.*
Page 184. for *Sterlin* read *Scone.*

It having been told me that the title-word of this book is absurd,
for that *auron* is not true Greek, I cannot verily think it much
amiss, for undeceiving rather of the reader then to vindicate
myself, to shew that although αὖρου do probably seem to have
been a Greek word of old, in that very same signification
wherein it is here taken, and that *aurum* by the Latines was
from thence borrowed, as it evidently appeareth by the word
thesauron thereof composed, *inde thesaurum*, now commonly
written θήσαυρος, *thesaurus*, as likewise by the word *aurochalcum*,
which some spell *aurichalcum* or *orichalcum* (as if its origine had
been from the Greek word 'ορείχαλκος); yet do I in sincerity
profess, without grounding any reasons of mine upon such
obselete warrants, that it was my intention (as the authentick
manuscript could, if extant, have testified) it should in the title-
page have been written *Exskybalaurum*, and no otherwise. The
corrector nevertheless of the press took occasion, because *k* was
no Latine letter, and that the greatest part of the word, at best,
was made out of the Greek, to put it into Grecian characters,
and give it accordingly a termination befitting that language,
thus: 'Εκσκυβαλαύρον, pretending that to the Greek tongue
should be allowed no less priviledge upon the Latine -*um* then to
the Latine speech on the Greek -*ov*, as is manifest in the words
symbolum, epimythium, epinicium, which are Latinized with many
hundreds of other such like dictions by changing meerly the final
-*ov* into -*um*, the remanent of the word continuing still the same
in both languages; and this custom of altering the termination
according to the propriety of the *idiome* whereunto the word is
to be translated seeming to be *juris Gentium*,[306] as by the words

Desinences: *endings*

211

prioridad, priorita, priorite and *prioritie*, which in the Spanish, Italian, French and English are words of several desinences, in the same sense borrowed from the Latine *prioritas*, differing in termination from all and agreeing in signification with each of the other four: he was thereby emboldened to the literation of this book's inscription as aforesaid, the which in a matter of so mean concernment I will neither justifie nor condemn.

Some others, little wiser than the former, are displeased with it, for that to them it appeareth to be a *Hybrid* or mungrel word composed of Greek and Latine, they not minding that *epitogium* and *mustela*, mentioned by Julius Scaliger in his *Causis Linguae Latinae*,[307] are of the same nature, together with many other such more emphatick words, very necessarily made use of by myself in the *Lemmas* of several Epigrams. But whatever exception any take at the like freedom of coining words, I hold it not much more important in the intitulation of a book, by what name it shall pass, then whether in a christening an infant be called Peter or Patrick, Joane or Jeane, provided the childe be thereby sufficiently designed for himself and distinguished from others.

Yet, seeing there is no remedie but that some critical censurers must still be gaping and bawling at both the doings and writings of others, although possibly in either they be nothing concerned, I have thought it expedient for my better riddance of such turbulent cattel to throw into their yawning mouths this hard bone of a Cyfral Octastick, with its appendix, to gnaw upon.

THE CYFRAL OCTASTICK

25.11.39.4.4.10.3.54.50.19.1.18.1.5.9.58.15.1.4.17.1.42.32.77.23.75.6.
     3.18.20.36.8.21.
4.10.22.3.5.11.3.162.18.21.44.79.42.2.17.61.32.7.7.107.8.59.28.54.31.113.42.
     31.5.19.32.3.115.3.22.
1.16.96.31.87.5.88.1.4.30.10.15.8.47.28.17.139.17.69.5.29.9.9.1.51.6.114.8.
     34.30.2.18.24.41.33.74.93.8.
5.12.58.162.12.44.1.66.9.15.100.42.2.28.16.6.27.4.196.70.53.7.1.69.2.15.89.
     34.11.13.12.29.15.76.40.22.8.24.75.
3.58.15.2.1.4.5.56.5.5.2.4.12.20.19.14.80.37.45.34.3.95.6.38.1.18.11.27.4.13.
     7.24.

Lemmas: themes   Octastick: *a group of eight lines of verse*

212

5.20.5.87.40.25.9.56.21.29.2.81.50.147.2.6.16.15.14.9.13.27.3.16.14.7.6.2.10.
16.69.1.44.
38.3.3.2.10.34.8.18.9.28.2.4.6.2.201.10.13.6.1.36.1.31.4.17.54.16.5.22.11.5.
31.
71.96.15.45.19.6.64.10.42.7.83.37.6.3.7.74.4.14.8.91.27.12.11.2.28.50.68.3.2.
12.1.5.49.3.
7.7.95.66.1.11.33.51.50.6.

To this *Octastick* if you will subjoyn
A *Decagram* of this same stuff of mine,
All gather'd out of my *Exskybalorum*,
You'll finde a Rule, by which, with great decorum,
You may most comfortably regulate
Your actions, thoughts and speeches; and know that
I love an *Aphaeresified* treason
Better then any *Prosthesized* Reason.

London, March $\left\{\begin{array}{l} 7, 1651 \quad \textit{Stilo veter, quoad mensem, et novo, quoad annum} \\ \\ 17, 1652 \quad \textit{Stilo novo quoad mensem, et veteri quoad annum.} \end{array}\right.$

Aphaeresified: suppressed   *Prosthesized: added*

213

COMMENTARY

1. *EKSKUBALAURON*: A portmanteau word invented by Urquhart, made up from the Greek ἐκ σκυβάλου ('out of dung') and the Latin *aurum* ('gold') modified by the substitution of the Greek noun ending *-on* for the Latin *-um*. For Urquhart's justification of this formation, and an account of his difficulties with the printer, see the note which he added during publication, here printed on pp. 211–12. This piece of creative philology is fairly typical of Urquhart, and combines the notion of the jewel hidden in the dunghill, as in the Aesopic fable to which he later alludes, with the alchemical process of converting base metal into gold. The 'jewel' is, of course, the Universal Language.

2. 'six before the Autumnal Aequinox': The Battle of Worcester was fought on 3 September 1651. The continued operation of the Julian calendar had by the mid-seventeenth century led to a discrepancy of some ten days with the solar date, so that the equinox would have occurred on 10 September, rather than on 21/22 September.

3. 'Distichon ad Librum . . .': 'The prefatory couplet follows, which equates the number of the Muses (nine) with the number of cases and articles.' The analysis of the syntax in the couplet appears to correspond to the rules of neither Latin nor English.

4. '*Efficiens et finalis sunt sibi invicem causae*': 'The efficient and final causes are reciprocal'. The logical tag, one of the many in *The Jewel*, is too general to be attributable to a single source. The 1652 edition prints '*finis*', but it is clear that '*finalis*' is the correct reading.

5. 'the phrase of their patron Knox': Urquhart refers to Knox's *First Blast of the Trumpet against the Monstruous Regement of Women*, an attack on Mary of England and Mary of Lorraine, published at Geneva in 1558.

6. 'honest Sir John': i.e. (ironically) Knox himself. 'Sir' was a courtesy title for clergymen in the sixteenth century.

7. 'there is at this present an English garrison': According to the account in *Logopandecteision* (*Works*, pp. 380–2), Robert Leslie of Findrassie had been responsible for arranging the quartering in

Urquhart's house of a troop of horse. Urquhart was apparently able to secure their removal on his return to the estate in 1652.

8. 'proceedings of the Presbytery of Aberdeen against Sir Alexander Irvin of Drum': Sir Alexander Irvin (c. 1600–1658), a leading northern Royalist, was excommunicated by the Session of Aberdeen on 1 February 1652, as a result of his refusal to subscribe to the Covenant (v. *Selections from the Ecclesiastical Records of Aberdeen*, ed. J. Stuart [Spalding Club, Aberdeen, 1846], p. 117; *Miscellany of the Spalding Club*, iii [Aberdeen 1846], pp. 205–7).

9. 'a petition or greivance of the commons of Scotland': Probably a reference to a broadside, published at Leith on 2 January 1652, *To the very honorable the Repesentative of the Commonwealth of England The humble Petitione and Remonstrance of such in Scotland who are clear in, and willing to close with the designe of advancement of Christ's Kingdom, and the just Freedom and Liberty of the People*. This pamphlet, which attacks 'Malignant and Presbyterian Confluences' in the Scottish government, is preserved in two copies in the National Library of Scotland.

10. 'I usually afforded the setter copy': The description of the printing process which follows is detailed and well-informed. 'Pica' is a printing term of Italian origin, denoting the size of type and attested in England by the end of the sixteenth century; 'gally' and 'form', referring to successive states of the set type, are current in English from Caxton's time on. The contemporary allusions noted above indicate that the Epistle Liminary was composed in the first weeks of 1652; the whole work was in type (and some copies presumably made up) by early March, when Urquhart added his comment about the title-page.

11. 'I care neither for Zoil nor Momus': Zoil, a cynic philosopher of the fourth century B.C., author of bitter attacks on Plato, Homer and others; Momus is a character in Lucian's *Jupiter Tragoedus*, a carping critic of legendary ferocity, and hence a personification of fault-finding.

12. 'Virgil said "*Ille ego qui quondam*"': 'I am he who once ...', the opening words of the apocryphal proemium often attached to texts of the *Aeneid*.

13. 'and Scaliger the younger, "*Ego sum magnus ille Josephus*"': 'I am that great Joseph ...'. J. J. Scaliger (1540–1609), a prominent Dutch philologist and Catholic propagandist.

14. 'Christianus Presbyteromastix': i.e. 'a Christian eater of Presbyterians'.

216

15. 'The names of the chiefs': Much of what follows is, of course, pure invention, but the first eleven names are drawn from the genealogy in Genesis, 5:1–32 and the twelfth from Genesis 10:2. The same information, with a good deal of bogus commentary, is given in *A peculiar Promptuary of Time*. The part of the genealogy which is supported by historical evidence begins with No. 143, Adam, who lived in the mid-fourteenth century.

16. *PANTOCHRONOCHANON*: Another conflation of several Greek works, including παντ- ('all'), ὁ χρόνος ('time') and χανδάνω (? from 'to hold, contain').

17. 'Master Spilsbury's house': It is not possible to identify this citizen of Worcester with any certainty, but Spilsbury occurs quite frequently as a Worcestershire surname at this period.

18. 'by the command of one Master Braughton': In *A peculiar Promptuary*, Urquhart states that his papers were rescued by 'a surpassing honest and civil officer of Colonel Pride's regiment' (*Works*, p. 151).

19. 'lest they should have been altogether lost at Sterlin': A clear indication that Urquhart was present with the Scottish army at the siege of Stirling immediately before the expedition which culminated at Worcester.

20. 'The effigies of Jupiter ... the image of Thersites': For Jupiter's adoption of the disguise of a bull in order to pursue Europa, see Ovid, *Metamorphoses*, II, 833–75; the story of Io is told, ibid., I, 583–681. Bucephalus was the legendary horse of Alexander the Great. Alcibiades (c. 450–404 B.C.), an Athenian general and statesman, and Coriolanus, a Volscian hero, are conventional stereotypes of nobility, while Thersites (cf. *Iliad*, II, 212ff.) was a Greek warrior whose twisted railing was developed by Shakespeare in *Troilus and Cressida*.

21. 'which hardly have any flection at all': The grammatical notion of inflection, deriving from Latin grammarians, occurs in such works by English writers as Paul Greaves, *Grammatica Anglicana* (Cambridge 1594).

22. 'the agglutinative faculty': Although *agglutinare* ('to join') is a well-known Latin verb, its application to grammar is rare, and Urquhart's is the only such use in English recorded before 1850 (*OED*).

23. 'The French, Spanish and Italian are but dialects of the Latine ...': We can perhaps see the influence here of J. J. Scaliger's *De*

Europaeorum linguis, published in 1610; cf. Comenius, *Panglottia* (1669), and John Wilkins, *An essay towards a real character* (London, 1668), p. 3.

24. 'as Diogenes of old was of the other': Diogenes of Sinope (c. 400–c. 325 B.C.), founder of the cynic school, was famous for his asceticism; v. Diogenes Laertius, *Lives of Eminent Philosophers*, VI, 20-81.

25. '*Quod ita dixerim parcant Ciceronianae manes, ignoscat Demosthenis genius*': 'May the ghost of Cicero, so to say, spare me and the guardian spirit of Demosthenes pardon me'. The source of this remark, if it is not Urquhart's own, has not been identified.

26. 'The "bonification" and "virtuification" of Lully, Scotus's "hexeity" and "albedineity" of Suarez': Raman Llull (c. 1232–1316), a Franciscan philosopher, apparently coined the terms *bonificatio* ('a turning into goodness') and *virtuificatio* ('making virtuous'); John Duns Scotus (c. 1265/6–1308), also a Franciscan, was responsible for the notion of *heccitas* ('thisness', the principle of individuation), v. *Opus Oxoniense*, II, dist. 3, qu. 6, n. 12; Francisco Saurez (1548–1617), a Jesuit philosopher and theologian, used the term *albedineitas*, denoting the quality of whiteness.

27. 'Ennius and Livius Andronicus': Quintus Ennius (239–169 B.C.) and Lucius Livius Andronicus (*flor.* 240–200 B.C.) were early Latin authors, of whose works fragments survive; cf. Cicero, *Brutus*, 72–9.

28. '*philosophia sunt res, non verba*': 'things, not words, are the subject of philosophy'. This tag contains the essence of the Realist doctrine, with which Urquhart clearly associates himself. It is too widespread a notion, and its expression here too general, to be attributable to a single source. The use of the plural verb with *philosophia* appears to be an error.

29. 'not much unlike the Innes-a-court-gentlemen at London': The Inns of Court were at least as much finishing-schools for the gentility during the early seventeenth century as they were institutions for legal training. R. R. Pearce, *History of the Inns of Court and Chancery* (London, 1848), refers to the 'full social and fashionable life' enjoyed by their members, while more detail is given by Wilfrid R. Prest, *The Inns of Court under Elizabeth I and the Early Stuarts 1590–1640* (London, 1972), esp. pp. 40–6.

30. 'at the confusion of Babel': cf. Genesis 11:1–9.

31. 'the statute called *scandalum magnatum*': A succession of English acts of Parliament, the first dating from 1275, establishing heavy penalties for the making of defamatory statements against persons of high rank.

32. 'gowns and beards longer than ever did Aristotle and Aesculapius': There is no difficulty about Aristotle, but he is paired rather oddly with Aesculapius, who was the Roman god of healing rather than a classical philosopher.

33. 'Here is the number of twelve articles wanting': For this section, omitted from *The Jewel* but included in *Logopandecteision*, see Appendix II, and the discussion above, pp. 21.

34. '*Laborant penuria verborum*': 'They are in difficulty through a poverty of words'; Seneca the Elder, *Controversiae*, 7.1.27: '*verborum inopia laborasse*'.

35. '*Quia plures sunt res quam verba*': 'Because there are more things than there are words'. Another Realist doctrine.

36. '*ad pauca respicientes facile enuntiant*': 'Those who take little into account find it easy to make pronouncements'. No authority has been found for this proverb-like remark.

37. 'as, according to Aristotle, there can be no more worlds but one': v. Aristotle, *De caelo*, I, 8–9, 277b9–279a11 (this is the most fully-developed statement of this doctrine in Aristotle's extant works, but there is a shorter version, possibly an interpolation, in *Metaphysics*, XII, viii, 1074 a 31–38).

38. 'Nothing is impossible to God that implies not a contradiction': This assertion in logical terms of divine omnipotence is a commonplace of medieval theology.

39. 'those exotick proverbs': For 'there is no new thing under the sun', see Ecclesiastes 1:8. Terence's remark that '*Nihil dictum quod non dictum prius*' ('Nothing has been said which has not been said before') occurs in *Eunuchus*, prol. 41, though in somewhat different words. For Paul's dictum about philosophers, see Colossians 2:8: 'Beware lest any man spoil you through philosophy and vain deceit, after the tradition of men, after the rudiments of the world, and not after Christ'.

40. 'how comes the invention of syllogisms to be attributed to Aristotle ... gunpowder and the art of printing': Aristotle's logical system was indeed founded on the syllogism (cf. *Prior Analytics*, 24b 18); while it may not be true that Archimedes was the discoverer of the sphere, he was one of the fathers of spherical geometry. John Napier of Merchiston (1550-1617), of whose name 'Neper' is a current seventeenth-century form, was the inventor of logarithms and the author of *Mirifici Logarithmorum Canonis Descriptio* (1614), in which he published his logarithmic tables and promised a description of the

methodology: it is probable that this approach influenced Urquhart's strategy in the presentation of his Language. 'Swart' is Berthold Schwartz, the fourteenth-century German monk to whom the invention of gunpowder was traditionally attributed, while Johann Gutenberg (named by Urquhart as 'Gertrudenburg') developed printing by moveable type about the middle of the fifteenth century.

41. 'Rehoboam by all appearance would have made use of them': For the rebellion of Israel against the rule of Rehoboam, son of Solomon, see 1 Kings 12:1–14:31.

42. 'Pancerola's Treatise, *De Novis Adimpertis*': i.e. Guido Panciroli, *Rerum memorabilium jam olim deperditarum* (Amberg, 1599), a work on Classical antiquity, which is contrasted by Urquhart with the historical writings of Polydore Vergil, whose *Historia Anglica* deals with more recent British history.

43. 'so that the allegation of Bliteri by the Summulists will be of small validity': The Summulists were logicians, commentators on the *Summulae logicales* of Peter of Spain, notorious for their pedantry. 'Bliteri' (cf. 'blitery', p. 89) is apparently derived from the MSc. verb 'bluiter' (also used as a noun), meaning 'to talk foolishly or outspokenly'; cf. Alexander Montgomerie, Sonnet xxiv, *Poems*, ed. James Cranstoun (STS, Edinburgh, 1887), p. 100, 'A Baxters bird, a bluiter beggar borne'; Patrick Hume of Polwarth, *The Flying betwixt Montgomery and Polwart*, 141, ibid., p. 64, 'Bot, Lord! I laugh to see the bluiter'.

44. 'as when we see my Lord General's picture': This seems to be an attempt at flattery on Urquhart's part, since the General is presumably Cromwell himself.

45. 'plural and redual': 'Redual' is scarcely intelligible, corresponding to no grammatical category in any language — perhaps Urquhart was thinking of a separate number for two squared, or perhaps he was merely indulging in a flight of fancy.

46. 'all the results of the Cephalisme from ten to eighty-one inclusively': The 'Cephalism' (from Gk. κεφαλισμος) was a form of multiplication table of single numbers, alluded to by Aristotle, *Topica*, 8.14.5, and also mentioned by the lexicographer Suidas.

47. 'that dexterity which Mithridates, King of Pontus, was said to have': The reference is probably to Mithridates VI, the Great (c. 120–63 B.C.), who fought prolonged campaigns against Rome and was eventually defeated by Pompey.

48. 'they are till this houre called by the name of Nominal Philosophers': i.e. Nominalists, the term applied by medieval philosophers to the school which emerged in the fourteenth century, its most prominent exponent being William of Ockham, which held to the doctrine that abstract terms refer to mental concepts and that existence consists entirely of particulars.

49. 'because there is an Act of Parliament for it': Urquhart is presumably referring to the Statute of Monopolies (1623), which established the rights of inventors and became the foundation of patent law.

50. '*quae non fecimus iste*': 'which we did not make ourselves'.

51. '*Vix ea nostra voco*': 'I scarcely call them our own'.

52. '*si ab inaequaibus inaequalia demas, quae restant sunt aequalia*': (The laws of mathematics require us to read '*inaequalia*' in the first clause, although the 1652 text prints '*aequalia*') 'if you take odd numbers from odd numbers, that which is left is even'.

53 'the Act for Discoveries maintaines the truth thereof': Apparently another reference to the Statute of Monopolies, although Urquhart's reference is inexact. This Act gave the Crown the right to grant in inventors a monopoly on the exploitation of their inventions for periods up to fourteen years.

54. 'I appeal to Scipio': The story of Publius Cornelius Scipio Africanus (236–184/3 B.C.), who was disgraced as a result of attacks by Cato and others, is told by Livy (38, 53, 8), who states that '*moriuntem rure eo ipso loco sepeliri se iunisse ferunt monumentumque ibi aedificari, ne fumus sibi in ingrata patria fieret*' ('when he was dying he instructed that he should be buried in the country and his tomb built there, so that he should not be buried in his ungrateful homeland').

55. 'twitted the Athenians with ingratitude for the ostracizing of Aristides': For an account of the disgrace of Aristides, owing to the animosity of Themistocles, see Plutarch, *Aristides*, 7.

56. '*contrariorum eadem est ratio*': 'and the same applies to the opposite'.

57. 'Ahab's case in Naboth's vineyard': The story of the seizure by Ahab, king of Samaria of the vineyard of Naboth, and of God's stern response, is told in 1 Kings 21.

58. '*quia violenti non fit injuria*': 'Since an injury is not done to a willing victim'.

59. '*pactum hominis tollit conditionem legis*': 'agreement by an individual removes the force of the law'.

60. 'and a hay-mow then the meadow': In this and the following six lines of the 1652 edition, the letters 'i', 'u', 'l', 'a', 's', 'i', and 'n' have been wrongly set at the end of the line. Only the last misreading is listed among Urquhart's Errata (see *A Note on the Text*, above, p. 47); all have been silently corrected in the present edition.

61. 'Mammona': The personification of covetousness, mentioned in Matthew 6:24 and Luke 16:9–13 and hence becoming widely referred to as the demon of worldliness. The word is derived from the Aramaic *mamon*, 'riches'.

62. 'their synagogical Sanhedrins': The Sanhedrin were the supreme council and judicial tribunal of Old Testament Israel.

63. 'Plautus' exolet phrases . . . the eloquent orations of Ciceron': The fanciful style of the dramatist Plautus (2nd cent. B.C.) is naturally contrasted with Cicero's more restrained manner, generally adopted in the Renaissance as a model of good Latin style.

64. 'the tribe of Levi': The descendants of Levi were the priestly tribe of Israel (v. Joshua 18:7, 1 Chronicles 23:2–32); the term is here used ironically and dismissively of the Presbyterian clergy.

65. 'trace the foot-steps of Zedekiah's fellow captives': Zedekiah was king of Judah at the time of the Babylonian captivity (v. Jeremiah 27:3–39:9).

66. '*nobilius dare quam accipere*': 'It is more noble to give than to receive' (cf. Acts 20:35, '*Beatius est magis dare quam accipere*').

67. 'this mnemoneutick hexameter': Such verses were immensely popular in the Middle Ages, and continued in currency into the seventeenth century.

68. 'I heard once a Maronite Jew': There does not seem to have been any such sect. Maronite *Christians* were (and are) a Syrian sect linked with the Catholic Church and living mainly in the Levant: but the point of the story (attributed to a mysterious Rabbi Esra) is that Jewish commentators will go to absurd lengths to explain away inconvenient features of the New Testament. Perhaps the whole thing is Urquhart's invention. For the underlying reference to Malchus, the servant of Caiaphas whose ear was cut off by Peter, v. John 18:10.

69. 'a knot of Scotish bankers': This was in fact the period during which the elements of a banking system were emerging in London, but

there is little evidence that it was dominated by Scots. It was the London goldsmiths who appear to have formed the nucleus of the English banks.

70. 'look so idolatrously upon their Dagon of wealth': Dagon was a deity of the Philistines, and hence comes to refer to any idol: cf. Dunbar, *Flyting*, 66 (*Works*, ed. James Kinsley [Oxford, 1979], p. 78): 3e dagone, dowbart, thairof haif thow no dowt.

71. 'like so many wolves, foxes of Athenian Timons': For the tale of the misanthropic Timon who lived a solitary life, see Plutarch, *Antony*, 70 (the source of Shakespeare's play), and Lucian, *Timon*.

72. 'in a book in the last edition of a pretty bulk, written in the Latine tongue by one Dempster': i.e. Thomas Dempster's *Historia Ecclesiastica Gentis Scotorum*, first published in Bologna in 1627 (ed. David Irving [Bannatyne Club, 2 vols, Edinburgh, 1829]), a curious mixture of complete fabrication and useful biographical and bibliographical information, upon which much of Urquhart's subsequent account of Scottish writers and scholars abroad seems to have been based.

73. 'several of them have for their fidelity, valor and gallantry ...': Much valuable information about the military exploits of Scottish expatriates in northern and eastern Europe can be found in the successive volumes of Th. A. Fischer, *The Scots in Germany* (Edinburgh, 1902), *The Scots in Eastern and Western Prussia* (Edinburgh, 1903), and *The Scots in Sweden* (Edinburgh, 1907).

74. '*Scoticani foederis* [1652 *faederis*] *supremus dux*': 'supreme commander of the Scottish Covenant'. Alexander Leslie, later Earl of Leven (c. 1580–1661), organised the signing of the Covenant by Scottish soldiers in Europe, returning to lead the Covenanting forces at Duns Law (June 1639) and to campaign continuously on the side of the Covenant.

75. 'a book in folio, intituled *Monroe's Expedition*': i.e. *Monro his expedition with the worthy Scots regiment* (London, 1637).

76. 'Colonel James Seaton and Colonel James Seaton': The repetition of the name is confirmed by there being two colonels of that name in the list at the end of the work.

77. 'for his service done at the Bridge of Dee near Aberdeen against the Earl of Montross': The engagement at the Brig o'Dee on 18 June 1639, which paved the way for Montrose's recapture of Aberdeen the following day, is described with some attention to its defence by Gunn in James Gordon's *History of Scots Affairs* (Spalding Club, 3 vols,

Aberdeen, 1841), II, 274–83. The Aberdeen campaign of May–June 1639 (in the first stages of which Urquhart himself participated) is also described in Spalding's *Memorialls of the Trubles in Scotland and in England* (Spalding Club, 2 vols, Aberdeen, 1850), I, 193ff.

78. 'Gustavus the Caesaromastix': Gustavus Adolphus, king of Sweden (1611–32), who fought successful campaigns against the Emperor Ferdinand III from 1630 to 1632.

79. 'the battel at Leipsich': i.e. the battle of Breitenfeld (17 September 1631), which resulted in a decisive victory by the Swedish army over the Imperial forces.

80. 'the Duke of Wymar, Gustavus Horne, Baneer and Torsisson': Bernhard, duke of Weimar, Gustav Horn, Johann Baner and Lennart Torstensson were all prominent commanders of Gustavus Adolphus' army.

81. 'Mowat living in Birren': Axel Mowat (1592–1661), the son of a Scot who emigrated to Norway, became a captain in the Danish navy in 1628 and subsequently was appointed admiral. His base was in Bergen (Urquhart's 'Birren'), and he held substantial estates in western Norway. There is, however, no evidence that he ever held a position approximating that of Danish regent in Norway.

82. 'colonels under the pay of Lewis the Thirteenth of France': Louis XIII (1601–43) maintained, like his predecessors, a Scots Brigade in his army.

83. 'Colonel Leslie and Colonel Gordon': For the careers of Walter Leslie and John Gordon, about which Urquhart's information is essentially accurate, v. Fischer, *The Scots in Germany*, pp. 113–16.

84. 'the ever-renowned Earl of Bodwel': The account given by Urquhart of Bothwell's service abroad seems to fit neither the life of James Hepburn, fourth Earl and husband of Queen Mary (d. 1578) nor that of Francis Stuart, fifth Earl (d. 1624).

85. 'Gasconads of France, Rodomontads of Spain, Fanfaronads of Italy': These are all mocking terms for soldiers' bragging. *OED* gives as the earliest occurrence of 'Gasconade' (from the reputation of Gascon soldiers) an article by Steele in *The Tatler* (No. 115, 1709). 'Rodomontade' is derived from the name of a Saracen leader in Ariosto's *Orlando Furioso*.

86. 'Spadassins and Acuchilladores': 'Spadassin' (not in *OED*) is derived from Italian *spadaccino* (cf. Spanish *espadachin*), and ultimately

from French *espadid*, a light sword. 'Acuchillador' is a Spanish term, meaning 'knife-wielder'.

87. 'like those of Amades de Gaule, Esplandian and Don Sylves de la Selve': Amadis of Gaul is the hero of a popular romance, and Esplandian his son. The reference to Don Sylves de la Selve is more obscure, but may relate to Feliciano de Silva, the author of a chivalric romance.

88. 'under the command of Spinola': Ambrosio Spinola, a Genoese, was the commander of the Imperial forces in the Low Countries during the war of 1603–8.

89. 'it was the old Earl of Argile': Archibald Campbell, seventh earl of Argyll (c. 1576–1638) had been a prominent supporter of the policies of James VI and I, but in 1618 he joined the forces of the Catholic Philip III of Spain in the Low Countries, and was branded a traitor the following year. His son, also Archibald, was created Marquis by Charles I.

90. 'like Ismael': cf. Genesis 16:12.

91. 'several Scotish colonels under the command of the Prince of Orange': For details of the Scottish participation in the Dutch wars, v. *Papers Illustrating the History of the Scots Brigade in the United Netherlands*, James Ferguson (SHS, 3 vols, Edinburgh, 1899–1901), vols I and III. All those named by Urquhart appear there.

92. 'admirable inventions made use of by Archimedes in defence of Syracusa': See Plutarch, *Marcellus*, 14–19.

93. 'so compleatly praised in that Preface of the author's': cf. *Works*, pp. 59–60.

94. 'not much unlike that of Archita's dove': Archytas (4th cent. B.C.) was reputedly the founder of the science of mechanics. For his mechanical dove, see Aulus Gellius, *Noctes ambrosianae*, 10.12.

95. 'his compatriot Crichtoun': The historical figure of James Crichton (1560–1582) is well attested from contemporary sources, and there is unquestionably a basis in fact for Urquhart's hyperbolic praise. Dempster gives an extended notice in his *Historia ecclesiastica*, ed. cit., I, 187–8; for a relatively modern attempt at a substantive biography, v. P. F. Tytler, *The Life of the Admirable Crichton* (Edinburgh, 1823). John Willcock, *Sir Thomas Urquhart of Cromartie* (Edinburgh, 1899), pp. 161–3, considers and rejects the view of J. H. Burton that, because there are strong resemblances between Urquhart's account of

Crichton's career and a passage of Rabelais concerning the feats of Pantagruel, the former should be taken ironically.

96. 'at the Duke of Mantua's court': Guglielmo Gonzaga, Duke of Mantua (1550–1587) was one of the leading princes of later sixteenth-century Italy, and a prominent patron of the arts and learning.

97. 'Tramonti': lit. 'those from across the mountains', i.e. foreigners from northern Europe.

98. 'like another Romulus or Marcellus in triumph': Romulus was the legendary founder of Rome; for his triumphant return after defeating the Caeninans, see Livy, I, 10. Marcius Claudius Marcellus (consul in 222 B.C.) was received in triumph after the defeat of Viridimarus.

99. 'like another Prothee': For the legendary ability of Proteus to change his form, see Homer, *Odyssey*, IV, 385ff., and Virgil, *Georgics*, IV, 387ff.

100. 'the gratious proclamations of Paulus Æmilius in favour of their liberty': In the supplementary Errata added by Urquhart during the printing of *The Jewel*, this reference is corrected. He had apparently confused Paulus Æmilius Macedonicus (d. 160 B.C.), who defeated Perseus at Pydna, with Titus Quintus Flamininus (named by Urquhart as Flaminius), victor over the Macedonians at Cynos-cephalae, of whom the story of the birds falling from the sky when he received the applause of the crowd at the Isthmian games is told by Plutarch, *Flamininus*, 10.

101. 'as Sir Philip Sydney says, that a wonder is no wonder in a wonderful subject': The reference is to *Arcadia*, II, 7, 2.

102. 'since the days of Alcibiades': Alcibiades (c. 450–404 B.C.) was an Athenian leader, a brilliant disciple of Socrates, whose life is recounted by Plutarch and who also receives favourable attention from Plato, Xenophon and Thucydides.

103. 'to the common schoole of the Colledge of Navarre': The College of Navarre, founded by Joanna of Navarre in 1304, was one of the leading institutions within the University of Paris, with a particular reputation in the later Middle Ages for theology.

104. 'trou-madam': or troll-madam, a bagatelle-like game, recorded as early as 1572 and apparently played mainly by women: it remained in currency as late as the nineteenth century.

105. '*ultro citroque habitis*': 'bandied back and forth' (cf. Cicero, *De republica*, 6, 9).

106. 'went to the Louvre in a buff-suit': More usually described as a buff-coat, a stout leather garment worn by soldiers (from *buff*, 'buffalo').

107. 'broke as many lances on the Saracen': The Saracen was a Turk's head used in the seventeenth century as a target for jousting.

108. 'on that day of carnavale, as they call it': The Italian feast of Shrove Tuesday was well known in Britain from the mid-sixteenth century, and *carnavale* had become a fairly familiar term. The practice of riotous celebration before the beginning of Lent was widespread in later medieval Europe, and Fastern Eve had been the Scottish equivalent before the Reformation.

109. 'in the disguise of a Zanni or Pantaloon': Both are figures from the *commedia de l'arte*; the *zanni* were clowns, the *pantalone* a foolish old man.

110. 'to prank it *a la Venetiana*': The Venetian style of acting was particularly famous, and stylized in a particularly elaborate way; cf. R. D. S. Jack, *The Italian Influence on Scottish Literature* (Edinburgh, 1972), p. 196.

111. 'like another Sejanus with a periwig daubed with Cypres powder': Sejanus is the tragic hero of Jonson's play of that name, first performed in 1603; the story derives from Tacitus, *Annals*, III, iv. Cypres powder, used in the treatment of the elaborate wigs which were a feature of fashionable dress in the seventeenth century, was powdered galingale, from the aromatic herb *Cyperus longus* (Sweet Galingale).

112. 'a Monmouth-like cap on his head': Such round caps were much worn by soldiers and sailors; cf. *Henry V*, IV, 7, 104.

113. 'come in pilgrimage from Saint Michael': i.e. (presumably) Mont-St-Michel, the island abbey in Normandy.

114. 'he honderspondered it': cf. Urquhart, *Rabelais*, III, 42: 'Finding that none would make him any Answer, he passed from thence to that part of the Leaguer, where the huff, snuff, honder-sponder, swash-buckling High-Germans were . . .', translating Rabelais' '*il passe on camp des Hondrespondres* . . .' (*Oeuvres*, ed. A. Lyrne *et al.* [Paris, 1912–], V. 308). *Hondrespondre*, derived from the German slang phrase *honder ponder* ('a hundred pounds'), was a nickname of the German mercenaries.

15. 'his arms a kenbol': The origin of this expressive phrase is obscure; the earliest recorded forms are *in kenebowe* (in the fourteenth-century

Tale of Beryn) and similar variants, but a number of writers in the seventeenth century use *kenboll/kemboll*.

116. 'plaies the Capitan Spavento': A braggart Spanish captain, a figure in the *commedia dell'arte* created by the famous Francesco Andreini, founder of the leading *Gelosi* company, who published *Le Bravure del Capitano Spavento* (Venice, 1607 and frequently republished). The name is derived from the Italian *spaventare*, 'to frighten'. Cf. G. Senigaglia, *Capitan Spaventa* (Florence, 1899).

117. 'the Heliconian nymphs': Helicon is the mountain of the Parnassus traditionally said to be the home of the Muses.

118. 'like that angel in the Scripture': The angel is Gabriel, whose voice is so described in Daniel 10:6.

119. 'the supremest Lydian note': A musical mode, soft and effeminate, derived from the region of Lydia in Asia Minor.

120. 'a transendencie overreaching Ela': *Ela* was the highest note in the Gamut, the upper E which is the highest note of the seventh hexachord according to the musical system of Guido d'Arezzo (early 11th century).

121. 'as the manna of the Arabian desarts': v. Exodus 16: 10–35.

122. 'in an Alcoranal paradise': An account of the sensual pleasures awaiting the true believer in Paradise is found in the Islamic scripture, *Al-Koran*.

123. 'the young Adonises and fainthearted initiants in the exercises of the Cytherean Academy': 'Cytherean' refers to Venus, to whom the island of Cythera was sacred, while Adonis was a handsome young man loved by Venus.

124. 'Pindarising their discourse': Pindar (5th cent. B.C.) was a Greek lyric poet, author of odes in a lofty style.

125. '*a la Cypriana*': 'in the Cypriot style'. Cyprus was the traditional birthplace of Venus.

126. 'the thin cawle of her Idalian garments': Idalion was a mountain-city in Cyprus, sacred to Venus.

127. '*puris naturalibus*': 'natural purity', here with a fairly impure connotation.

128. 'like that of Aeneas to Dido': Cf. Virgil, *Aeneid*, I, 588–9: 'restitit Aeneas claraque in luce refulsit/os umerosque deo similis'.

228

129. 'as to the female deities did Ganimed': Ganymedes was a beautiful youth carried off by Zeus to become his cup-bearer; cf. Ovid, *Metamorphoses*, X, 155–61.

130. *'definitiones logicae verificantur in rebus'*: 'logical definitions are verified by objects' (another Realist doctrine!).

131. 'Septembral juyce': A characteristically periphrastic phrase, meaning 'wine'.

132. 'Morphee': Morpheus was the Greek god of dreams, the son of Sleep.

133. 'for the discharge of Hymenaean rites': Hymen (or Hymenaeus) was a Greek deity of doubtful origin, the patron god of marriage.

134. 'to the oracle of Pallas Armata': The armed Pallas is one of the aspects of the goddess Athena, patroness of war.

135. 'that followed the Purification Day': i.e. Candlemas (2 February).

136. 'the Lyaean god': i.e. Bacchus, who was sometimes known by this surname (e.g. Ovid, *Amores*, 3, 15, 17).

137. 'to make his tith outvy their stock': Urquhart is here punning on terms from swordsmanship and usury. 'Tith' and 'stock' are types of sword, but they also relate to money-lending, where 'tith' ('a tenth') has the sense of a share or interest, and 'stock' of capital.

138. *'kardagas'*: This astronomical term, meaning a sector of $15°$ and hence equal to the part of the earth's rotation which occupies one hour, was imported into Latin from Sanskrit via Arabic, and is attested as early as the thirteenth century; cf. *Richard of Wallingford: An Edition*, ed. J. D. Worth (3 vols, Oxford, 1976), II, 46–8.

139. 'thurst in quart': The metathesis of 'thurst' is a Scotticism, one of the few indications in the text of Urquhart's linguistic background (cf. Introduction, pp. 35–6).

140. 'a whole brigade of Paphian archers': i.e. from Paphos, a city in Cyprus where Venus was worshipped.

141. 'Arachne-like': Arachne was a woman of Lydia, whose weaving rivalled that of Athena and who hanged herself after the goddess had destroyed her work. She was then turned into a spider by the penitent Athena; cf. Ovid, *Metamorphoses*, VI, 5ff.

142. 'all the excellencies of Juno, Venus and Minerva': i.e. the three goddesses who were the subject of the Judgment of Paris.

143. 'or azimuth and almicantar circles intersecting other': These are astronomical terms deriving from the Arabic (*al-zimut* and *al-macantar*), which in medieval and Renaissance usage referred to lines of longitude and latitude respectively.

144. 'the Pierian Muses': Pieria, in northern Thessaly, was the reputed home of the Muses.

145. 'secret mines of greater worth than those of either Tibar or Peru': Tibar is a problem. The only geographical name to which it bears any obvious resemblance is the home of the Tibareni, i.e. Pontus (Asia Minor), referred to by Xenophon and other Greek writers. But this does not seem to fit the context, while there are no familiar areas of mining which recall Urquhart's form.

146. 'as did Cato Uticensis': Marcus Procius Cato, Uticensis (95–46 B.C.) committed suicide after the defeat of the Pompeian forces as Thapsa; v. Plutarch, *Cato Minor*, 67–70.

147. 'to turn his own Atropos': Atropos was one of the Three Fates, the one who cut the thread of life.

148. 'Baptista Mantuanus': Baptista Spagnuoli Mantuanus (1448–1516), General of the Carmelite Order, whose Latin verses (especially the *Eclogae* and *Fasti*) enjoyed enormous popularity during the Renaissance. It is, nevertheless, a little surprising to find him being linked with Virgil in this way!

149. 'had quit the Elysian fields': In Greek legend the fields of Elysium were the abode of the virtuous dead.

150. 'Ariosto, Dante, Petrark and Bembo': The acknowledged masters of Italian literature, only Boccaccio's name being omitted from the list. Ludovica Ariosto (1474–1533), author of *Orlando Furioso*, and Pietro Bembo (1470–1547) were writers of great current popularity, whose works in the high style ensured that their reputations rivalled those of Dante and Petrarch.

151. 'so cleared the archipelago of the Mussulmans': The Venetian state was perennially troubled with Turkish pirates in the Adriatic in the earlier seventeenth century. The *Calendar of State Papers: Venetian* contains no reference to Urquhart's vice-admiral William Scott: there was a Captain Robert Scott in the Venetian service around 1624, but he was a land-based mercenary rather than a sea-captain.

152. 'another Don Jean d'Austria or Duke d'Orea': John of Austria (1629–1679) was the illegitimate son of Philip IV of Spain, who put down the Neapolitan rebellion against Spanish rule in 1647. Andrea

Doria (1466–1560) was an outstanding Genoese *condottiere*, prince of Melfi and one of the great military leaders of the first half of the sixteenth century.

153. 'the very Scyths and Sarmats': Warlike nomadic tribes of western Asia, described by Herodotus, IV, 1–144. The names were still used in the seventeenth century, although they were, strictly speaking, obsolete.

154. 'the great Duke of Muscovy': Michael Romanov, czar of Russia (1613–45) founder of the Romanov dynasty, who fought to establish Muscovite power in eastern Europe.

155. 'was elected King of Bucharia': Bokhara, now part of the Uzbek SSR, was from c. 1505 a khanate of the Uzbek Tartars, the subject after the reign of Abdullah Khan (1556–98) of bitter internal conflict between the Shaibani dynasty and the Ashtarkhanides, descendents of Tamburlaine. There may, therefore, be some element of truth in this apparently fantastic story of their election as Khan of a Scot in the service of the Muscovites.

156. 'in that service against the Crim Tartar': After a brief period of independence, the Crimean Tartars were dependent on the Ottoman Turks, and hence natural enemies of the Russians, from 1475 until the annexation of the region by Russia in 1783.

157. 'Vienne': i.e. Vienna.

158. 'High-Dutchman': 'Dutch' was often used to refer to the whole Germanic-speaking area of Europe except Scandinavia, thus including both the Low Countries and Germany (from 'Deutsch'). 'High-Dutchman', therefore, means someone from Germany proper.

159. 'after the fashion of a Charlewaine': Charlewaine, corrupted *via* 'Charles's wain' from OE. *ceorles wæn*, 'a farmer's wagon', was an alternative name for the Great Bear, or Plough.

160. 'the Archduke Leopoldo's court': Leopold William (1614–1662) was the second son of the Emperor Ferdinand II; he was the holder of several episcopal sees in succession, and served from 1647 to 1655 as Stadholder of the Spanish Netherlands.

161. 'they all had but Toledo-blades': Toledo was famous from medieval times for the high quality of its sword-blades.

162. 'such as the Robert Scot who was the deviser of leathern guns': The first inventor of leather guns was probably Melchior Wurmprandt, an Austrian officer in the Swedish army; but Scott was

also working in this area while serving with the Swedish, and he was certainly the first to bring the new guns to Britain. It is claimed in his epitaph in Lambeth church that he 'invented the Leather Ordnance'. These guns were much in use during the Civil War; v. David Stevenson and David H. Caldwell, 'Leather guns and other light artillery in mid-seventeenth century Scotland', *PSAS*, 108 (1976–7), 300–17.

163. 'to the oracles of the Delphian presbytery': Delphi was the site of the oracle of Apollo, the most famous of its kind in antiquity and noted for the obscurity and ambiguity of its predictions.

164. 'did consist those fresh water officers': A current term in the sixteenth and seventeenth centuries for raw and unskilled soldiers; cf. Thomas North, *Plutarch* (1579–80), who uses the phrase 'freshwater Soldiers' which is also given by Gerard, *The Herball* (London: John Norton, 1597) as the popular name of *Stratiotes aloides*, still known as Water Soldier.

165. 'the new Diana of Ephesus': The temple of Ephesus (Asia Minor) was a famous shrine of Artemis, or Diana.

166. 'the committees of the shires of Innernass and Ross': Committees to organise the war effort in each county were set up by the Scottish parliament on 26 August 1643, ten days after the drafting of the Solemn League and Covenant, and reappointed at intervals thereafter (v. *APS*, VI, i, 52–6 etc.), until as late as 1650.

167. 'like good Simeons of iniquity': Simeon and Levi were sons of Jacob by his wife Leah (Genesis 29: 33–4); for his curse on their wrong-doing, v. ibid., 49: 5–7.

168. 'to give it the title of Neroniana': Urquhart has here confused two rather similar points in Suetonius' account of the reign of Nero: *Neroniana* was the name of the quinquennial games he instituted in A.D. 60 (*Vitae Caesarum*, Nero, 12.3), while the name which he proposed to substitute for Rome was *Neropolis* (ibid., 55).

169. 'Master Alexander Ross': Ross (1591–1654) was one of the outstanding scholars among Urquhart's contemporaries, successively schoolmaster in Southampton and vicar of Carisbrook (Isle of Wight), and chaplain to Charles I. Urquhart's account of his published works is impressively up-to-date: the *Arcana Microcosmi* did not appear until 1651.

170. 'every whit as useful as Sir Edward Cook's reports are to the lawyers': Sir Edward Coke CJ (1552–1634) was one of the founders of English legal reporting, his reports appearing in successive editions from 1600.

171. 'according to the metempsychosis of Pythagoras': That a belief in the transmigration of souls was a central feature of the Pythagorean system is attested by as early an authority as an elegy by his contemporary (late 6th-early 5th century B.C.), Xenophanes.

172. 'the souls of Socrates, Chrysostome, Aristotle, Ciceron and Virgil': A list which neatly combines Greek philosophy (Socrates and Aristotle) with Latin eloquence (Cicero and Virgil) and with Christian wisdom (St John Chrysostom, bishop of Constantinople and one of the principal Patristic writers).

173. 'as Danae was by Jupiter': For the story of Danae, seduced by Zeus in the form of a shower of gold and thus the mother of Perseus, see Ovid, *Metamorphoses*, IV, 610 and elsewhere, and Apollodorus, *The Library*, II, iv, 1.

174. 'as much of Maecenas' soul': Caius Maecenas (d. 8 B.C.) was the patron of Virgil, Horace, Propertius and other writers.

175. 'under the reproach of ignorance which the Oriental nations fixe upon them': Urquhart apparently refers to the supposed intolerance of the Christians, who accepted the authenticity only of Jesus, and not of Mahomet.

176. '*laus* ought to be *virtutis assecla*': 'praise should be the servant of virtue'.

177. 'one Sinclair': David Sinclair appears in Dempster's *Historia Ecclesiastica*, II, 595. Peter Ramus, or de la Ramée (1515–72), was a prominent Parisian teacher, whose elaborate logical system was intended to supersede the Aristotelian logic which was the foundation of scholastic philosophy.

178. 'one Anderson': For Alexander Anderson, v. Dempster, op. cit., I, 63–4.

179. 'another called Doctor Seaton': i.e. William Seton, for whom see Dempster, II, 591.

180. 'chief professor of the Sapience': The University of Rome, founded by Boniface VIII in 1303, had since the early sixteenth century been housed in a building known as La Sapienza ('The Palace of Wisdom').

181. 'Il Collegio Romano': This important seat of Jesuit learning, the first modern seminary, was established in 1551, eleven years after the foundation of the Society of Jesus.

233

182. 'those Teatinos': The Theatines, or Congregation of Regular Clerics, took their popular name from the Latin form of the diocese of their founder, Gian Petro Carffa, bishop of Chieti (Theate), who later became Pope Paul IV. Established in 1524, the Theatines resembled the Jesuits in being a new order, which may explain the euphemistic allusion attributed to Seton by Urquhart.

183. 'like a Hercules amongst so many Myrmidons': The Myrmidons were a warlike tribe from Thessaly, who accompanied Achilles on his expedition to Troy (cf. *Iliad*, II, 684).

184. 'being possessed with the Chair of Lipsius': Justus Lipsius (Joest Lips) (1547–1606) was a Netherlandish scholar who, after teaching for a time at Leiden and in a number of other universities, ended his career as professor of Humanity at Louvain.

185. 'for, as sayes Aristotle': The assertion that 'all men by nature are desirous of knowledge' forms the opening sentence of Aristotle's *Metaphysics* (I.1, 980a21).

186. 'as if he had been another Livy or Salustius': Titus Livius (59 B.C.–A.D. 17) and Caius Sallustius Crispus (86–34 B.C.) were Roman historians, generally regarded as masters of Latin prose style.

187. 'le Sieur de Balzak': Jean Louis Guez de Balzac (1594–1654) was the author of two celebrated volumes of *Lettres* (1624, 1636) and other literary works, including essays on style.

188. 'Romancealists': i.e. authors of romances, who would be expected to write in a particularly elegant style.

189. 'another Scotish man named Cameron': Urquhart is presumably referring to John Cameron (c. 1579–1625), regarding whom see G. B. Maury, 'John Cameron: A Scottish Protestant Theologian in France', *SHR*, 7 (1910), 325–45. But while a number of Cameron's works survive, we have found no evidence of his being known as *Bibliotheca Movens*, nor of the existence of a book with that title, either in Latin or English.

190. 'their compatriot Barclay': John Barclay (1582–1621) is mentioned by Dempster, op. cit., I, 126–7. His *Argenis* was, as Urquhart indicates, extraordinarily popular, and was frequently reprinted in the course of the seventeenth century.

191. 'there was a Scottish man named [Colvil]': The 1652 edition gives the name as Melvil, but John Durkan, 'Three Manuscripts with Fife Associations: And David Colville of Fife', *Innes Rev.*, 20 (1969),

47–58, has amply demonstrated that the correct name is Colvil. David Colville (c. 1581–1630) was a noted expatriate scholar, and was for a time associated with the Barberini circle, on whom v. below, no. 202.

192. 'taken by Don Juan of Austria at the Battel of Lepanto': On 7 October 1571, a combined Christian fleet under the command of Don Juan of Austria won a remarkable victory over the Turks off Lepanto in the Gulf of Corinth.

193. 'These four eminent Scots': Hugh Sempill (1594–1654), the author of a number of mathematical works, the two James Gordons (d. 1620 and 1641) and George Turnbull (d. 1633) were all early Scottish members of the Jesuit order.

194. 'a learned addition to Rossinus': Dempster produced an enlarged edition of Johannes Rosinus' *Antiquitatum Romanorum Corpus Absolutissimum*, which had first appeared at Basel in 1583. Dempster's edition was published at Paris in 1613 and was dedicated to James VI and I, who invited him to come to London as royal historiographer.

195. 'Balfour, a professor of philosophy in Bourdeaux': i.e. Robert Balfour (d. 1610), mentioned by Dempster, *Historia Ecclesiastica*, I, 119.

196. 'Primrose, a Scotish man who was a preacher in French at Bordeaux': Gilbert Primrose of Dalmeny (c. 1580–1641) was a prominent member of the Protestant community at Bordeaux, and subsequently became minister of the Huguenot church in London.

197. 'Pontaeus': i.e. Robert Pont (d. 1606), whose career is described by David Buchanan, *De scriptoribus* (Bannatyne Club, Edinburgh, 1837), pp. 126–8.

198. 'a professor of the Scottish nation within these sixteen years in Somure': Saumur was a Protestant theological academy, founded in 1599, which acquired a reputation as 'the second Geneva'. Many Scots taught there, including William Geddie, Robert Boyd of Trochrig, and Zachary Boyd; Urquhart is referring to Mark Duncan, who taught Greek at Sedan before moving to Saumur in 1606, where he was professor of Philosophy and later (1627–40) of Greek, as well as serving as Principal; v. Marguerite Guignet Campbell, 'Mark Duncan, Professor at Saumur 1606–1640', *Recs. of the Scottish Church Hist. Soc.*, 5 (1935), 73–80.

199. 'then Philip was of Aristotle, or Tullius of Cratippus': Aristotle was employed by Philip of Macedon as tutor to his son Alexander, an arrangement which lasted from c. 343/2 to 335 B.C. Cratippus was a Greek teacher to whom Cicero sent his son Marcus, who wrote of his

tutor 'non ut discipulum, sed ut filium esse coniunctissimum' ('I am linked to him not as a pupil, but as a son') (Cicero, *Epistulae ad Familiares*, XVI, 21.)

200. 'such as the Bishop of Vezon': Urquhart means either William Chisholm II, bishop of Dunblane until the Reformation and later (1570–85) bishop of Vaison in France, or his nephew William, who succeeded him at Vaison and remained bishop until 1623; cf. A. Ritchie, 'The Character and Career of William Chisholm II', *Procs. Soc. of Friends of Dunblane Cathedral*, 6 (1950–3), 83–9.

201. 'and Chalmers, Bishop of Neems': Here Urquhart's information seems to have been inaccurate, since there was no bishop of Nimes of this name. Perhaps Thomas Chalmers, who served as almoner to Cardinal Richelieu, is intended.

202. 'Signor Georgio Con': George Conn (d. 1640) was successively a student at Douai, Paris and Bologna, and later became a member of the circle around Cardinal Francesco Barberini (whose envoy to the court of Henrietta Maria of England he was in 1636), his brothers Cardinal Antonio Barberini, and Taddeo, prince of Palestrina. The Barberini were nephews of Pope Urban VIII (Maffeo Barberini).

203. 'his compatriot Cardinal Betoun': David Betoun (c. 1495-1546) was archbishop of St Andrews from 1539, and created Cardinal in 1543. He was assassinated by a small band of Protestants in his own castle of St Andrews on 29 May 1546; the story is told with much circumstantial detail by John Knox, *The Historie of the Reformatioun in Scotland*, ed. W. Croft Dickinson (2 vols, Edinburgh, 1949).

204. 'whether Periscians, Heteroscians or Amphiscians': These are terms applied to those who live beyond the polar circles, in the temperate zones, and near the Equator respectively, derived from the supposed position of their shadows (it was believed that the shadows of people near the Poles fell around them like a wheel!). The words are found in John Bullokar, *An English Expositor* (J. Leggatt: London, 1616; J. Leggatt: London, 1641), and in Henry Cockeram, *The English Dictionarie* (For Nathaniel Butler: London, 1623; Isaac Jaggard for Edmund Weaver: London, 1626).

205. '*ex malis moribus bonae oriuntur leges*': 'Good laws come from bad morals'. Cf. Macrobius, *Saturnalia*, 3.17.10: '*Leges bonae ex malis moribus procreantur*'.

206. 'for so begins the Covenant': Urquhart is thinking of the National Covenant of 1638, which had first appeared as the 'Negative Confession' in 1580. It begins with a denunciation of 'the usurped

authority of that Roman Antichrist' and then lists in great detail the objectionable features of Catholic doctrine.

207. 'of the opinion of Tamarlain': Cf. Samuel Purchas, *Purchas his Pilgrimes* (4 vols, London, W. Stansby, 1625), II, 142: 'Now he had all Religion in reuerence, so as it did worship one onely God, Creator of all things. He often said, that the greatnesse of Diuinitie consisted in the sundry kindes of people which are vnder the Cope of Heauen, who serued the same diuersely, nourishing it selfe with diuersitie, as the nature was diuers where it had printed his Image, God remayning, notwithstanding, one in his Essence, not receiuing therein any diuersitie.'

208. 'Tyry of the House of Drumkilbo, Mackbrek and Brown': James Tyrie (1543–1597) was a prominent Jesuit theologian, while Macbreck and Gilbert Brown (d. 1612) were also notable Catholic exiles and controversialists.

209. 'the great traveler Lithco': William Lithgow (1582–c. 1645) was the author of several works, the best known of which was *A most delectable and true discourse of an admired and painefull peregrination from Scotland to the most famous kingdomes in Europe, Asia and Affrike*, first published in London in 1614 and frequently reprinted.

210. 'so was Simon Graham': Graham (c. 1579–1614) was the author of *The anatomie of humors* (Edinburgh, 1609) and other works; cf. the edition by R. Jameson (Bannatyne Club, Edinburgh, 1830).

211. '*Nullum magnum ingenium sine mixtura dementiae*': 'There can be no great genius without some element of madness'. The quotation is actually from Seneca, *Dialogues*, 9.17.10.

212. 'Doctor John Forbas': Forbes (1593–1648) was an Aberdonian who studied at Aberdeen and Heidelberg, taught at Sedan, Leiden and elsewhere, who was in exile in Holland 1644–46, and whose *Irenicum amatoribus veritatis et pacis in ecclesia scoticana* was published at Aberdeen in 1629.

213. 'Doctor Robert Baron': Baron (c. 1593–1639) was Professor of Divinity at St Andrews and later at Marischal College, Aberdeen, where he subsequently became known as one of the episcopalian 'Aberdeen doctors'. His attack on George Turnbull SJ was published at Aberdeen in 1631.

214. 'Doctor William Lesly': Another of the 'Aberdeen doctors', Leslie (d. 1654) taught at King's College, Aberdeen from 1603, and was Principal 1632–40, at which date he was deposed by the General Assembly because of his episcopalian views.

215. 'Anits, Lycons and Melits': The accusers of Socrates.

216. 'some honest Lysias': Lysias (c. 459–c. 380 B.C.) was a noted Athenian forensic orator.

217. 'Doctor William Guild': Guild (1586–1657) was Leslie's successor as Principal of King's College, Aberdeen before he was, in his turn, deposed in 1651. The Aberdonian emphasis in this list of scholars is, of course, largely a reflection of Urquhart's north-eastern origins and contacts.

218. 'Master William Seaton': Urquhart's tutor is not to be confused with the legist mentioned earlier; there were several Aberdeen graduates of this name in the seventeenth century, of whom the one referred to here is possibly the MA of 1612. He does not appear to have made a mark outside Aberdeen.

219. 'Master William Lauder, preacher at Ava': William Lauder (1614–c. 1672) took the degree of MA from Aberdeen in 1632 and was minister of Avoch in Ross from 1642; he was suspended on 22 May 1647 for subscribing to the Earl of Seaforth's Remonstrance, but was subsequently restored.

220. 'that worthy gentleman, Master David Leech': Leech was a regent at King's College from 1628, and was sub-principal from 1632.

221. 'an elder brother named John': John Leech (fl. 1594–1616) was the author of a notable collection of *Epigrammata*, published several times in the seventeenth century.

222. 'One Master Andrew Ramsay': Ramsay (1574–1659) was Professor of Theology at Saumur, and was subsequently a minister and Professor of Divinity in Edinburgh (1620–27). He was the author of sacred poems in an Ovidian style. Ramsay was condemned as a 'Malignant' in 1649.

223. 'Doctor Arthur Jhonstoun': Arthur Johnston (1587–1641) is now best remembered as the collector of the *Deliciae Poetarum Scotorum* (Amsterdam, 1637), but he was also a Latin poet of considerable merit; his *Parerga* were published at Aberdeen in 1632 and his psalm translations in 1637.

224. 'Master Robert Gordon of Straloch': Gordon (1580–1661) was a noted geographer, who was involved in the revision of the Scottish maps for Blaeu's *Atlas*. He also wrote a number of minor historical works.

225. 'a disciple of the most excellent astronomer Tycho Brahe and condisciple of that worthy Longomontanus': Duncan Liddell had studied with Tycho Brahe (1546–1601), the Danish astronomer, and with his associate Christian Severin (1562–1647), 'Longomontanus'. Brahe's discovery, on 11 November 1572, of a 'new star' in the constellation Cassiopeia was signalled in his treatise *De nova stella* (Copenhagen, 1573); there is no trace of Liddell's critique of this work.

226. 'he bequeathed fourty pounds English money a yeer': Liddell endowed a chair in mathematics at Marischal College in 1613.

227. 'when Doctor William Jhonstoun dyed': Johnston died in January 1641, and the younger Liddell who has obtained the MA degree from Marischal in 1634, was not given the chair in mathematics, which passed instead to William Moir. Liddell did, however, succeed Moir in 1661.

228. 'whether Xantippe or Myrto': Xantippe was certainly Socrates' wife, but there is a rival tradition that he was married to Myrto, the granddaughter of Aristides. This is chronologically improbable, and doubt is cast by as early an authority as Plutarch, *Aristides*, 27. Nowhere, however, does it seem to be suggested that Socrates was actually guilty of bigamy.

229. 'the colour of the Duke of Vandome's cloak': This seems to be a topical joke, the basis of which is now unclear. Cesar, duc de Vendome (1594–1665) was the illegitimate son of Henry IV of France and Gabrielle d'Estrees, and played a prominent part in mid-seventeenth century French politics.

230. 'Sir William Alexander, afterwards created Earle of Sterlin': William Alexander of Menstrie (c. 1567–1640) began his literary career as one of the poets at the court of James VI, publishing his tragedy *Darius* at Edinburgh in 1603 and then writing three more before 1607. His addition to Sidney's *Arcadia* was printed in London in 1613, while he marked his involvement with the project to settle Nova Scotia by producing *An encouragement to colonies* (London, 1624). He was made a baronet in 1609, and Earl of Stirling in 1633.

231. 'so dearly have they bought their orange riban': The order of Knights Baronet of Nova Scotia was founded by Charles I in 1625 as part of the promotion of the new colony; its insignia included a ribbon of tawny orange.

232. 'Drummond and Wishart': The Drummond so tersely commended is presumably William Drummond of Hawthornden (1585–1649); Wishart is otherwise unknown.

233. 'nor is Master Ogilvy to be forgot': Ironically, no seventeenth-century vernacular poet of this name is now recorded, and neither the Virgilian nor the Aesopic translations survive.

234. 'Master David Chalmers': The work in question is *De Scotorum fortitudine, doctrina et pietate* (Paris, 1631).

235. 'one Simson': Archibald Simson (c. 1564–1628), minister of Dalkeith, published *Hieroglyphica animalium terrestrium* (2 vols, Edinburgh, 1622–24). 'Hieroglyphicks' is not used in the strict Egyptological sense, but as a general term for symbolic representations; Simson's *Hieroglyphica* is an exegetical work.

236. 'one Hart in the city of London': John Hart's *Fort Royal of the Scriptures* (London, 1649) was a Biblical concordance.

237. 'the chief favourite and the only trustee of the Grand Mareshal de Criky': Charles de Crequi de Blanchefort et de Canaples, duc de Lesdiguieres (d. 1638) was created Marshal of France in 1622. Urquhart does not appear to have been aware of his death.

238. 'Doctor William Forbas': Forbes (1585–1634) was Principal of Marischal College in 1620–1, and was made the first bishop of Edinburgh by Charles I in 1634; he lived only for a few months after his elevation.

239. 'which . . . were bought at a good rate by Doctor Laud': William Laud (1573–1645) was a noted book collector, who donated most of his library to the Bodleian between 1635 and 1640. For lists of the books and discussion of their provenance, see the *Summary Catalogue of Western Manuscripts in the Bodleian Library*, II, 12–69; and *Bodleian Library, Quarto Catalogues*, II, *Laudian Manuscripts*, ed. H. O. Coxe, Rev. R. W. Hunt (Oxford, 1973). No manuscript has so far been attributed to Forbes' collection, and the cataloguers appear to have ignored Urquhart's statement.

240. 'whose spiritual brother, Spotteswood': John Spottiswoode (1565–1639) became Charles I's chancellor in 1635; his *History* was not published until 1655.

241. 'William, Earl of Lanerick by name': James Hamilton (1606–1650), first Duke of Hamilton, was succeeded after his execution by his brother William, Earl of Lanark, secretary of state for Scotland from 1640. William, second Duke, died at Worcester.

242. 'What became of that manuscript': This most authoritative MS. of Spottiswoode's *History* is now Trinity College, Dublin MS 531, and

was used as the basis of the Bannatyne Club edition of 1850 (3 vols, Edinburgh, 1850) for a discussion of the text see I, viii–xiii).

243. '(for the author dyed but the very day before)': The date of Spottiswoode's death was 26 November 1639; it follows that Urquhart was in London (and at the Court) by that date. See Introduction, p. 5.

244. 'Andreas Rivetus': Rivet (1572–1651) was professor of theology at Leiden 1619–32, and subsequently Principal of the college at Breda. He was the author of numerous theological and controversial treatises.

245. '*praefervido Scotorum ingenio, et ad audendum prompto*': 'the hot-blooded temperament of the Scots, ready to perform deeds of daring'. The source of this allusion to Buchanan and Knox has not been identified.

246. 'for want of able and skillful printers': There is some justice in Urquhart's condemnation of contemporary standards in Scottish printing. In his day, the Scottish printers were Tyler and Lithgow in Edinburgh, George Anderson and Heve in Glasgow, and Edward Raban and then James Brown in Aberdeen. None of these achieved a high standard of craftsmanship, and it is understandable that Urquhart published all his works in London.

247. '*non facile emergunt quorum virtutibus obstat res angusta domi*': 'People whose domestic poverty impedes their merits do not easily rise to the top.' Cf. Juvenal, 3.164, '*Haute facile . . .*'

248. 'sing out aloud and cheerfully with Martial, "*Sint Maecenates non deerunt, Flacce, Marones!*"': 'Provided Maecenases are not lacking, there will be Horaces and Virgils' (Martial, 8.55.5), i.e. the appearance of poets is dependent on the presence of patrons.

249. 'Duns Scotus, Sacroboscus, Reginaldus Scotus': Duns Scotus and Sacrobosco (thirteenth century) are both well known scholars, although it is not absolutely clear that Dempster, *Historia*, II, 578–9, and David Buchanan, op. cit., pp. 75–7, are correct in their assertion that the astronomer Sacrobosco (John of Holywood) was a Scot. By Reginaldus Scotus, Urquhart presumably means the first abbot of Arbroath (?d. 1241), who is mentioned by Fordoun and (on that authority) by Dempster, II, 562–3.

250. 'the Scots under the conduct of Godfrey de Bullion': Godefroy de Bouillon (c. 1060–1100) was one of the leaders of the First Crusade, recapturing Jerusalem and becoming its king in 1099. The chronicler Guibert de Nogent refers to Scottish participation in the Crusade, but does not associate the Scots specifically with Godefroy.

251. 'the Dukes of Chasteau le Roy and Dukes of Aubigny that were Scots': Urquhart here seems a little confused. By 'Chasteau le Roy' he perhaps means Duke of *Chatelherault*, the title conferred on James Hamilton, earl of Arran (d. 1575) by Henry II of France in 1549. Jean Stuart (1365–1429) became *seigneur* d'Aubigny in 1425, and the title descended through three generations as far as Jean III (1519–67); but Urquhart may also be thinking of Alexander Stewart, brother of James III, who had the Scottish title of Duke of Albany, which passed to his son, John, Governor of Scotland during the minority of James V.

252. 'Count Betun and Count de Mongomery': Henry II of France was accidentally killed by Gabriel Montgommery, seigneur de Lorges (d. 1574) at a tournament in Paris on 30 June 1559. One of the French noble families of Bethune does seem to have been descended from a Scottish mercenary named Betoun, and to be distinct from those deriving their name from the place in north-eastern France.

253. 'I appeal to Sir Oliver Fleemin, Master of the Ceremonie, and to Master Dury': Fleming was Master of Ceremonies both under parliamentary rule and during Cromwell's Protectorate, and served in a quasi-diplomatic capacity. John Durie (1596–1680) was a noted Presbyterian divine, whose negotiations for Christian unity had the approval of Cromwell and the support of the English universities. Urquhart's appeal to them may owe something to the fact that they were the only Scots with influence in the Cromwellian government.

254. '*Amicus certus in re incerta cernitur*': 'A friend in need is a friend indeed' (Ennius, *Scenica*, 210, as quoted by Cicero, *De amicitia*, 17.64).

255. 'then Massala Corvinus was subject to, who forgot his own name': Massala Corvinus was a friend of Horace, and patron of Tibullus (cf. Tibullus, I, vii, 57).

256. '(Solomon and Alfonso of Aragon being laid aside)': Solomon was the reputed author of the Song of Songs and Ecclesiasticus, while Alfonso V of Aragon (1416–58) was a noted patron of humanist scholarship, whose court at Naples was an important literary centre.

257. '*King James his Works*': A collected edition of works by James VI and I appeared in London in 1616 and was reprinted four years later.

258. 'his motto of "*Beati pacifici*"': 'Blessed are the peace-makers' (Matthew 5:9). This motto was associated with James VI and I at least from 1616, when it appeared in the portrait by Simon van de Passe which served as a frontispiece to the *Works*, and was frequently alluded to by later writers such as Sir John Stradling, whose *Beati Pacifici: A*

Divine Poem written to the Kings Most Excellent Maiestie was published in 1623. It also occurs on the statue of James at the Bodleian Library in Oxford. Urquhart's most likely source is the 1616 *Works*, mentioned just above.

259. 'for the title of *"Sylla Felix"'*: i.e. Lucius Cornelius Sulla (c. 138–78 B.C.), famous for his exploits against Jugurtha, German tribes, in the Bellum Sociale and the civil war against Caius Marius, and against the army of Mithridates.

260. '*τὸ οὗ ἕνεκα*': 'the beneficiary', lit. 'the thing for whose sake (something is being done)'. 1652 reads '*τὸ ᵬ...*', an archaic ligature for '*οὗ*'.

261. 'the wars betwixt the Venetians and Genois': The dominance of Venice in the Mediterranean was established by the war with Genoa of 1377–81. For the relative poverty of individual Venetian citizens, on which Urquhart is well informed, see Philip Longworth, *The Rise and Fall of Venice* (London, 1974), pp. 118–20.

262. 'Captain John Mercer': Although several military figures of this surname occur in seventeenth-century records, none of them is certainly Scottish, and Urquhart's reference is insufficiently specific to make the identification straightforward.

263. 'Anancharsis, though a native of Scythia': Anacharsis (6th cent. B.C.) was a Scythian prince who was accepted in Greece and included among the Seven Sages (v. Herodotus, 4, 76f.; Diogenes Laertius, 1, 10ff.).

264. 'Oxales': For an account of the exploits of Oxales, or Axalla, v. *Purchas his Pilgrimes*, II, 155–60. Purchas states that he was born in Greece 'of the Genuois race'.

265. 'neither in Duke Hamilton's engagement nor at the field of Dunbar': Two decisive defeats of the Scottish 'moderate' army, the first at Preston on 17–19 August 1648 under the command of the Duke of Hamilton, the second at Dunbar on 3 September 1650.

266. '*idem est non esse et non operari; non entium nullae sunt affectiones* and *sublato fundamento tolluntur et omnia quae illi superstruuntur*': 'non-existence is the same as non-activity', 'things which do not have being do not have feelings', and 'when the foundation is removed everything built upon it is removed also'. Three maxims from scholastic philosophy.

267. 'a malignant or a sectary': These are terms from the religious controversies of the period. 'Malignant' was the name applied by the

Covenanters to their Episcopalian opponents, while the 'Independents' mentioned by Urquhart immediately below were the extreme wing of the Covenanting movement.

268. 'the story of Geneva, the civil wars of France and Bohemia and history of Queen Mary of Scotland': Urquhart identifies four areas of conflict in which the Calvinist influence was particularly strong. Geneva was, of course, the centre of Calvin's religious and political revolution, and was a theocratic republic from 1541, while the wars of religion in France (1562–98) and in Bohemia (1618–48) involved an inextricable blend of religious fractionalism and dynastic rivalry. Mary of Scotland was similarly embroiled in religous conflict from her return to Scotland in 1561 until her deposition in 1567.

269. 'you may perceive by King James his *BAΣIΛIKON ΔOPON*, the late king's *EIKON BAΣIΛIKE* and this young king's *BAΣIΛIKOΣ AΔYNAΣTEΣ*': As David Reid has recently pointed out, this is a learned joke; cf. *The Party-Coloured Mind*, ed. David Reid (Edinburgh, 1982), p. 208. James VI published his *Basilikon Doron* ('The Royal Gift') in 1599, while *Ikon Basilike* ('The Royal Image') was the political testament attributed to Charles I. *Basilikos Adynastes* is a mock-title, and means 'The Royal Non-king' (i.e. Charles II).

270. 'as the Kings of Lacedemon whom the Ephors presumed to fine': The Ephors were magistrates in a number of Dorian states, including Sparta; the constitutional balance gave them some powers over the kings. Cf. W. den Boer, *Laconian Studies* (Amsterdam, 1954), pp. 197–212.

271. 'in playing at the hundred': The Hundred was a card-game, otherwise known as *cent*, resembling piquet.

272. 'or as the French on their Epiphany day use the *Roy de la Febve* or King of the Bean': The practice of electing a festive king on Epiphany or Twelfth Night (6 January) was widespread: the British and French names of King of the Bean (Lat. *faba*, 'a bean') derived from the method of election, whereby it was the person whose portion of cake contained the bean who was chosen. Cf. William Lauder, *The Office and Dewtie of Kyngis*, l. 29: 'Thir kyngs thai ar bot kyngs of bane'.

273. 'whom they crowned their king at Sterlin': It was actually at Scone that Charles II was crowned on 1 January 1651, and Urquhart corrects his slip in the supplementary Errata (see p. 211).

274. 'like Achan's wedge': Achan, son of Carni, looted a golden wedge and other objects after the fall of Jericho, which brought punishment on the whole of Israel (see Joshua 7).

275. 'then those of Gideon ... and Jonathan': Cf. Judges 7 and 1 Samuel 14:1–17.

276. 'against the Sennacheribs': For the prayers of Hezekiah against Sennacherib king of Assyria, see 2 Kings 18–19.

277. 'contrary to Saint Paul's admonition': Cf. 1 Timothy 5:8: 'But if any provide not for his own, and specially for those of his own house, he hath denied the faith, and is worse than an infidel'.

278. '*Aures verbis ditant alienas, suas ut auro locupletent crumenas*': 'They enrich the ears of others with their words, so that they may fill their own purses with gold' (Aulus Gellius, *Noctium Atticarum*, 14.1.34, quoting Accius, *Tragedia*, 169 R[3]).

279. 'I will not say, "*κακοῦ κορακος κακὸν ᾠον*"': 'The egg of a bad crow is bad' (The text of the 1652 edition is corrupt, apparently because the printer confused Urquhart's writing of Greek κ with χ, producing a piece of nonsensical Greek). The remark is applied to 'people born of evil parents' (v. Diogenianus, *Centuria*, V, 39); its origin may lie in the reputed inedibility of both the crow and its egg.

280. 'Sir Francis Bacon': Bacon (1561–1626) was created Baron Verulam in 1618 and Viscount St Albans in 1621. His speech on the subject of the *postnati* (those Scots born after the union of the crowns in 1603) was made in the House of Commons on 17 February 1607, and was printed in London in 1641, appearing again the same year as one of *Three Speeches*. The relationship between Urquhart's text and the various versions of Bacon's speech which were in circulation is not altogether clear, but it is apparent that he did not use either of the editions of 1641; his text is much closer in a few significant details to that given by John Blackbourn in his edition of Bacon's *Works* (4 vols, London, 1730), derived from the *Resuscitatio* published by William Rawley (London, 1657) (see notes 286, 289 and 293 below). It seems, therefore, that Urquhart's source was a manuscript close to that subsequently used by Rawley.

281. 'which Demosthenes did ... make to the people of Athens': Demosthenes (c. 383–322 B.C.), the great Athenian orator, frequently urged the setting-aside of self-interest. Bacon may have been thinking in particular of *Philippic*, IV, 35–45, a text of doubtful authenticity but believed in the seventeenth century to be genuine.

282. 'said Alexander to Parmenio': See Arrian, *Anabasis of Alexander*, II, 25.

283. 'the memorable union which was between the Romans and the Latines': The people of Latium were defeated by the Romans at the battle of Regilla (c. 496 B.C.) (Livy, 2.21), and the Latin were subsequently subject to Roman rule.

284. 'that war which was called Bellum Sociale': The 'Social War' (91–87 B.C.) was a rebellion of the Italian cities against Roman rule, leading to the granting of Roman citizenship to the people of the rebel towns. The Consuls are not named in the first printed version of Bacon's speech, but the names do appear in *Three Speeches* and elsewhere, including Rawley-Blackbourn; they are actually incorrect (v. Livy, 8.3–5).

285. 'the example of Sparta and the rest of Peloponnesus': Theban forces under Epaminondas defeated the Spartans in 371 B.C., a setback from which Sparta never recovered and which led eventually to the destruction of Laconia by Philip of Macedon and the fall of Thebes to the Macedonian army in 335.

286. 'the kingdome of Aragon had, in the persons of Ferdinand and Isabella, been united with the rest of Spain': Aragon was united with the kingdom of Castile and Leon as a result of the marriage of Ferdinand V of Aragon and Queen Isabella in 1479. The rebellion to which Bacon refers took place in 1591, beginning with a riot in Zaragoza in May. The printed texts of 1641 have a lacuna where Urquhart prints '*Libertad, Libertad*', but Rawley-Blackbourn give '*Fueros Libertad, Libertad*' ('*Fueros*' was the correct name for the liberties guaranteed to the Aragonese at the time of the union).

287. 'Pisa likewise being united unto Florence': The Pisans were defeated by Florence in 1406 and incorporated into the Florentine state. Both Pisa and Florence were occupied by Charles VIII on his southward march in 1494.

288. '*opposita juxta se posita clarius elucescunt*': 'opposites become clearer when they are set against one another'. The printed Bacon texts, including Rawley-Blackbourn, give 'magis' where Urquhart reads 'clarius'.

289. 'Granada, Murcia, Toledo': These names do not appear in the 1641 editions, but they are given by Rawley-Blackbourn.

290. 'whether the Heptarchy was a true story or a fable': The term used for the seven Anglo-Saxon kingdoms of Northumbria, Mercia, Wessex, East Anglia, Essex, Kent and Sussex, as they existed in the seventh and eighth centuries.

291. *'maneat nostros ea cura nepotes'*: 'Let this task await our descendants' (Virgil, *Aeneid*, III, 505).

292. 'it was well said by Titus Quintus the Romane': Bacon paraphrases Livy, 36.32.6, who quotes Titus Quinctius Flamininus: *'ceterum sicut testudinem, ubi collecta in suum tegumen est, tutam ad omnes ictus video esse'* ('like a tortoise, which I see to be secure against all attacks when its parts are drawn up inside its shell').

293. 'the convenient situation of the west of Scotland': Both the printed texts of 1641 and other early versions have 'the north of Scotland', but Rawley-Blackbourn give the same words as Urquhart.

294. 'a true answer that Solon of Greece made to rich King Croesus of Lydia': Solon (c. 698–558 B.C.) was a generation later than Croesus, but there was a persistent ancient tradition that there had been a link. Cf. Herodotus, I, 32.

295. 'the authority of Machiavel': Niccolo Machiavelli (1469–1527) was one of the most influential political writers of the Renaissance. For his remark about 'the sinews of war', see *Discorsi*, II, 10, *Opere*, ed. A. Panella (2 vols, Milan/Rome, 1938), II, 273–4, where the refuted remark (which actually occurs in Cicero, *Philippics*, 5.5) is attributed to Quintus Curtius; cf. also *Dell'Arte della Guerra*, vii, ed. cit., II, 657.

296. 'Catalonia, a word composed of Goth and Alan': The etymology of the name 'Catalonia' (Sp. *Cataluna*) is uncertain, and the speculation that it was derived from the Visigothic kingdom of Spain, via some such form as 'Gothalaunia', is of an early date. It is much more likely that its fortified character led to the association with the region of the Latin word *castellanus*.

297. 'Anduluzia, a name corrupted from Vandalitia': There are similarly two theories concerning the origin of this name; Bacon espouses one, but other writers more credibly derive *Andalucia* from Arabic *Andalus* ('land of the west').

298. 'after the battel near Granson': The battle of Grandson was fought on 2 March 1476 between Charles the Bold of Burgundy and a confederation of Swiss cantons. For the Burgundian treasure plundered after the battle, see F. Deuchler, *Die Burgunderbeute* (Bern, 1963), and R. L. Wyss *et al.*, *Die Burgunderbeute und Werke burgundischer Hofkunst* (Bern, 1969).

299. 'then did Aesop's cock': The fable of the Cock and the Jasp, or jewel, occurs in the major medieval fable collections, and is used by Urquhart as part of the complex resonance of his title. For Henryson's version, see *Poems*, ed. Denton Fox (Oxford, 1981), pp. 5–9.

300. 'the ruine of the Frenche king's affaires in Italy, Lowis the Twelfth': Louis XII of France (1498–1515), who claimed the title of Duke of Milan, was heavily defeated at Novara in 1513 and forced to abandon his pretensions, largely as a result of the efforts of Swiss mercenaries.

301. *'Credidi, propter quod loquutus sum'*: 'I believed so, and that is why I spoke' (Psalms 115:10, quoted by Paul, 2 Corinthians 4:13).

302. *'dulcis tractus pari jugo'*: 'Hauling is pleasant when the yoke is shared equally'. This is clearly proverbial, although the exact phrase is not found in H. Walther, *Lateinische Sprichworte und Sentenzen des Mittelalters* (6 vols, Gottingen, 1963–9); cf. however, E.617: *'Equale iugum nulli quoque opprimit dorsum'* ('An equal yoke does not weigh down the back').

303. 'in Robert Calvin's case': A celebrated case in which Robert Calvin, a Scot, established his entitlement to own land in England. Part VII of Coke's *Reports* was published in London in 1608: see now *The English Reports*, 77 (Edinburgh/London, 1907), pp. 377–411.

304. *'divisos orbe Britannos'*: 'Britons, divided from the world' (Virgil, *Eclogues*, I, 66).

305. 'an inundation of greater eloquence': Urquhart's list of rhetorical figures is clearly derived from one of the several textbooks on the subject, such as J. C. Scaliger's *Poetices libri septem* (Lyons, 1561) or Henry Peacham's *The Garden of Eloquence* (London, 1577; second edition London, 1593). It is interesting that he generally gives the Greek name for the various figures. For a useful guide to this material, see Lee A. Sonnino, *A Handbook to Sixteenth-Century Rhetoric* (London, 1968).

306. 'seeming to be *juris Gentium*': 'according to the laws of nations'.

307. 'mentioned by Julius Scaliger in his *Causis Linguae Latinae*': Julius Caesar Scaliger's *De causis linguae Latinae*, a humanist study of the Latin language which reflects much of the current interest in Greek and in philology, was published by Sebastian Gryphius at Lyon in 1540.

Appendix II

[The following text of the articles omitted from *The Jewel* is taken from the 1653 edition of *Logopandecteision*.]

38. I saw once a young man who, for his cunning converance in the feats of Leger Demaine, was branded by some of that fry for sorcery; and another for being able, by vertue of the masson word, to make a masson whom he had never seene before, without speaking or any other apparent signe, come and salute him, reputed by many of the same litter to have had a familiar; their grosse ignorance moving them to call that supernaturall or above the naturall reach of meere man, whereof they knew not the cause.

39. By which meanes, mathematicall thaumaturgies, opticall magick, secrets of nature and other philosophicall mysteries, being esteemed to be rancke witchcraft, they ruine the best part of learning and make their own unskillfullnes supreame judge, to pass an irrevocable sentence upon the condemnation of knowledge.

40. The matter, notwithstanding, would be lesse danger were this the worst; but to this ignorance of theirs is concomitant so much wickednes, that when an action of any extraordinary performance is done, although by a man of a most approvable conversation, and to a very good end, such as the curing of the diseased or releeving men out of apparent peril, yet if the cause thereof be unknowne to them, they will not be so charitable as to attribute the effect to a good angel, albeit their faith obliege them to beleeve that the spirits belonging to any of the nine celestiall orders are, for the atchievement of such masteries, in nothing inferior to the infernall demons; but instead of Gabriell, Raphaell, Michaell and such good spirits, by whom, I think, it is more probable an honest man would be assisted in works of a strange and hidden operation then by the bad ones, they ascribe the wonderfullnes of the exploit to the inspiration of Beelzebub, Abadon, Lucifer or some other of the fiends of hell; so malevolently they asperse the reputation of gallant men, whose deeds surpass their capacity.

41. Truly those two qualities of ignorance and wickednes conjoyned are of such pernicious consequence that no nation or commonwealth

249

wherein they get footing is able long to subsist; for rapine, covetousnes and extortion flowing from the one, as from the other doth all manner of basenes, pusillanimity and cowardize, ignorance affecteth the braine and wickednes the heart; yet both the braine and heart of a common weale by the mischeivously unskilfull and illiterately malicious are equally depraved.

42. For remedy of so generall a calamity, seeing universality hath its existence in individualls, would each amend but one, the totall would be quickly rid of this lamentable infection.

43. Therefore since ever I understood any thing, knowing that the welfare of the body of a government consisteth in the intirenes of its noble parts, I always endeavoured to employ the best of my brain and heart towards the furtherance of the honour of that country unto which I did owe my birth.

44. In prosecuting whereof, as the heart is *primum vivens*, so was it my heart which, in my younger years, before my braines were ripened for eminent undertakings, gave me the courage for adventuring in a forrain climat, thrice to enter the lists against men of three severall nations, to vindicate my native country from the calumnies wherewith they had aspersed it; wherein it pleased God so to conduct my fortune that after I had disarmed them, they in such sort acknowledged their error and the obligation they did owe me for sparing their lives, which justly by the law of arms I might have taken, that in lieu of three enemies that formerly they were, I acquired three constant friends both to my selfe and my compatriots, whereof by severall gallant testimonies they gave evident proofe, to the improvement of my country's credit in many occasions.

45. As my heart hath been thus devoted to the love of my native soile, so have my braines to the honour thereof discharged so much duty, that betwixt what is printed and what ready for the presse, I have set forth above a hundred severall bookes on subjects never hitherto thought upon by any.

44. Let no man think that I have spoke this in hope of future benefit or by way of regret I should have faild therof in times past; vertue, in my estimation, whether morall or intellectuall, carrying alwayes along with it a recompence sufficient; not yet out of pride or vaine glory in extolling of my own praises, which, as willingly as to live, I would have smothered but that the continuall receiving of bad offices for my good intentions hath wrought this excursion out of my pen.

47. Could any man imagine I should have been singled out amongst all those of Scotland to suffer most prejudice without a cause; that the wickedest of all the land should be permitted to possesse the best part of my inheritance, under colour of a law, by meer iniquity; and other, little better then he, to gape after the remainder without any fault of mine?

48. Who would think that some of my tenants, whilst I was from home, being killed and neer upon three thousand pound sterlin worth of goods taken from them by a pack of villaines, who could pretend for their robery no other excuse but that they had been plundered by others, no reparation or justice should be granted, although oftentimes demanded; that I should be extorsed in matter of publique dues beyond any of my neighbours; that a garrison should be placed within my house and kept there ten months together, to my almost utter undoing, upon no other pretence but that the stance thereof is stately and the house it selfe of a notable good fabrick and contrivance; and in the mean while a party both of horse and foot remain nevertheless quartered upon my lands till the remotest Highlands should pay their sesse-mony; that neighbor garisons besides my own should by parties inforce me, upon their governours' bare tickets, to furnish them with what provisions they pleased, and yet nothing thereof be allowed unto me, although I presented a bill to that purpose to the Scots Committee of Estates, as I did for the quartering of severall troops of horse, for many months together, without any allowance.

49. These grievous pressures, with many other and as many more, I have sustained by the ministry of the land, whereof I make account in the large treatise of my Aporrexises to give notice more at length, have occasioned this digression in a part; which likewise having proceeded from a serious consideration of the two aforesaid scurvie qualities, that move the inhabitants of the Ile to run every foot to supernatural causes, engageth me to say that as it is a maxim in philosophy that *entia non sunt multiplicanda sine necessitate*, so that it is no lesse incongruity to avouch that a thing hath miraculously been done by God or that for atchievement thereof the help of an evill spirit, because of his being reputed of more experience then man, hath been required thereto, when in the mean while, perhaps, the performance of it by secondary means of an ordinary working, is obvious to any that have the dexterity to open his eyes to see the truth.

[In addition to the above articles omitted between paragraphs 37 and 50, the following three articles are introduced in *Logopandecteision* at the end of the list of advantages of the Universal Language.]

251

134. Sixtie fourthly, negative expressions are more compendiously uttred in this language then in any other in the world.

135. Sixtie fifthly, the infinitant terms by this tongue are in one single word expressed, which succinctness is by no other language afforded.

136. Lastly, there is not any phrase whatsoever, which, for being peculiar to one speech and consequently in all other to be improperly taken (wherewith each known tongue in the world is most variously stored) hath, when translated from its original idiome, the denomination of Graecism, Latinism, Scotism, Anglicism and so forth; but in this universal language is so well admitted that, in losing nothing of its genuine liveliness, it beareth along with it, without any diminution either of sense or expression, the same very emphasis in the stream which it had at the spring, the like whereof is in no other language to be found.